Gary L. Ruff

THE
LORD'S
SUPPER

WHAT THE
BIBLE SAYS
ABOUT
THE
LORD'S
SUPPER

Andrew Paris

College Press Publishing Company, Joplin, Missouri

Scripture quotations,
unless otherwise noted,
are from the
NEW AMERICAN STANDARD VERSION

Copyright © 1986
College Press Publishing Company

Printed and bound in the
United States of America
All Rights Reserved

Library of Congress Catalog Card Number: 86-071103
International Standard Book Number: 0-89900-253-6

TO

THE TWO DEAREST PERSONS THAT
THE LORD HAS GIVEN ME:

Carol (my lovely wife) and Tim (my precious son)

Who make it impossible for me to have a
mid-life crisis and whose encouragement and support
made this book possible!

ALSO TO

John Abbott and Jack Wingate

whose expertise in computer science and electronic wizardry
taught me how to write a book with a computer!!!

Table of Contents

PART III: THE MEANING OF THE LORD'S SUPPER

PART IV: THE IMPORTANCE OF THE LORD'S SUPPER

Yes, I know exactly what you might be thinking: "What? Another book about the Lord's Supper? Hasn't enough been written already? Come on, Andy, what could you possibly say about the Lord's Supper that we don't already know?"

Although many have written about this sacred feast, no one yet has written the "last word" on it. The subject is so large that it cannot possibly be exhausted.

Also, I find that many elders and deacons (and not a few preachers as well) often lament that there are few good books in print to guide them in preparing their Sunday Communion meditations. They feel a real need for such devotional resources.

Even Christians who sit week after week in the church pews and partake of Holy Communion find that they need to improve and enrich their worship experiences. They sense a feeling of "lameness, sameness, and tameness" that descends upon the Communion services like a dismal fog. New life, refreshing insights need to dispel the fog and revive the church's Communion services.

Let's face it; the proper observance of the Lord's Supper involves the highest responsibilities; to reap marvelous blessings from it is not as easy as some might think. It requires diligent labor and the purest desire. And the themes surrounding it are simply tremendous: The love of God in sending His only begotten Son into the world to save sinners, the love of Christ that led Him to die on the cross to achieve our salvation, and the glorious resurrection of Jesus that guarantees forever the infinite power of that death. And when we think of these two issues—our responsibilities at the Lord's Table and the gravid themes surrounding this feast, our souls must cry out for more light upon it. What is the nature of the Lord's Supper? How is Christ present in it? What should the Supper mean to us? How can we use this holy time of communion with the Savior to benefit these weak souls of ours? How can we improve and enrich our worship time as we partake at the Table of the Lord? We need such help and guidance. But where do we turn for it? These are searching questions that must be answered!

Yes, there is a crying need for a book about the Lord's Supper that will equip us to worship acceptably by reverently remembering our Savior's death for us.

Therefore, I here humbly offer you some assistance in that great and good work, which you have to do, and are concerned to do well, when you gather around the Lord's Table. I have written it out of the sincere desire to aid my fellow Christians who seek to glorify their Master and to get more out of Communion.

Especially, I wish to give the reader numerous devotional resources to which he or she can go to find even more depth and meaning to the Lord's Supper.

I believe it was Bernard, the celebrated philosopher and theologian of the Catholic cathedral at Chartres, France, during the twelfth century (he probably died 1130), who said that we are like dwarfs on the shoulders of giants, so that we can see more than they, and things at a greater distance, not by virtue of any sharpness of sight on our part, or any physical distinction, but because we are carried high and raised up by their giant size (*Metalogicon*, 3:4). And that is certainly true of this present book. I feel a deep sense of indebtedness to many: my godly mother who raised me to love the Supper of the Lord; Jack Cottrell, my esteemed colleague and teacher, who was of inestimable help to me as I wrote my M.A. thesis at the Cincinnati Christian Seminary on the theme, "The Manner of Christ's Presence in the Lord's Supper" (1975); the works written by numerous beloved men of God in the past generations of church history—especially Matthew Henry (*The Communicant's Companion*, 1704) and Edward Henry Bickersteth (*A Treatise on the Lord's Supper*, 1825), both of whom have helped me appreciate the Lord's Supper all the more; and finally, Thomas More College, a Roman Catholic institution that invited me to be guest lecturer in a religion class in 1973 concerning the Protestant view of the Eucharist, which provided me with the impetus to get involved in this pleasant study.

Most of all, I praise and magnify the glorious Name of Jesus Christ whose Death and Feast this little book is all about. His grace has greatly strengthened me to write.

No one is more aware of this book's shortcomings and failings than I. For I write it with a sense of my own unworthiness and unfitness to bear the holy vessels of the Lord and to do service in His sanctuary. When anyone writes upon such a magnificent theme as the Supper of the Lord, the writer must exclaim with the beloved Apostle to the Gentiles: "Who is adequate for such things?" (2 Corinthians 2:16). But I am what I am by the grace of God (1 Corinthians 15: 10). And my only aim is to help the Body of Christ—His glorious Church—to get more out of the Lord's Supper. If God, by His mercy, will help me produce that goal, I have what I prayed for.

Just a word about Bible versions. I have used throughout this work the New American Standard Bible. Its accuracy is unparalleled. However, I have from time to time quoted from the New International Version when I felt its rendering of a text was clearer and more helpful. When I did so, I included an abbreviation (NIV) after the Scripture citation.

I have enjoyed every minute of studying this subject and writing upon it; it has richly blessed me and revived my love for the Savior whose death cleanses me from all sin (1 John 1:7).

PART I

THE
FOUNDATIONS
OF
THE LORD'S SUPPER

1

INTRODUCTION

THE IDEA OF THE LORD'S SUPPER

When Christians partake of the Lord's Supper, what are they doing? What is the primary concept that is involved in the phrase, "The Lord's Supper"?

By definition, this sacred meal is the act of remembering Christ's death on the cross for our sins; the bread reminds us of His body broken, and the fruit of the vine reminds us of His blood shed. Thus, this is primarily a memorial feast by which Christians remember a past historical event to edify and to strengthen their lives; this provides food for the soul.

Our Savior knew that our treacherous minds are apt to forget Him (Deuteronomy 6:12). And so He instituted this simple but profound banquet of souls to revive in our memories the very center of our Christianity: the death of Jesus our Lord.

The Supper of the Lord is thus an emblematic representation of all the grand truths of the Christian System. For truth may be brought before the mind in two ways: by verbal statement or by emblematic representation. The first is best suited for conveying new information; but the second is beautifully fitted for recalling to the mind information formerly presented to it. The first method of presenting the leading truths of Christianity is adopted in the written and spoken word of God. The second method is found in the Lord's Supper.

Upon closer examination of this sacred feast, we find it is a miniature picture of the major teachings of the gospel of Jesus. Since the bread and the fruit of the vine symbolize Christ's body and blood, the Supper represents the incarnation of our Lord. The Son of God took on the nature of humanity to be the God-Man; He never lost His deity, but He added to it a human nature (Hebrews 2:14-17), Philippians 2:5-11). Thus, in a most eloquent manner, the Lord's Supper recalls to our minds the immortal words of John 1:14, "the Word became flesh and dwelt among us."

Also, since the bread is broken and the fruit of the vine is poured out, this reminds us that the God-Man Jesus suffered a most violent death in our place for our sins. His death was vicarious or substitutionary; that is, He died not for His own sin, because He was perfect. No, He died for our sins. When he died, He endured the wrath of God in our place. He takes our sins and we receive His righteousness by faith at the time we are immersed for the forgiveness of sins. Therefore, with one glance of the eye, as we gather around the Table of the Lord, we behold the wondrous plan of human redemption through the work of God the Son in

16

His incarnation and sacrifice. The Lord's Supper tells us more touchingly than words could do that "Christ died for our sins according to the Scriptures" (1 Corinthians 15:3-4); "He was pierced through for our transgressions, He was crushed for our iniquities" (Isaiah 53:5); "in Him we have redemption through His blood, the forgiveness of our trespasses" (Ephesians 1:7).

Also we see in this feast the social nature of Christianity. The Supper is a social gathering of Christians together to remember their Savior's death. It is a symbol of our common Christianity. Unity is the keyword here. Unfortunately, what was originally designed as a unifying rite by the Lord, has been corrupted into an occasion for division and destruction by the sinful heart of man. The communion feast has been turned into a battle ground full of envy, strife, and hatred among fellow members of the church. However, the original intention of our Savior was to make the Supper a feast of love and warmth among Christians of like precious faith.

Yes, in this simple meal, we see the grand truths of the gospel proclaimed to our minds deeply and beautifully as we partake in faith; it is a living Bible.

This is the idea of the Lord's Supper. It is a precious memorial of the greatest event in all gospel history: Christ's sacrificial death for sinners such as we.

THE NEED FOR STUDYING THE LORD'S SUPPER

We need to study the Lord's Supper today because of two evils that have arisen among us: the famine of good books that discuss it, and the "ho-hum" attitude of indifference concerning it that too many Christians have.

The Famine of Good Books Today

Having seen what the Lord's Supper is, you would think that many today would be writing about such an all-important topic. But such is not the case at all. Not only are there few good books that deal with it, but there are not many books at all that discuss it. Just go to your neighborhood Bible book store and check this out for yourself. You will find to your utter chagrin that—much like the fabled Mother Hubbard of old—the shelves are bare. Books abound on church growth and discipleship; but when it comes to the Lord's Supper, it seems no one is home!

And this is especially so among the churches within the Restoration Movement ("Christian Churches/Churches of Christ"). We, more than most other churches, have emphasized the meaning and frequency of the Lord's Supper. We preach and teach it. We strive to restore it to its rightful place in our worship services. Yet, strange as it may seem, even we have written few books about it.

This fact is confirmed by looking at one of the best works ever produced on this topic in the Restoration Movement: *The Lord's Supper* by John L. Brandt (1889). He gathers the finest examples of Baptist, Catholic, Episcopal, Methodist, Presbyterian, and Christian Churches/Churches of Christ thoughts on the Supper. When it first appeared, B. V. Watkins reviewed it favorably in the August 24, 1889 issue of the *Christian Standard* periodical. He proclaims:

> That we as Disciples of Christ, who have undertaken to restore the spiritual symbols of the gospel to the place and intents of their original position, it is wonderful how long we have been without an extensive treatise on the Lord's Supper. We have learned works on baptism and its consequences; learned disquisitions on the views of all churches on the form and design of baptism; all of which we have eagerly read. Then why should we not have one standard work on the Lord's Supper? While baptism with its accessories, is essential to our putting on Christ, the supper is essential to our life in the church, to our growth in grace, and to our Christian perfection.

Yes, even in 1889, our people had not seen much written on this important subject. And on into the twentieth century, as we today can testify, the situation has not improved but rather has worsened.

The famine of good books about the Lord's Supper shows the need for studying anew this all-important theme.

The "Ho-Hum" Attitude of Indifference Toward It

On numerous occasions when people found out that I was teaching an undergraduate course on the Lord's Supper, almost all of them gave the same response: "An entire course just about the Lord's Supper? What could anyone possibly say about it for a full fourteen-week semester? Do we have to spend all semester on merely the Lord's Supper?"

And the more I thought about it, the more I came to realize that this flippant, "ho-hum" attitude towards the Lord's Supper raises its ugly head in some churches. Many of us do not expect anything marvelous or blessed to happen at the Lord's Table. Content to sit, soak, and sour, some Christians just go through the motions each Lord's Day morning of eating a little bread and drinking a little grape juice in a superficial and mechanical way; they rarely realize how extremely important Communion ought to be. It tends to become the low point in our worship services. Few get really excited about taking the Lord's Supper. Think of the blessings missed! Some seldom enjoy sweet communion and fellowship with their Lord around His Table. "Many Christians do not expect enough at the Lord's Table, and thence lose much of the benefits to be there obtained. We should have a large expectation, and we shall receive largely."[1]

---

1. Edward H. Bickersteth, *A Treatise on the Lord's Supper* (London: L. B. Seeley and Son, 1825), p. 118.

And some of the communion meditations we hear on Sunday mornings also reflect this "ho-humity." They are usually some last-minute thoughts that the speaker put together; most of the time these little devotionals all sound the same no matter who might be giving them. Occasionally, they will read some "canned" meditations from a little booklet in a monotone speaking style that puts us all to sleep. This is so tragic. If the Supper is really all that important to us, we should prepare fresh, exciting messages that thrill the soul and revive the heart of all who hear them.

Few Bible Colleges (if any!) teach extensively on the Lord's Supper. The subject is usually tucked away as one little part of a much larger theme ("the Church," "The Ordinances," or "Salvation"). The teacher ends up lecturing on it for a relatively short time, while baptism and other topics get almost exhaustive treatment.

Therefore, these things point to one evident fact. To revive our spirits from such ho-hum indifference towards the Lord's Supper, we need to study it deeply.

And when we do, we will find that it is truly one of the divinely-ordained means of grace by which we grow up in Christ. It will empower us to live the victorious Christian life. It will be a reviving power-house designed to equip our souls with divine strength. Remember the words of Watkins:

> . . . the supper is essential to our life in the church, to our growth in grace, and to our Christian perfection.

Consider carefully the following words of Bickersteth:

> Yet it has been justly remarked, that in the accounts which we have of those most distinguished for piety, never anyone excelled in the virtues of the Christian life, but was accustomed

frequently to nourish his soul with "the banquet of this most heavenly food."[2]

Since it is one of the keys to living the abundant life, let us study Holy Communion to become zealous servants of the Master who instituted this sacred feast.

THE ORIGIN OF THE LORD'S SUPPER

This may seem a technical, academic question to some of those who read this book. Most Christians, of course, accept the Biblical view that God gave us the Supper. And I boldly declare that He truly did. The Supper is of divine origin.

However, at the risk of boring you out of your mind, I would like to spend just a few pages discussing the issue anyway. For I believe it is vital. Serious issues rest upon it. If the Supper is not from God, if it comes from fallible men, then why observe it? It then becomes no better than any pagan rite or ceremony. And the New Testament is a liar when it declares that Jesus revealed the Lord's Supper to His Church. Besides all this, it will do our souls much good to see how the skeptical theories of unbelieving theologians have been exploded as more evidence pours in; this study can strengthen our convictions even more.

The Answer Prior to the Nineteenth Century

The verdict of church history is clear. From the dawn of the Christian era until the early nineteenth century, few even questioned the fact that Jesus Christ Himself had

---

2. Bickersteth, p. 2.

instituted the Lord's Supper as a memorial for His Church. All agreed that the holy meal is from God alone.

Then the age of skepticism began. Motivated by the cold air of unbelief that blew its chilling breath throughout the eighteenth century and was known as the "Enlightenment Period" in Europe, the beginning of the nineteenth century witnessed the rationalist Heinrich E. G. Paulus pollute the waters of faith's fountain by denying the divine origin of the Lord's Supper.[3]

But the point here is that for about 1800 years all accepted the divine origin of the Lord's Supper. That was the view of all early Christians; that was the position of all Roman Catholics during the Medieval Age; that was the faith of the Protestant Reformation, led by such giants as Luther, Zwingli, and Calvin, as well as those who followed them during the sixteenth and seventeenth centuries.

The Influence of the Mystery Religions

While loyal Christians were doing "battle royal" against the unbelievers who denied with Paulus the divine origin of the Supper, the "Liberals" adopted a new tactic. They claimed that the Apostle Paul had copied his view of this meal from the pagan Graeco-Roman "mystery religions."[4]

---

3. Heinrich E. G. Paulus, *Commentar uber das Neue Testament*, 4 volumes, 1800-1804; also see his *Leben Jesu*, 2 volumes, 1828. He was soon followed by another German scholar, Kaiser, *Biblische Theologie*, 2 volumes, 1813-1821. See John Cairns, *Unbelief in the Eighteenth Century* (the Cunningham Lectures; New York: Harper and Brothers, 1881), pp. 134-136.

4. Otto Pfleiderer, *Das Urchristentum* (1887), later translated as *Primitive Christianity: Its Writings and Teachings in Their Historical Connections*, translated by J. W. Montgomery and edited by W. D. Morrison (first published 1906-1911; Clifton, N.J.: Reference Book Publishers, 1965 reprinted), 1:61-63, 413-426; Wilhelm Heitmuller, *Taufe und Abendmahl bei Paulus* (Gottingen: Vandenhoeck and Ruprecht, 1903), p. 35; Richard Reitzenstein, *Die hellenistichen Mysterien-religionen* (Leipzig: B. G. Teubner, 1910), pp. 55-60;

Not only was it of human origin, but it was of pagan human origin at that. This view began in the year 1887 when Otto Pfleiderer made it popular in Germany and America. And it remained strong well into the middle of the twentieth century.

What were "mystery religions"? When Roman armies in the first century B. C. conquered the East, they brought back the Eastern religions with them. These included such deities as Cybele, Osiris, Isis, Attis, Mithras, Demeter of the Eleusinian mysteries, Dionysus, and Serapis.[5] Since the classical Graeco-Roman religions had failed to meet the needs of the people (it was truly an age suffering from "failure of nerve"[6]), many sought satisfaction in these foreign religions. Such cults stressed secret ceremonies, and thus were called "mystery" religions. They promised individual salvation and deliverance from fate and death.

At first glance, these appeared to be quite similar to Christianity, especially Baptism and the Lord's Supper. For

---

4. (continued) all three are discussed briefly in Stephen Neill, *The Interpretation of the New Testament 1861-1961* (London: Oxford University Press, 1964), pp. 158-160; see also H. A. A. Kennedy, *St. Paul and the Mystery Religions* (London: Hodder and Stoughton, 1913), pp. 256ff.; C. C. Clemen, *Primitive Christianity and Its Non-Jewish Sources,* translated by Robert G. Nisbet (Edinburgh: T. and T. Clark, 1912), pp. 257-266; A. E. J. Rawlinson, *The New Testament Doctrine of the Christ* (the Bampton Lectures of 1926; London: Longmans, Green and Co., 1926), pp. 270-284.

5. See S. Angus, *The Mystery-Religions and Christianity* (New York: Charles Scribner's Sons, 1925); M. P. Nilsson, *Greek Piety* (New York: W. W. Norton, 1968), pp. 150-161; Arthur Darby Nock, "The Development of Paganism in the Roman Empire," *The Cambridge Ancient History,* edited by S. A. Cook and others (Cambridge: At the University Press, 1956), 12:409-449; J. Gresham Machen, *The Origin of Paul's Religion* (Grand Rapids: Wm B. Eerdmans Publishing Company, 1973 reprinted), pp. 211-290.

6. Gilbert Murray, *Five Stages of Greek Religion* (London: Watts and Company, n. d.), pp. 123-172.

some of these cults did emphasize a sacred meal by which the initiates were inducted into the "mystery religion." They even talked about the "Table of the Lord." Their god was considered the host, as well as sometimes the guest. For instance, we read in one ancient letter: "Chaeremon invites you to dine at the table of the Lord Serapis, tomorrow, 15th, at nine o'clock."[7] After the worshippers offered an animal sacrifice to the god Demeter at Eleusis, they ate a meal of the victim's flesh.[8] Tertullian tells us the followers of Dionysus ate of "chosen food."[9] In fact, the ancient worshippers of Dionysus actually believed "they were killing the god, eating his flesh, and drinking his blood" when they savagely devoured the raw meat of bulls, calves, goats, and fawns.[10] Justin Martyr reports that "bread and a cup of water are offered and eaten in the rites of initiation" into the Mithras cult.[11] All this seems similar to the Lord's Supper.

Therefore many liberal theologians from the year 1887 onward claimed that the Bible writers had copied their Lord's Supper ideas from the mystery religions.

Today, however, few scholars of any persuasion would maintain such a notion. It has been crushed by the sheer weight of abundant evidence to the contrary. As they critically investigated the mystery religions, the following facts emerged to refute that skeptical position:

---

7. *Oxyrhynchus Papyri,* 1:110; cited by Angus, p. 128.

8. Angus, p. 129.

9. Tertullian, *Apology,* 39; cited by Angus, p. 129.

10. Sir James George Frazier, *The Golden Bough: A Study in Magic and Religion* (second edition revised and enlarged; London: Macmillan and Company, 1900), 2:15ff.; see also Arthur Darby Nock, *Early Gentile Christianity and Its Hellenistic Background* (New York: Harper and Row, 1962), pp. 73-74.

11. Justin Martyr, *Apology,* 166; cited by Angus, p. 129.

1. We are not sure what these sacred meals meant to the mystery religions.[12] The evidence we have is too obscure for us to ascertain the precise significance of the first century A. D. cultic meals. Their meaning is now lost to us. If we could find out from the ancient inscriptions that the pagans believed they were actually receiving the life-force of the deity by eating and drinking, then at least some parallel with the Lord's Supper could be made. But we do not even know that. When the initiate to the Eleusinian Mysteries said, "I have fasted, I have the kykeon (a kind of soup made with milk), I have taken (the sacred object) from the box, I performed the act, I put the things in the basket and out of the basket into the box,"[13] what did that all mean? What significance did any of it have? Or when the initiate to the mysteries of Attis and Cybele said, "I have eaten out of a timbrel, I have drunk out of a cymbal, I have become an initiate of Attis,"[14] what did that eating and drinking really mean to him? And did he eat bread and drink from a cup anyway, as a model from which supposedly the Christians copied for their eucharistic doctrine? All we can say with assurance is this: we just do not know.

With such uncertainty abounding, we would do well to keep from making dogmatic statements that assume the Christians copied from the mystery religions. As the eminent Arthur Darby Nock expresses it, "There is then, as far as we can see, nothing in this which can well have contributed to the genesis of the Christian rite, still less to its central position and soteriological significance."[15] And Nock

---

12. Nock, *Early Gentile Christianity*, pp. 74-76.
13. According to the early Church father, Clement of Alexandria, *Exhortation to the Greeks*, 2:21; cited by Nock, *Early Gentile Christianity*, p. 74.
14. According to the early Church father, Clement of Alexandria, *Exhortation to the Greeks*, 2:15; cited by Nock, *Early Gentile Christianity*, pp. 74-75.
15. Nock, *Early Gentile Christianity*, p. 76.

possessed amazingly wide knowledge of all Hellenistic religion. His precise and careful mind could not accept the Liberal position here, even though he himself was a liberal who taught at the Unitarian divinity school at Harvard University. The evidence would not let him.

2. Great differences exist between the Christian feast and the pagan mystery meals. The meaning of the mystery meals is uncertain, as far as we know right now. But the precise interpretation of the Lord's Supper by the early Christians of that time is clear. Also, the pagan meals prepared the people for initiation into the cult. But the Lord's Supper was never designed for those who were to be initiated into Christianity; rather it was to be observed weekly by those alone who had already become Christians. True, both pagan mystery cults and Christians in their sacred feasts remembered a dying and triumphant deity. However, only Christians remembered their Lord's death as a victory over the forces of evil and darkness; Christ's death possessed a moral value all its own (Colossians 2:14-15; 1 John 3:8). But in the mystery religions, their god's death was merely a bare event; it had very little moral value.[16]

The only mystery religion whose sacred meal even came close to the Lord's Supper was Mithraism. Those in it partook of bread and cup in a way so similar to the Christians' sacred meal that Justin Martyr, the early Christian writer/philosopher, said the demons had copied from the Lord's Supper and had given the counterfeit banquet to the Mithraic devotees.[17] They even believed that eating it gave them supernatural results and powers.[18] Such close parallels

---

16. Nock, *Early Gentile Christianity*, p. 76.

17. Justin Martyr, *Apology*, 166; Irenaeus, *Prescriptions Against Heretics*, 40.

18. J. Greshem Machen, *The Origin of Paul's Religion* (Grand Rapids: Wm. B. Eerdmans Publishing Company, 1973), pp. 281-282.

between it and the Lord's Supper caused men like Heitmuller to claim the Christians had copied from Mithraism. And this now brings us to the most important point of all: the issue of dating. Who came first, Christianity or Mithraism? And who copied from whom? The mystery religions, including Mithraism, came forth at a very early date; so it is possible that the Christians could have copied from them. On the other hand, it is just as possible that the mystery religions, including Mithraism, copied from the Christians. Our third point will seek to answer this question.

3. Mithraism became a notable force in the ancient world too late to exert any influence upon early Christianity.[19] This famous cult was too weak during the first century A. D. to make a lasting impression upon the majority of people in the Graeco-Roman world. Here the matter of accurate dating is of first importance. It makes any alleged influence of Mithraism upon Christianity highly improbable. And for this reason most modern New Testament scholars would agree in part with Justin Martyr: Mithraism copied its sacred meal theology from the Christians and not vice versa.

This issue of precise dating also applies to the very famous quotation about Chaeremon inviting someone to the "Table of the Lord Serapis." The fact of the matter is that when we pay careful attention to the chronological data, we will find this quotation comes from the third century A. D.[20] Again, it comes too late to claim the Christians copied from the Serapis mystery cult for their view of the Lord's Supper. Of course, one might assume that this cult arose much

---

19. Nock, *Early Gentile Christianity*, p. 133; Machen, pp. 281-282.
20. Stephen Charles Neill, *The Interpretation of the New Testament 1861-1961* (London: Oxford University Press, 1964), pp. 170-171.

earlier than Christianity did, but we have no record of that yet. Yes, that is possible; but again, let me stress that all our evidence points in the opposite direction: it is more probable to declare that the followers of Serapis imitated the Christian view of the Lord's Supper and not vice versa. All we can say right now is that there is no trace of a Pre- Christian use of the expression, "Table of the Lord." It may have been used earlier; but we just do not know.[21]

When the Liberal theologian claims that the Christians copied from the pagan mysteries for Lord's Supper ideas, this seems the best illustration I know of where the wish becomes father to the thought.

But the issue of dating comes up for discussion not only when the mystery religions are too late, but also when they are too early. As we shall see next.

4. The cannibalistic practices of the followers of Dionysus, who ate their god's own flesh and blood literally, cannot have influenced the early Christians, since that pagan religion does not seem to have survived in the Hellenistic mystery religions.[22] It came too early to exert any god-eating ideas upon the early Church. Again, we see how dating becomes very crucial. Anyway, why would the Christians resurrect the out-moded ideas of god-eating from the Dionysians, when even the first century pagans had rejected such ideas?

For these four reasons, the modern theological world rejects the "history-of-religions" school's notion that the origin of the Lord's Supper lies in pagan mystery religions.

---

21. Hans Leitzmann, *Handbuch zum Neuen Testament*, volume 9 (1931), in a special excursus on this subject; cited by Neill, p. 171.

22. Machen, pp. 282-283.

The Skepticism of Rudolf Bultmann

Having given up on the mystery-religions approach to the origin of the supper, some modern scholars followed Rudolf Bultmann, the eminent German theologian of Marburg University (1884-1974). His numerous writings have influenced many to reject the historical value of much in the Bible. His ideas fell like a plague upon the modern theological world, causing scholars to explain away the supernatural elements of the Scriptures.

He clearly denied that Jesus ever intended to establish a "Church" that would regularly observe the "Lord's Supper." Bultmann felt that these two things were merely invented by the early Christian community when it realized Jesus would never arise from the dead.[23]

The Approach of Modern Theology

Most theologians today, however, have rejected such a skeptical approach. They declare that Jesus certainly did establish both His Church and His Supper.[24] The origin of the Lord's Supper, therefore, is to be found in the creative teachings of Jesus Himself. He invented it so that His People would faithfully celebrate His death through its weekly observance.

Angus J. B. Higgins, a British scholar of Liberal persuasion, represents the attitude of most New Testament scholars today when he declares that the way Christ used the two titles together, "Son of Man" and "Kingdom of God/Heaven," proves that He surely intended to build a "Church" who would remember His death through the Lord's

---

23. Rudolf Bultmann, *The Theology of the New Testament*, translated by Kendrick Grobel (New York: Charles Scribner's Sons, 1951), 1:10, 57-58, 144-151.

24. For an excellent critique of the death of Bultmannianism, see Carl F. H. Henry, *Frontiers in Modern Theology* (Chicago: Moody Press, 1972), pp. 9-29.

Supper.[25] For our Lord used that exalted name—"The Son of Man"—more than any other title to show His relation to the coming Kingdom of God/Heaven. That was precisely why He used it so much. It stressed the glorious kingdom imagery found in Daniel 7. And He employed it in a Messianic sense. Through its use, Jesus proclaimed that He is the Savior-Messiah-Lord who will build His Church. That Kingdom will observe the Lord's Supper faithfully until He returns on the clouds of heaven. Therefore, Higgins argues, as the Son of Man and Kingdom of God/Heaven are inseparable, so the Messiah must have His own Messianic Church.

In similar fashion the German New Testament scholar K. L. Schmidt writes:

> For the Son of Man in Daniel is not a mere individual: he is the representative of "the people of the saints of the Most High" and has set Himself the task of making this people of God . . . a reality. From this point of view the so-called institution of the Lord's Supper can be shown to be the formal founding of the Church.[26]

One cannot separate the Church of Jesus from the Lord's Supper. They form one grand theme in Christianity. And informed Biblical scholars and theologians of various schools of thought agree that Jesus truly founded His Church and the Lord's Supper.

Nowadays most New Testament scholars, even Liberals, contend that Jesus and Paul received their Lord's Supper ideas from the Old Testament and especially the Passover feast.[27]

---

25. Angus J. B. Higgins, *The Lord's Supper in the New Testament* (London: SCM Press, 1952), pp. 1-10; "The Origin of the Eucharist," *New Testament Studies*, I (1954-1955), pp. 200-209.

26. K. L. Schmidt, *"Ecclesia"* (Church), *Theological Dictionary of the New Testament*, edited by Gerard Kittel and others (1968), 3:521.

27. Vincent Taylor, *New Testament Essays* (London: Epworth Press, 1970), pp. 48-59; Joachim Jeremias, *The Eucharistic Words of Jesus* (London: SCM Press, 1973), pp. 118-127.

In conclusion, we have seen that the Lord's Supper comes from God and is intended for God's people—the Church. The numerous attempts by unbelievers to deny this fact shatter upon the rocks of evidence. The pagan mystery religions cannot be the source of such ideas. Bultmann's view that Jesus never established a Church or the Lord's Supper has been shown to lack solid evidence; most scholars today have rejected it. Jesus Himself gave us this glorious gift of the Lord's Supper to nourish our souls and to strengthen our faith. Its origin lies in our Master and Lord and nowhere else. This is the faith of the Church and the facts of history.

THE RELATIONSHIP BETWEEN THE PASSOVER AND THE LORD'S SUPPER

In this section, we discuss the historical background of the Lord's Supper. To understand the things that Jesus did at the Last Supper, we must first study the details of the Jewish Passover, for He celebrated His Supper after He and the disciples had eaten the Passover meal. The Passover sheds light upon the Last Supper.

The Lord's Supper as the New Passover

By reading the accounts found in Matthew, Mark, and Luke (called the "synoptic" gospels because they discuss similar material from the life of Jesus and thus they can be "seen together") we find that Jesus institutes His own Supper along some of the same lines as the Passover meal. Therefore, according to them at least, the Lord's Supper is the "New Passover" for the Church—the "New Israel of God." Many similarities exist between the two meals. What

31

the Passover means can aid us in seeing the meaning of the Lord's Supper. Let us see how closely related they really are.

The Synoptics record that the Last Supper is a Passover meal. This fact appears in the following passages:

> Now on the first day of Unleavened Bread the disciples came to Jesus, saying, "Where do You want us to prepare for You to eat the Passover?" And He said, "Go into the city to a certain man, and say to him, The Teacher says, My time is at hand; I am to keep the Passover at your house with My disciples." And the disciples did as Jesus had directed them; and they prepared the Passover (Matthew 26:17-19).

> And on the first day of Unleavened Bread, when the Passover lamb was being sacrificed, His disciples said to Him, "Where do You want us to go and prepare for You to eat the Passover?" (Mark 14:12).

> And the disciples went out, and came to the city, and found it just as He had told them; and they prepared the Passover (Mark 14:16).

> And He said to them, "I have earnestly desired to eat this Passover with you before I suffer" (Luke 22:15).

Such passages reveal to us that the Synoptics believed Jesus instituted His Supper alongside the Passover and along the same lines as the Passover meal.

Also, there are the following additional similarities that connect the Lord's Supper with a "New Passover" idea: 1) Only the Passover was a night meal; all other Jewish feasts occurred during the daylight hours. And the Synoptics record that the Last Supper of Jesus took place at night. 2) Only the Passover meal had a dish preceding the breaking of the bread; and the Synoptics report that the Last Supper of Jesus had the dish preceding the breaking of the bread (Mark 14:20-22; Matthew 26:23, 26). 3) The Last Supper ended with the singing of a hymn, which may very well have been the famous "Hallel" (Psalms 113-118) which was always sung at the Passover meal alone. 4) After the meal, Jesus went to Gethsemane—not to the usual spot called Bethany, which was outside the area to which one might go on Passover night (Talmud, *Pesachim,* 63b; 91a; *Menahim,* 78b, 11:2). 5) The words of institution that Jesus spoke at the Last Supper ("This is My Body," "This is My Blood") remind us of the Jewish custom that the one presiding at the Passover feast explained its meaning. 6) Both meals stress the covenant idea. The Passover was primarily a "covenant-sealing feast" which both commemorated and renewed the original Sinai pledge. The Qumran documents—the Dead Sea scrolls—have shown this idea to be very much alive at the beginning of the Christian era. 7) At both the Passover feast and the Last Supper the blood was emphasized. 8) Both meals stressed "remembrance."[28]

For these reasons, many contend that the Lord's Supper is really a "New Passover" meal for the Church. Support for this comes from the accounts given in the Synoptic Gospels.

The Passover Ritual

What really happened when a Jewish family gathered together on the fourteenth day of Nisan and observed the Passover feast? What was the Passover like during the first century A. D. when our Lord took it with His disciples in the upper room? To answer such questions, I will first explain the six indispensable things necessary for having a "Kosher" Passover banquet; then I will list the eighteen

---

28. Throughout this section about the similarities between the Passover and the Lord's Supper, I am greatly indebted to Leon Morris, *The Gospel According to John. The New International Commentary on the New Testament* (Grand Rapids: Wm. B. Eerdmans Publishing Company, 1971), pp. 774-775.

parts of the Passover feast itself, and how they fit in with the Last Supper.

The Passover feast must include at least the following six items: the lamb, the unleavened bread, the bowl of salty water, the bitter herbs, the sweet paste (charosheth), and the four cups of wine. We will study these more carefully.[29]

1. *The Lamb* (Exodus 12:21-23). The first requirement of any true Passover meal was the sacrificing and the eating of a lamb. This would remind the Israelites of their fore-fathers in Egypt who were delivered from the angel of death by smearing the lamb's blood upon their door posts. All other houses in Egypt, however, would suffer God's wrath; their first-born sons would die. The lamb eloquently pictured salvation by God.

This lamb had to be prepared in a very special way. It could not be boiled or stewed. Nothing could touch it—not even water or the sides of a cooking pot. It must be fastened upon a skewer which pierced through it from mouth to vent, and then it must be roasted over an open flame. The whole animal was to be roasted—even its head, legs, and tail.

The minimum number of people who could celebrate the Passover together was twelve. If one's family had less than that amount, he should join another family and both together would partake of the roasted lamb (see Exodus 12: 4). Also, they must eat the entire lamb, leaving nothing.

2. *The Unleavened Bread* (Exodus 12:8, 15-20; Deuteronomy 16:3-4; Numbers 9:11). The second require-ment was a special kind of bread. It could not contain any leaven in it whatsoever. Thus, it was not like bread as we know it, but actually much like a water biscuit. The

---

29. Throughout this section about the Passover's details, I am greatly indebted to William Barclay, *The Lord's Supper* (Nashville: Abingdon Press, 1967), pp. 20-22.

unleavened nature of it would symbolize the fact that their forefathers were in such a hurry to leave Egypt that they did not have time to leaven the loaf (Deuteronomy 16:3; see Exodus 12:11).

3. *The Bowl of Salty Water.* This third requirement is not found in the Old Testament, but it was later added by the Jews. All Passovers of the first century A. D. included this. It reminded them of the tears their forefathers shed while in the rigors of Egyptian slavery, and also of the waters of the Red Sea, through which they had been brought to safety.

4. *The Bitter Herbs* (Exodus 12:8; Numbers 9:11). This fourth item was a collection of such bitter herbs as horseradish, chicory, endive, lettuce, horehound; these remind the Israelites of the sorrows and griefs they bore as slaves in Egypt. Throughout the Passover, they were to recite this: "And you shall remember that you were a slave in the land of Egypt, and the Lord your God redeemed you" (Deuteronomy 15:15).

5. *The Charosheth Paste.* This fifth item is also not found anywhere in the Scriptures, but the Jews added it later. It was a sweet-tasting paste called charosheth. It was prepared by mixing together bits of apples, dates, pomegranates, nuts, with sticks of cinnamon running through it. This symbolizes the clay (paste) from which their forefathers made the bricks, and the straw (cinnamon sticks) they needed to make those bricks. They also remembered how the Egyptians withheld the straw from the Jews (Exodus 5:7-9).

6. *The Four Cups of Wine.* This last part of a first century A. D. Passover is also not found in Scripture, but was added in subsequent times by the Jews. In some ways it was

the most important ritual of all. The four cups of wine, each one containing one-sixteenth of a hin (a little more than 1/2 a cup), consisted of two parts wine to three parts water. It was considered so important to the observance of this feast that if a Jew were too poor to obtain the wine, he must get it by one of the following three methods: receive help from the Temple fund for the poor, pawn his own garments, or hire himself out.

The meaning behind these four cups: they symbolize the four beautiful promises found in Exodus 6:6-7 "I am the Lord, and I will bring you out from under the burdens of the Egyptians, and I will deliver you from their bondage. I will also redeem you with an outstretched arm and with great judgments. Then I will take you for My people, and I will be your God."

By seeing the six parts of the Jewish Passover ritual, we understand that it was a feast of remembrance. It reminded the Jews of salvation, deliverance, and freedom from God's enemies. It was the high point in the Jewish year. It commemorated God's grace and love for His people. These grand motifs were surely running through the mind of Christ and His disciples as they partook of the Passover meal just before He instituted the Lord's Supper.

But how did these six items fit into a formal Passover service in the first century A. D.? The following eighteen parts of that ritual emphasize remembrance of God's salvation for Israel at the Exodus.[30]

1. The "kiddush" ("consecration") cup. In later times, probably during Jesus' earthly ministry, the presider at the meal offered a prayer of thanksgiving to God for this memorial of salvation, and for accepting Israel as His own.

2. The presider washes his hands three times.

---

30. Barclay, pp. 22-25.

3. The worshippers eat a piece of lettuce or parsley that had been dipped into the salt water (Exodus 12:22). The greens represented to the Israelite the hyssop which was dipped in the blood of the Passover lamb, and with which the lintel and the doorposts were smeared; then the salt water stands, as we have already observed, for either the tears of Egypt or the waters of the Red Sea.

4. The bread is now broken. Three flat rectangular-shaped cakes of unleavened bread were placed upon the table, heaped one on top of the other. They were positioned in front of the presider. He takes the center cake and then breaks it into smaller pieces. These wafers symbolized the bread of suffering that their forefathers ate in Egyptian bondage; and the broken nature of the bread represented the poverty of their forefathers in Egypt; they never possessed a full loaf. They had only fragments to eat.

At this point in the Passover the presider says, "This is the bread of affliction which our forefathers ate in the land of Egypt. Whosoever is hungry, let him come and eat; whosoever is in need, let him come and eat the Passover with us."

Notice the high degree of symbolism in the broken bread. It truly is the bread of affliction, but only in a symbolic or representative manner. It reminded the present worshippers that their forefathers ate the bread of suffering in Egypt. But not for one minute did they entertain the notion that the bread really and literally changed into the bread of affliction that their forefathers ate in Egypt. Instead the Jew who ate the Passover bread would in his own mind make the broken bread of the meal represent or symbolize the spiritual things of the Exodus. He turned the bread he ate into the vehicle of remembering his forefathers in Egypt and how God saved them. He acted just as if he was back there in the year 1447 B. C. in Egypt, suffering along with the fathers of Israel. Therefore, in that phrase, "This is the bread of affliction," it meant to him: "This bread symbolizes the suffering and the salvation that our fathers experienced in the land of Egypt." In his meditation around the Passover table the Jew was, so to speak, transported in some celestial time-machine back to the fifteenth century B. C. He was there when the Israelites suffered under the Pharaohs; he was there when they cried out to God for deliverance; he was there when the ten plagues brought the might and splendor of Egypt to its knees; he was there when they walked out of Egypt, freed by God their Savior; he was there as God delivered them from the power of the Egyptians at the Red Sea. The Passover brought the glorious truths of redemption right before the worshipper's eyes.

5. The Proclaiming was intended to be a running explanation or narrative of what the Passover meal represented (Exodus 13:8). This was the solemn duty of every father. He explained to his son in the presence of all gathered together what the Passover meant. This is strictly commanded of every Jewish father in Exodus 13:8.

Then the son would respond:

> Why is this night different from other nights? For on all other nights we eat leavened or unleavened bread, but on this night only unleavened bread. On all other nights we eat any kind of herbs, but on this night only bitter herbs. On all other nights we eat meat roasted, stewed or boiled, but on this night only roasted.

The father would answer:

A wandering Aramaean was my father (Deuteronomy 26:5).

And then, beginning with the story of Abraham, he would tell the history of the Jewish nation all the way down to the deliverance from Egyptian bondage.

38

6. They all join in singing Psalms 113-114, the first part of the "Hallel" (which means "praise God" and is made up of Psalms 113-118). This whole section of Scripture is truly a rich portion of God's Word. All Israelites had to memorize these seven Psalms from youth, never to be forgotten.

7. The second cup, called the "Proclaiming" cup, was received. It was called this because it always followed the Proclaiming portion of the ritual. This may very well have been the cup mentioned in Luke 22:17.

8. All who wish to partake of the Passover meal now wash their hands. Everything before this was merely pre-paratory; now the meal proper begins.

9. The presider offers this prayer of thanksgiving: "Blessed art Thou, O Lord our God, who bringest forth fruit from the earth. Thou who hast sanctified us with Thy commandment, and enjoined us to eat small pieces of unleavened bread." Now they all eat the little pieces of unleavened bread that have been distributed by the presider.

10. More bitter herbs are eaten (see point number 3).

11. They now eat the "sop". That is, some bitter herbs were put between two pieces of unleavened bread and dipped into the charosheth and eaten. This item figures pro-minently in the Last Supper of Jesus (see John 13:26ff.; Matthew 26:23; Mark 14:20).

12. The Passover lamb is now eaten. This meal was often called the feast for hungry men, for no one was al-lowed to eat any food from the time the priests in the Jeru-salem Temple sacrificed the Passover lambs—which could be as early as midday—until the time the Passover meal began—which must be after 6:00 P. M. And the entire lamb had to be consumed; they could leave nothing for the next

day. If any portions remained after the Passover ended, they must be burned up (Exodus 12:10). For the Passover lamb could not be used for any common purposes; it was very sacred and holy.

13. After the lamb is eaten, the worshippers wash their hands again (see point number 8).

14. The rest of the unleavened bread is now broken (see point number 4). This fact appears in the Last Supper of Jesus (see Matthew 26:26; Mark 14:22; Luke 22:19). It is the bread that is broken by our Lord to begin the Lord's Supper.

15. The presider offered to God a lengthy thanksgiving prayer for the entire meal. This most probably was the prayer that our Lord gave as He broke the bread in the Lord's Supper. "And when He had taken some bread and given thanks" (Luke 22:19). The Jews from the first century A. D. onward would always end this portion of the Passover with a petition that God would send the promised Elijah to herald the coming of the Messiah (Malachi 3:1; 4:5). Our Lord, however, did not do that, for He had declared that Elijah had already come in the person and ministry of John the Baptist (Matthew 11:14; Mark 9:13; see Luke 1:17). Jesus proclaimed that He Himself is the Messiah promised of old in the Prophets. The Jews, to this present day, still retain this petition for God to send Elijah, since they reject Jesus as the Messiah; this prayer not even God will answer for He has already sent the Messiah Jesus.

16. The third cup, called the "Thanksgiving" cup, was now given to the Passover company to drink. Then the presider would offer this prayer: "Blessed art Thou, O Lord our God, King of the universe, who hast created the fruit of the vine." Most probably this third cup is the one that our

Lord used as the cup of the Lord's Supper (see Matthew 26:27-29; Mark 14:23-25; Luke 22:20). It was often called the "cup of blessing" or the "cup of thanksgiving" by the Jews. And the Apostle Paul called the cup of the Lord's Supper the "cup of blessing which we bless" (1 Corinthians 10:16-17; or the "cup of thanksgiving for which we give thanks"—NIV).

17. The worshippers now sing the rest of the Hallel, Psalms 115-118, and the "Great Hallel" (Psalm 136). Then the fourth and final cup was received. This singing may be what the Synoptics refer to when they say that Jesus and His disciples sang a "hymn" and then went out to the Mount of Olives (Matthew 26:23; Mark 14:20).

18. Finally, two prayers are offered, the second of which is as follows: "The breath of all that lives shall praise Thy name, O Lord, our God. And the spirit of all flesh shall continually glorify and exalt Thy memorial, O God, our King. For from everlasting to everlasting Thou art God, and beside Thee we have no king, redeemer, or savior."

In summarizing the relationship between the Passover and the Lord's Supper, we see that both stressed a memorial meal that caused the worshippers to remember how God had saved them in the past. And the more we study the elements involved in the Lord's Supper, the more we can see how much Jesus used the Passover motif in the Lord's Supper. Truly the Lord's Supper is the "New Passover" for the Church—God's "New Israel." This will have great importance later on when we look at the proper interpretation of the words, "This is My body," and "This is My blood."

THE TIME WHEN JESUS INSTITUTED
THE LORD'S SUPPER

Here we are concerned with chronology, the time when Jesus instituted the Last Supper. There is a problem that arises when one compares the statements of the Synoptic Gospels (Matthew, Mark, and Luke) with those in the Gospel of John. They appear to contradict each other, and scholars for centuries have tried to resolve this difficulty. Well, what is the problem and how can it be solved?

We have already seen the clear-cut testimony of the Synoptics: Jesus took the Passover when all the Jews in Jerusalem took it.

However, John seems to say that the Jews had not yet eaten the Passover when Jesus was on trial. For instance, he says, "They led Jesus therefore from Caiaphas into the Praetorium, and it was early; and they themselves did not enter into the Praetorium in order that they might not be defiled, but might eat the Passover" (John 18:28). Jesus had already eaten a sacred meal with His disciples the night before, but the Jews had not yet eaten the Passover; that seems to be what John means here. Furthermore, John 19:14 states that it was "the day of preparation for the Passover" when Jesus appeared on trial before Pilate; that is, the trial of our Lord occurred on the day before all Jerusalem ate the Passover.

Some scholars have maintained that John deliberately plays loose and easy with the historical sequence here so he can make Jesus die on the cross as the Lamb of God (1:29) at the very same time that the Passover is sacrificed by the High Priest in the Jerusalem Temple (John 19:36).

Now that we have seen the problem, let us look at the options we have for possible solutions.

42

Some maintain that both accounts are not trustworthy and must be rejected, leaving us with little knowledge of what really happened.

Others declare that the two accounts hopelessly contradict each other, but John is correct; the Synoptics are wrong.

Finally, we are told that there are two different calendars in Judea; the Synoptics follow one and John the other.

Frankly, I am turned off by all these so-called solutions. The last one mentioned has some merit, but the evidence seems weak. However, I would like to offer a possible solution that does enjoy adequate evidence, and also harmonizes the seeming contradiction.

I believe that the Passover occurred as the Synoptics say it did, that Jesus and His disciples observed the Passover at the very same time all the other Jews did, and John really does not contradict these facts. One needs to understand what John means when he talks about the "Passover" and "the day of preparation for the Passover." And then the problem goes away. The Synoptics and John harmonize perfectly.

First, the witness of the Synoptics is quite definite. They proclaim that the Jerusalem priests killed the Passover lambs in the Temple on Thursday afternoon (3:30-5:50 P. M.) on the fourteenth day of Nisan. Then on Thursday evening (6:00 P. M. to midnight), all Jerusalem eats the Passover meal on the fifteenth day of Nisan at the very same time Jesus and His disciples do. On Friday morning, they begin to eat the seven-day "Feast of Unleavened Bread" (see Leviticus 23:5ff.).

The clear-cut statement of Mark 14:12; Matthew 26:17; and Luke 22:7 that the Passover lamb was slain on the day Christ made preparation to eat in the upper room, together

43

with the repeated declarations that Jesus died on "Preparation" day before Sabbath or Saturday (Matthew 27:62; 28:
1; Mark 15:42; Luke 23:54; John 19:31, 42; 20:1) and
that the day following this Sabbath was Sunday, establishes
Thursday night as the time when Christ ate the Last Supper
during the Passover Feast, and Friday as the day of His
crucifixion. Thus, the Last Supper that Jesus celebrated
with His disciples in the upper room was truly a Passover
meal and was observed while all other Jews in Jerusalem
were keeping their Passover meals. Jesus died the day after
the Passover meal.

And John really does not differ with these facts. The
term "Passover" can mean any one of the following three
things: 1) the lamb slain (Exodus 12:21; Deuteronomy
16:5; Mark 14:12; Luke 22:7); 2) the meal itself that
occurred after sunset on the fifteenth day of Nisan (Exodus
12:21; Leviticus 23:5; Numbers 28:16; Matthew 26:2, 17-
19; Mark 14:1, 14-16; Luke 22:8, 11, 15; John 12:1; 13:
1) and finally 3) the seven-day Feast of Unleavened Bread
(John 2:13; 6:4; 11:55; 18:39; Luke 22:1; Acts 12:1).
And it seems to me that John 18:28 and 19:14 refer to
"Passover" in that third meaning. John does not mean
Jesus died the day before all Jerusalem ate the Passover
meal itself (the second "Passover" meaning); rather he
means Jesus died the day before the seven-day Feast of
Unleavened Bread began (the third "Passover" meaning).
John agrees with the Synoptics that all Jerusalem, including Jesus and His disciples, had already eaten the Passover
meal itself (the second "Passover" meaning) on the night
before He died. The New International Version reflects this
view by translating the word "Passover" as "Passover week"
in John 19:14.

In John 19:31, 42, the Apostle explains what he means by that term ("preparation"). He means Friday, the day just prior to the Sabbath day, just as the Synoptics do.

The meal referred to in John 18:28, which kept the Jews from entering the Praetorium lest they might be defiled, is not the Passover feast itself (the second "Passover" meaning). For they had already eaten it the night before. But it is most probably the "chagigah" feast which would occur before sunset on the next day after the Passover meal and during the Feast of Unleavened Bread (Numbers 28: 16-23; Leviticus 15:1-24; 16:26-28; 17:15-16).[31]

Therefore John is harmonized with the Synoptic Gospels. There is no need for us to look at the meal Jesus and His disciples ate as some kind of "kiddush" or "haburah" or special pre-Passover Passover (Christ's own "do-it-Yourself") meal. Jesus simply ate the Passover with His disciples at the same time that the rest of the Jews ate it.[32]

Only one difficulty exists with this proposed solution: there is no evidence in Scripture that the word "Passover" was ever used to mean the Feast of Unleavened Bread

---

31. For more information about this controversial topic, see Leon Morris, "Additional Note H," *The Gospel According to John. The New International Commentary on the New Testament* (Grand Rapids: Wm. B. Eerdmans Publishing Company, 1971), pp. 774-785; N. Geldenhuys, *Commentary on the Gospel of Luke. The New International Commentary on the New Testament* (Grand Rapids: Wm. B. Eerdmans Publishing Company, 1950), pp. 649-670; Theodor Zahn, *Introduction to the New Testament* (Edinburgh: T. and T. Clark, 1909), 3:272-283, 296-298; A. J. B. Higgins, *The Lord's Supper in the New Testament* (London: SCM Press, 1952), chapter two; Joachim Jeremias, *The Eucharistic Words of Jesus* (Philadelphia: Westminster Press, 1955), chapter one; George Ogg, *Historicity and Chronology in the New Testament* (London: S. P. C. K., 1965); Rupert Clinton Foster, *Introduction and Early Ministry* (Grand Rapids: Baker Book House, 1966), pp. 199ff.

32. Jeremias, chapter one; Morris, pp. 779-782.

alone without the Passover meal; the word "Passover" in its third meaning always refers to the Passover meal itself plus the Feast of Unleavened Bread.[33] In spite of this weakness, I still maintain that this solution offers fewer difficulties than any other. It offers a far more reasonable way of harmonizing the Synoptics and John.

_____

33. Morris, p. 779.

2

THE NAMES FOR THE LORD'S SUPPER

We gain a much better view of the meaning of the Lord's Supper when we inquire into its names. They reveal to us what God Himself thinks of this sacred feast. They also help us to keep our own language pure, calling Biblical things by Biblical names.

THE LORD'S SUPPER

Paul himself, inspired by the Holy Spirit, calls it the "Lord's Supper" (1 Corinthians 11:20). As he condemns the Corinthian Christians for the selfish and irreverent manner in which they observed this feast, Paul declares: "This is not to eat the Lord's Supper." It was supposed to be the Lord's Supper; that was what God had called this feast. But they had so corrupted it that the meal they ate was

47

anything but "the Lord's Supper." The "Lord's Supper" is its divine name.

This is a most fitting title for this sacred meal. It shows us two things: it is a "supper," and it is Christ the "Lord's" supper. In order to understand this rite more fully, we need to look at this title more closely.

First, it is a "supper." As anyone knows, a supper is a stated meal for the body; it nourishes the body so that we can live and work. The soul needs its nourishment also. And God has graciously provided the Lord's Supper as the marvelous means of grace by which our souls are fed. It is food from heaven. When the Christian reverently eats the broken bread and drinks the fruit of the vine, he receives divine nourishment to his soul. It feeds and strengthens and edifies his spiritual life. He grows in the grace and knowledge of our Lord and Savior Jesus Christ through the Supper; of course, the Lord's Supper is not the only way we receive such blessing, but it is one of the most important.

Yes, the Lord's Supper truly feeds our souls. This idea must be maintained persistently, for some mistakenly think that the Supper is a "mere memorial." They claim that it carries no more meaning than, say, a wedding ring on the finger: a mere memorial that actually communicates nothing to the soul. But they err in this. It is truly a "supper" that gives the soul power for victorious Christian living.

Second, it is the "Lord's" supper; belongs to Christ. He gave it to us. He nourishes us through it. And if we would receive any benefit from it, we must recognize that Jesus is Lord of our lives. We must own Him as Lord and King, the sovereign Ruler of all we are. The sanction of this meal comes from the authority of Christ the Lord; and the substance of this meal comes from the grace of Christ the Lord. We celebrate it in obedience to Him, in remembrance of Him, and for His praise. Justly is it called the "Lord's Supper"! For it is the Lord Jesus who sends the invitation, who makes the provision, who gives the blessings. In it we feed upon Christ, for He is food for our souls; we feed with Christ, for He is our constant companion and friend; and He it is who graciously welcomes us to His banquet table. Truly He is the very center of this meal. Therefore, let us come to the Table with our eyes to Him, to the Lord Christ, and to the remembrance of His name. We see nothing here if we do not taste the love of Christ. We must behold the Lord Jesus as the Alpha and Omega, the First and the Last, the Beginning and the End, the All in All. If we do not meditate upon the Lordship of Jesus as we take the loaf and cup, we may have the supper—but not the Lord's Supper.

THE COMMUNION

In 1 Corinthians 10:16-17, we find that at the Lord's Supper we truly have a "sharing" in both the blood and the body of Christ. "Is not the cup of blessing which we bless a sharing in the blood of Christ? Is not the bread which we break a sharing in the body of Christ?" The Greek word translated "sharing" here also means "participation, fellowship, communion" (koinonia). So this feast may be Scripturally called the "Communion." As we gather around the Table of the Lord, we truly commune with Christ. However, it could just as accurately be called the "Fellowship," the "Participation," and the "Sharing." But we seem to enjoy using the title "Communion" or "Holy Communion" rather than these others.

The Lord's Supper is called "Communion" for two excellent reasons: in it we truly have communion with Jesus and with our fellow Christians. Let's look at this more carefully.

49

In this holy feast we have precious and sweet communion with the Lord Jesus. He here manifests Himself to us and gives to us His graces and blessings and comforts; we here set ourselves before Him, and offer Him the grateful returns of love and duty. As we partake, an intimate bond or "common union" develops between our Lord and us. We share things that we both have in common. Jesus dwells in us through His Holy Spirit; and we abide in Christ by faith and love. We are one. And the Supper knits us to Christ ever more strongly as we faithfully remember our Lord's death each Sunday. But this communion presupposes friendship; for how can two walk together unless they be agreed (Amos 3:3)? We must, therefore, in the bond of an everlasting covenant, join ourselves to the Lord, and combine our interest with His; and then make His concerns our own, His goals our own.

But this communion is not only with the Lord; it is also with our fellow Christians as we gather together around the Lord's Table each week. As Paul reminds us, in the Lord's Supper we remember that "since there is one bread, we who are many are one body; for we all partake of the one bread" (1 Corinthians 10:17). And we confess this grand truth every time we partake of the Holy Communion. Our love goes out to all fellow Christians, regardless of race, color, or location; we are united to all the Church, both past and present and future. The Supper of the Lord causes us to focus our minds upon that unity for which our Savior so earnestly prayed in John 17:20-21. We should be concerned to preserve and to increase and to improve Christian love and benevolence as we meditate on the Lord's Supper, making it truly a time of communion, fellowship, and unity.

EUCHARIST

When Jesus instituted the Lord's Supper, He offered to the Father a prayer of thanksgiving (Luke 22:17; 1 Corinthians 11:24). And this is the essential truth captured in this title. For the English word "eucharist" comes from the Greek word that means "thanksgiving."

I am well aware of the problem that some people have with this title. Since the Roman Catholics often use it, some people refuse to use it at all. Their idea seems to be that if the Catholics like it, then there must be something wrong with it. Well, just because the Catholics brush their teeth, does not necessarily mean that we must knock ours out! Although the New Testament never specifically calls the Supper by this name, I believe the idea of thanks giving in the title certainly appears throughout the pages of the Word. For Jesus definitely gave thanks for the Supper, and so should we. Therefore, "eucharist" beautifully describes the meaning of this feast.

Jesus gave thanks for the Lord's Supper. Though our Savior, when He instituted this feast, had full knowledge of the agonies and tortures He was about to endure at Calvary, yet He did not forget to thank God for this sacred meal. He was so confident of the victory He would win over Satan that Jesus gave thanks for the Lord's Supper—the holy "eucharist."

And we must also give thanks as we partake of the Supper. It is designed to be an ordinance of thanksgiving appointed for the joyful celebration of Christ's death and His power to save sinners. At the Passover meal, the Jews thanked the Father frequently, as we have already shown. And we should do no less than they. Therefore, let us come to the Table and sing to the Lord in this blessed feast. Let the high praises of our Redeemer be in our mouths and in our hearts. For thanksgiving is the very essence of the Lord's Supper. Let it do its wondrous work in these hearts of ours so that complaints turn into praises and grumbling is transformed into gratitude.

THE TABLE OF THE LORD

In the Old Testament the phrase, "the table of the Lord," appeared as a descriptive title for the Temple altar (see Malachi 1:7, 12; compare Ezekiel 41:22; 44:16). But in the New, this title is used only of the Lord's Supper. In 1 Corinthians 10:21, it is used to describe that feast in contrast to the table of demons or pagan idol-feasts.

And since the Old Testament used this title of the altar, some people have maintained that the Lord's Supper ought to be called an "altar." Lutherans often call it "the blessed sacrament of the altar." Roman Catholics usually speak of the table on which the Mass is performed as the "blessed altar."

However, such terminology is foreign to the New Testament. Nowhere does it call the Supper an "altar." Although some have claimed that Hebrews 13:10 so teaches it ("We have an altar, from which those who serve the tabernacle have no right to eat"), upon closer examination this text refers to the cross of Christ, as the context clearly shows.

But the essential truth revealed by the title, "the table of the Lord," is clear. The Lord's Supper, while not an altar, is the Lord's table, a sacred feast lovingly provided for us by our precious Savior Himself. He invites us to dine with Him. It is a high and holy privilege that we should never take lightly. Since it is His table, only those who belong to Him should partake.

52

THE FEAST

Although most Christians do not prefer to call the Lord's Supper by such a title as the "Feast," yet it is a fitting description of that holy banquet. In 1 Corinthians 5:7-8, Paul says: "Clean out the old leaven, that you may be a new lump, just as you are unleavened. For Christ our Passover also has been sacrificed. Let us therefore celebrate the feast not with old leaven, nor with the leaven of malice and wickedness, but with the unleavened bread of sincerity and truth." In this text, the Apostle is not limiting his discussion to the Lord's Supper; here Paul speaks generally of the entire Christian life: it is a "feast" which, much like the Passover meal, omits all leaven (that is, wickedness and malice) and includes only unleavened bread (that is, sincerity and truth). But, of course, included in the Christian life in general, we can see the Lord's Supper in particular. For the Supper is truly a feast that is eaten. Those who partake of it are said to feast with us. The guests are many, the invitation solemn, and the provision rich and plentiful, and so it may well be called a feast of souls. The entire nature of the Lord's Supper is wrapped up in this beautiful word, "Feast." It seems to be a Scriptural name for the Table of the Lord. We would do well to use this title more than we do to describe the Lord's Supper.

By comparing the Lord's Supper with the different feasts mentioned in the Old Testament, we gain a clearer idea what it is all about.

First, it is a royal feast, much like the one given by King Xerxes (or Ahasuerus) in the book of Esther: a magnificent banquet. According to Esther 1:4, the purpose of that royal Persian feast was to display the "riches of his royal glory and the splendor of his great majesty." And

53

in an even greater way, the Supper of the Lord is a royal feast, designed to display the unsearchable riches of Christ, the treasures hidden in Him and the glories of the Redeemer. At a royal feast the provisions, we may be sure, are plentiful and abundant, rich and noble, such as befits a king to offer his subjects. And so it is in the Lord's Supper: Christ gives like a king.

Therefore, let us remember that in this "Feast" we sit to eat with the Ruler and Sovereign of the entire universe, with a Ruler of rulers. He gives us all we need. Our need is great, but His royal feast is even greater. Truly Jesus is all we need. Let us behave ourselves well as we sit with the King; He is Lord!

Second, it is a memorial feast, much like the Passover meal, of which it is said: "Now this day will be a memorial to you, and you shall celebrate it as a feast to the Lord; throughout your generations you are to celebrate it as a permanent ordinance" (Exodus 12:14). The divine act of delivering Israel out of Egyptian bondage was a work of wonder never to be forgotten; the Feast of Unleavened Bread was therefore invented by the Lord to be observed annually throughout all the ages of the Old Covenant as a solemn memorial of that grand deliverance, that the truth of it being confirmed by this might never be questioned. But our redemption by Christ from sin and hell is a greater work of wonder than that was, more worthy of remembrance, and yet more apt to be forgotten. This sacred meal, the Lord's Supper, was thus instituted by Christ at the close of the Passover meal to be a standing memorial in the Church of the glorious achievements of the Redeemer's cross, the victories obtained by it over the powers of darkness, and the salvation produced by it for the children of light.

Third, it is a feast of dedication, much like the feast that Solomon made when the Jerusalem Temple was built

(1 Kings 8:65-66). And even when the second Temple was erected by Zerubbabel and Joshua (Ezra 3:2-13: 5:2; 6:16-22), the children of the Captivity "celebrated the dedication of this house with joy" (Ezra 6:16). In the Lord's Supper, we dedicate ourselves to God as living temples (1 Peter 2:1-6), temples of the Holy Spirit (1 Corinthians 6: 18-20), separated from all that is unholy, and entirely devoted to the service and praise of God in Christ. To show that we do this with cheerfulness and satisfaction, and that it may be done with all reverence, this feast is appointed. Then we shall go, like the children of Israel when Solomon dismissed them from his feast of dedication, "joyful and glad of heart for all the goodness that the Lord had shown to David His servant and to Israel His people" (1 Kings 8:66).

Fourth, it is a feast upon a sacrifice. The law and the custom of sacrifices, both among the Jews and in other nations, was to offer the beast that was slain, sprinkle its blood, burn the fat and other selected parts of it upon the altar, give the priest his share of it, then the remainder was given back to the offerer to eat as a feast upon a sacrifice. Paul refers to such sacrifices when he writes, "Look at the nation Israel: are not those who eat the sacrifices sharers in the altar?" (1 Corinthians 10:18). And the Lord's Supper is similar to such feasts. For Jesus Christ is the great and only Sacrifice, who by being offered once for all, perfected forever those who are sanctified (Hebrews 10:14); this offering need never be repeated; it is perfect and complete all by itself—once for all. And the Lord's Supper is a feast upon this sacrifice. That is, we give consent to and take sweet comfort in the method which infinite wisdom has taken for saving us by the blood of Jesus. That was the essence of the Old Testament feast upon a sacrifice: the worshipper received comfort and joy from it, knowing that his sins were gone by means of the blood sacrifice made. In feasting upon the sacrifice, we apply the benefit of it to ourselves and ascribe the praise of it to God with joy and thankfulness.

Finally, the Lord's Supper as the "Feast" is a feast upon a covenant. The covenant or solemn agreement between Isaac and Abimelech was made with a feast (Genesis 26:28-30). So was that between Laban and Jacob (Genesis 31:43-54). And in the Lord's Supper we are admitted to feast with God, in token of the reconciliation between us and Him through Christ. Though we have provoked God, and been enemies to Him in our minds by wicked works, yet He thus graciously provides for us, to show that now He has reconciled us to Him (2 Corinthians 5:19-21). Therefore, the Supper is a token and pledge that we stand in His sight as blameless and holy and forgiven. We are in the New Covenant.

THE BREAKING OF THE BREAD

The final name for the Lord's Supper in Scripture is the "Breaking of the Bread" (Acts 2:42; 20:7; see 1 Corinthians 10:16). This phrase is a specifically Jewish expression, meaning originally the beginning of a meal, and then the meal as such. After the head of the Jewish household gave thanks to the Lord for the food, he broke the bread (see Isaiah 58:7; Jeremiah 16:7; Lamentations 4:4) and then distributed the little pieces of it to the ones at the table with him. Since bread was the main food staple in the Old Testament times, the expression "to break the bread" meant "to share a common meal with him."

All of the accounts of the institution of the Lord's Supper (Matthew 26:26; Mark 14:22; Luke 22:19; 1 Corinthians 11:23ff.) stress the introductory phase of this sublime ordinance by saying that Jesus took bread, said thanks over it ("blessed" in Matthew and Mark), broke it, and gave it to His disciples. Since the breaking of the loaf became symbolic of the broken body of Jesus on the cross, it is therefore understandable that this general Jewish expression— "the breaking of the bread"—became a specific and technical term for the Lord's Supper alone in the early Church. Its appearance from the very beginning of the Christian Church's existence (Acts 2:42) shows that it was probably the oldest title for the Lord's Supper. By the year A. D. 110, it had become the primary name for this sacred feast (Ignatius, *Epistle to the Ephesians,* 20:2; and the *Didache,* 14:1).

The breaking of the bread I consider essential to the proper performance of this solemn and significant ceremony. Because this act was designed by our Lord to shadow forth the wounding, piercing, and breaking of His body upon the cross, and as all this was essentially necessary to the making of a full atonement for the sin of the world, so it is of vast importance that this apparently little circumstance—the breaking of the bread—should be carefully attended to, that the godly communicant may have every necessary assistance to enable him to discern the Lord's body, while engaged in this most important and divine of all God's ordinances. Since this is so, I do wish and pray that we would return to the excellent practice of having bread on the Lord's Supper tray for the worshipper himself to break with his own hands. To me that seems so much more meaningful than our present practice of taking these "celestial chiclets." They serve no worthy purpose other than they are convenient. They cannot easily be broken. The symbolism of Christ's broken body is ruined when we pick up one of these teeney-weeney little bits of hard dough and plop it into the mouth. And that is their main problem. I think that Christ wants the individual worshipper to see the bread actually broken right before the eyes—yea, verily, to break that bread ourselves. Then it will truly be called "the Breaking of the Bread." How can we call it that when we never actually break the bread? Who does not see that one small cube of bread, previously divided in some mechanical contraption in an unseen factory somewhere in the world, can never answer the purpose of the Lord's Supper? Mankind is naturally a dull and heedless creature, especially in spiritual things, and has need of the utmost assistance of his senses, in union with those expressive ceremonies which the Holy Scripture—not tradition—has sanctioned, in order to enable him to arrive at spiritual things through the medium of earthly symbols. Therefore, let us strive to restore to our churches the action of the breaking of the bread, and not merely the name itself. Let us actually do what the name says: break the bread. It will mean so much to us when we do.

The names for the Lord's Supper suggest grand spiritual lessons for us to ponder upon. Any one of these names might be used in our Communion meditations; they provide rich blessings.

PART II

CHRIST'S PRESENCE
AT
THE LORD'S SUPPER

3

THE UNBIBLICAL VIEWS

In this chapter we are concerned with the manner of Christ's presence in the Lord's Supper. Christianity has always believed that in some sense Jesus is present in this Feast. And the reason for this faith is found in the Words of Institution: "This is My body," and "This is My blood." Jesus called the bread and the cup His body and blood. So in some way He meant to show us that He is present at the Communion.

But how is He present? There is the real difficulty. How do we properly explain the nature of the Lord's Supper? Then we get into a lot of heated debate. This problem is so acute that it has been the battleground for numerous church controversies. It has become a source of disunity and contention among Christians throughout the centuries of church history. What was originally designed to be the mark of brotherly love and unity among Christians (1 Corinthians 10:16-17), has instead become the source of hostility and disagreement.

The battle lines have been drawn between three groups: the Roman Catholic, the Lutheran, and the Calvinistic interpretations of Christ's presence in the Lord's Supper.

We will study their views in this chapter. No attempt will be made to refute them here; that will occur in the next chapter. All we seek now is to discover what these church fellowships believe about Christ's presence in the Eucharist.

THE ROMAN CATHOLIC VIEW

The Eucharist holds a high place of honor in the Roman Catholic Church. In fact, the lofty doctrines of the Trinity and the Incarnation and the Eucharist form an inseparable triangle. The Supper of the Lord is thus equal in importance to these two other doctrines.[1]

This importance of the Supper in Catholic theology can also be seen in the fact that Christ's glorified humanity is communicated to the believer by this sacred feast. True, all seven sacraments in Catholicism do this. Yet, "the Eucharist is the sacrament par excellence . . . ."[2] The Supper could never be considered as merely equal with the other six sacraments of baptism, confirmation, penance, extreme unction, holy orders, and matrimony,[3] since it is esteemed a

---

1. Joseph Pohle, "Eucharist," *The Catholic Encyclopedia,* edited by Charles G. Herbermann and others (1913), 5:573.

2. Marie-Joseph Nicolas, *What Is the Eucharist?* Translated by R. F. Trevett (New York: Hawthorn Books, 1960, p. 121.

3. The term "sacrament" throughout this chapter means the same thing as it does in all of Catholicism: an outward sign of an inward grace given through Jesus to the soul. This outward sign has such inherent, objective power that it works *ex opere operato* (by the mere mechanical performance of the act itself) so long as the properly ordained Roman Catholic priest exercises the right "intention."

unique sacrament head and shoulders above all the others.[4]

The seven sacraments answer this question: how can the glorified, ascended Christ who is now bodily absent from His people come close to them on earth? But the Eucharist, according to Catholic theology, is really the Sacrament of sacraments. Through it "Christ makes His presence . . . actively visible and tangible too."[5] Through this meal, the Catholic believes he receives a true, bodily communication of Christ's presence.

When we understand this, we can easily see that the Roman Catholic affirms the physical presence of Jesus in the Eucharist. This is called the "central dogma" of the Lord's Supper.[6] Although their view is often misunderstood by non-Catholics, in this section we will attempt to be fair to them as well as accurate. It will discuss first the fact and then the evidence for the bodily presence of Jesus in the Eucharist, as proclaimed by Roman Catholicism.

The Fact of the Real Presence

Throughout this section and this chapter, the phrase "real presence" means only one thing: the physical body of Christ is really and truly present in the bread and cup.

Catholicism has authoritatively and definitely expressed its full explanation of Christ's presence in the Supper. They call their view "transubstantiation." It is found in the Council of Trent's decree on the Lord's Supper as stated in 1551. It says:

---

4. Wilfrid F. Dewan, "Eucharist," *The New Catholic Encyclopedia*, edited by William J. MacDonald and others (1967), 5:600.

5. Edward Schillebeeckx, *Christ the Sacrament of Encounter with God* (third edition; New York: Sheed and Ward, 1963), p. 49.

6. Pohle, p. 573.

In the first place, the Holy Synod teaches, and openly and simply professes, that, in the august sacrament of the holy Eucharist, after the consecration of the bread and wine, our Lord Jesus Christ, true God and man, is truly, really, and substantially contained under the species of those sensible things.

And because that Christ, our Redeemer, declared that which He offered under the species of bread to be truly His own body, therefore has it ever been a firm belief in the Church of God, and this holy Synod doth now declare it anew, that, by the consecration of the bread and of the wine, a conversion is made of the whole substance of the bread into the substance of the body of Christ our Lord, and of the whole substance of the wine into the substance of His blood, which conversion is, by the holy Catholic Church, suitably and properly called Transubstantiation.[7]

What does this authoritative decree mean? 1) The essence or "substance" or invisible inner nature of the bread and the wine (since Catholics rarely use grape juice in their Masses) are miraculously changed into Christ's physical flesh and blood after the Catholic priest properly consecrates the bread and the wine. 2) However, the accidents or "species" or outer physical properties of the bread and wine stay the same. They never change. Even after the priest consecrates the loaf and cup, the taste, color, smell, and appearance of bread and wine stay as they always were. 3) The basis of this view is the words that Jesus spoke during the institution of the Lord's Supper: "This is My body," "This is My blood."

Some well-meaning Protestants have claimed that if we put the consecrated bread and wine under a microscope, this "scientific test" would refute the whole Catholic

---

7. *The Council of Trent,* 13:1, 4; cited in Philip Schaff, *The Creeds of Christendom with a History and Critical Notes* (New York: Harper and Brothers, 1877), 2: 126, 130.

position. They assume that they have destroyed transubstantiation completely once they prove scientifically that the consecrated elements will possess the chemical properties of bread and wine—not flesh and blood. This argument, however, does not even put a tiny dent into the Catholic's armor. For he affirms that only the essence of the elements are changed—not the accidents. And all a scientific microscope can show is the outward properties of matter; no scientist can peer into the mysteries of the essence of things. All Catholics agree with us that the scientific analysis shows the chemical properties of bread and wine in the elements, before and after the priest has blessed them. Therefore, such an argument as advocated by some Protestants is simply wrong; we should never employ it.

The sixteenth century Council of Trent also declared that Christ's entire body and soul and spirit and divinity is eaten in the Eucharist. This view, which is called "Concomitance," forms a part of transubstantiation. The bread may be eaten all by itself alone—without the wine—and the worshipper will still eat the whole Christ, body and soul and spirit and divinity. Trent stated it as follows:

> If any one denieth, that, in the sacrament of the most holy Eucharist, are contained truly, really, and substantially, the body and blood together with the soul and divinity of our Lord Jesus Christ, and consequently the whole Christ; but saith that He is only therein as in a sign, or in figure, or virtue: let him be anathema.[8]

The doctrine of concomitance seems to the Catholic a logical conclusion of the words found in John 6:57, "he that eats Me, the same shall live by Me." Since Christ in this passage does not specify what part of Him is eaten (whether

---

8. *Council of Trent,* 13. canon 1; cited by Schaff, 2:137.

body or soul or divinity), the Catholic believes it refers to the entire Christ.[9] The doctrine of concomitance originated with Anselm of Canterbury, and then Thomas Aquinas formalized it. However, over a century before Trent ever came along, the Council of Constance (1415) had used concomitance to impose upon all true Catholics the "communion under only one kind (or species)." The "laity" could not receive the consecrated wine; they could eat only the bread. This council feared that since the bread and wine are "truly and really and substantially" the flesh and blood of Christ, what would happen if some clumsy peasant out there accidentally spilled the consecrated wine upon the ground and some mice came along and ate it? Why, it would be the epitome of sacrilege and blasphemy! And they were right, of course, if the dogma of transubstantiation was correct. So the Council of Constance decreed that only the officiating priest at the Mass will eat the bread and drink the wine; all other worshippers will be permitted to receive the consecrated bread alone—not the wine. And this council used the doctrine of concomitance to make this restriction legitimate. For someone can receive only the consecrated bread and not the wine, and still receive the whole Christ. That is the doctrine of concomitance in practical terms.

Needless to say, transubstantiation presented some problems for Catholics in the Middle Ages. For ever since it was first made a formal doctrine in 1215 by Pope Innocent III, transubstantiation caused several philosophical difficulties. First, how could the accidents or outward physical appearance (color, smell, shape, size of something exist without its substance or essence? Even to think of such a possibility

---

9. Pohle, p. 578.

boggles the imagination. Their only answer was that given by the great Medieval theologian, Thomas Aquinas: it is a miracle performed by God when the Catholic priest ministers at the Mass and at no other time. The second problem caused by transubstantiation was the question, "How can Christ's glorified human body, which is in heaven at the right hand of the Father, also exist everywhere in the world wherever Catholic Masses are performed? How can a local body possess omnipresence, the ability to exist everywhere at the same time, a characteristic that only a divine spirit has? The Medieval scholars of the Catholic Church adopted the view of Guitmund at Aversa and of Alger that the glorified body of Christ in heaven also possesses the ability to be everywhere at once. His flesh can be wherever He wants it to be.[10] And why not? He is God, isn't He? That was their argument. The presence of Christ in the Supper was a unique presence; His humanity could take on the ability of His divinity to be everywhere in countless pieces of bread and cups of wine all over the world at the same time. Just as the doctrine of transubstantiation is a unique miracle in which the accidents exist without their essence and vice versa, so the doctrine of Christ's omnipresent human body is a unique miracle occurring only at the Catholic Mass. In the words of the Council of Trent:

> For neither are these things mutually repugnant,—that our Savior Himself always sitteth at the right hand of the Father in heaven, according to the natural mode of existing, and that, nevertheless, He be, in many other places, sacramentally present to us in His own substance, by a manner of existing,

---

10. See Herman Sasse, *This Is My Body: Luther's Contention for the Real Presence in the Sacrament of the Altar* (Minneapolis: Augsburg Publishing House, 1959), p. 38, where the relevant quotations from Guitmund and Alger appear.

which, though we can scarcely express it in words, yet, can we, by the understanding illuminated by faith, conceive. . . .[11]

This is the Roman Catholic view of transubstantiation.

The Evidence for the Real Presence

The Roman Catholic does have evidences for his views about transubstantiation; they are from two sources: 1) Scripture, and 2) Tradition.

The Evidence from Scripture

The Roman Catholic uses the Words of Promise (John 6) and the Words of Institution (Matthew 26:26-28; Mark 14:22-25; Luke 22:20-22; 1 Corinthians 11:23-32) as his two primary Biblical sources for proving the Real Presence dogma in the Lord's Supper.

1. John 6. This chapter in the New Testament contains Christ's discourse on the Bread of Life given in the synagogue at Capernaum. Often the Catholic calls this chapter the "Words of Promise" or the "Words of Prophecy," to distinguish it from the "Words of Institution" in the Synoptics and Paul, because in John 6 Jesus promises or predicts the institution of the Supper before it actually occurred.[12]

---

11. *The Council of Trent,* 13:1; cited by Schaff, 2:126.

12. Nicolas, p. 20; Pohle, p. 582; Casimir Bernas, "Eucharist," *The New Catholic Encyclopedia,* edited by William J. MacDonald and others (1967). 5:598; *A Debate on the Roman Catholic Religion Between Alexander Campbell and John B. Purcell* (Nashville: McQuiddy Printing Company, 1914), pp. 363-364.

John 6 has two levels of thought: 1) in the first level, Jesus speaks of feeding upon Himself as the Bread of Life (vv. 26-50). Catholics and non-Catholics agree that this part of the sermon must be interpreted figuratively. Here Jesus meant that to feed upon Him is to believe in Him. No informed students of Scripture believe that in John 6:26-50 Jesus discusses the Lord's Supper. 2) However, in the second level, John 6:51-65, the Catholic theologian claims that Jesus changes the subject; He now begins talking about the Real Presence dogma in the Eucharist. Since this second level describes a Eucharistic eating, and since Jesus states such phrases as "unless you eat the flesh of the Son of Man and drink His blood" (John 6:53), the only type of presence Christ has in the Lord's Supper is a physical one, which can be called transubstantiation. That is the Catholic position. Thus, as the author of one of the most brilliant Catholic treatises on transubstantiation has declared, in John 6:51 the "Catholic maintains that, at this point, a total, though natural change of subject takes place, and a perfect transition is made from believing in Christ, to a real eating of His body and drinking of His blood, in the Sacrament of the Eucharist."[13]

What evidence exists in John 6 that leads to such a view? Although the Council of Trent never pronounced that this chapter concerns the dogma of the Eucharist, most Catholics give the following seven arguments for seeing a literal, physical eating of Christ's flesh and blood in the Mass.

a. The context and structure of John 6 demands such an interpretation. Jesus discusses three kinds of food that

---

13. Nicholas Patrick Stephen Wiseman, *The Real Presence of the Body and Blood of Our Lord Jesus Christ Proved from Scripture* (New York: O'Shea, 1874), p. 40.

are distributed to others by three different individuals. The foods consist of the manna eaten in the Old Testament era by the Israelites (John 6:31-32, 49, 59), the heavenly bread that Jesus gives to all who believe in Him (John 6:32-50; the first level of John 6), and the flesh and blood of Jesus that He will give at some future time (John 6:27, 52). Three persons give out these foods: Moses gives manna to the Israelites, God the Father gives Jesus as the Bread of Life to nourish man's faith, and then Christ Himself provides His own flesh and blood. Since Jesus will give to mankind a third and future food, this must be none other than the Eucharist. This food is His flesh and blood. So the words in John 6:51ff. "are in fact far too realistic and contain too many undertones of the words of Eucharistic institution to be merely a metaphor for faith in the person of Christ."[14]

b. The realistic expressions used in John 6 require a transubstantiation dogma. Nowhere does Jesus say that there is anything figurative or symbolic about His words throughout this chapter. Rather, so claims the Catholic, He used the most realistic expressions to make His point. These include such strong terms and phrases as "I will give" (v. 51; in the Gospel of John the verb "give" sometimes means "to give in sacrifice" as in 3:16; 6:27, 51; 10:28; 17:2; and therefore in John 6 this may be a hint of the Eucharistic sacrifice of the Mass), "drink My blood" (vv. 53-56), and "he who eats My flesh" (vv. 54, 56-58). And Jesus uses the Greek word *trogo* ("eat" in vv. 54, 56-58; see also John 13:18; Matthew 24:38), which means "munch," "crunch," "chew," and "eat audibly." This word never appears in John 6:32-50 (first level), but it does in verses 54-58 (second

---

14. Bernas, p. 598.

level), thus tending to confirm the Catholic position. For the Catholic affirms that if the view is right and John 6:32-50 is not about the Eucharist, then *trogo* should not occur in those verses. Also, he affirms that if his view is right and John 6:51-65 is about physically eating Christ's flesh and drinking His blood in the Eucharist (through transubstantiation), then *trogo* should occur in those verses. And this is exactly the way it really is; *trogo* is not in verses 32-50 but is in verses 51-65.[15]

Therefore the use of these strong, realistic expressions by Jesus in John 6:51-65 verifies the Catholic view. These verses teach the Real Presence dogma in the Mass.

c. The relationship between the Manna and the Eucharist throughout John 6 seems to prove the Real Presence doctrine. The contrast between the manna and the Lord's Supper appears to prove this. The manna is the type and the Supper is the anti-type. The Roman Catholic maintains that if Jesus viewed the manna in the days of Moses as a type of the future ordinance of the Lord's Supper, then "the latter must have been something more than merely blessed bread, as otherwise the prototype would not substantially excel the type."[16] What the Catholic means here is that throughout the Bible, the New Testament anti-type is always superior to the Old Testament type; Christ the anti-type is always superior to Moses the type. Therefore, there must be something about the Eucharist that is better than the manna. And that something is the Real Presence dogma of transubstantiation in the Lord's Supper.

d. A fourth argument used by Roman Catholics to prove that John 6:51ff. teaches transubstantiation is that all other

---

15. Pohle, p. 574; Bernas, p. 598; Dewan, p. 603.

16. Pohle, p. 574; the first one to use this argument was the great seventeenth century Catholic scholar, Robert Bellarmine, *On the Eucharist*, 1:3.

interpretations of the words, "eat My flesh and drink My blood," fail to make any sense; the figurative view, therefore, is wrong. For in the Bible the figurative meaning of such a phrase as this usually denotes the act of persecution, hateful murder, and vengeance. In Psalm 27:2 those who come to "devour" the "flesh" of David are called "evil-doers," "adversaries," and "enemies" (compare also Psalm 14:4). Micah 3:3 describes the vain, greedy leaders of Israel who afflicted the poor unjustly by these words: "And who eat the flesh of my people" (compare Ezekiel 34:3-5). And all commentators, both Catholic and Protestant, would agree that the figurative sense of the phrase, "eat my flesh," is the cruel and sinful actions of one's enemies against him.[17]

The same point appears from the way the Old Testament uses the phrase, "eat My blood." When God at times must severely chastise and punish certain people, He will make them "drunk with their own blood as with sweet wine" (Isaiah 49:26; see Revelation 16:6).

The Catholic now asks, "In John 6 is Jesus saying that His enemies, those who eat His flesh and drink His blood in a figurative manner by persecuting and hating Him, will reap the reward of eternal life, according to the promise revealed in John 6:54? Of course not. Such an interpretation would be absurd." Thus, since the figurative view of John 6:51-56 provides no rational meaning to Christ's words, the Catholic maintains the literal interpretation of these passages.

e. The Catholic claims that the early Christians and Ecumenical Councils of the first eight centuries held to the literal view of John 6:51-65.[18] The Council of Ephesus (431)

---

17. Pohle, p. 574: Wiseman, pp. 64-66.
18. Bernas, p. 598.

and of Nicea (787) adopted the Catholic meaning of these words in John 6. However, the Council of Trent never did dogmatically define this passage.

The witness of the early Christians and of the church councils forms an important basis to a Catholic, since he feels that these were led by the Holy Spirit to interpret the New Testament properly. "Tradition," that is, the writings of the venerable Fathers of the early church, is often considered as authoritative as Holy Scripture to the Catholics.

f. The Catholic points also to the reaction of those who heard Christ speak these words in the Capernaum synagogue. This one main argument is used most often by them to prove that John 6 teaches the doctrine of transubstantiation. In fact, this seems to be the main objection of the Capernaum multitude. They argued among themselves by saying, "How can this man give us His flesh to eat?" (John 6:52). The important point is that Christ, after hearing this objection, never watered down His previous statement; instead, He reinforced His discourse by emphasizing the literal eating of His flesh and drinking of His blood to receive eternal life (verses 52-56). This is the Catholic position. According to them, Jesus never said they had misinterpreted His words; He never admitted that He had been merely using figurative language in verses 50-51. Then, when the people further complained by saying, "This is a difficult statement; who can listen to it" (John 6:60), Christ "rather reproached them for their want of faith, by alluding to His sublimer origin and His future Ascension into heaven" (compare John 6:61-62).[19]

---

19. Pohle, p. 574; cf. *A Debate on the Roman Catholic Religion Between Alexander Campbell and John Purcell,* p. 365.

73

Often the following points will be added by the Catholic. Several times during the personal ministry of Jesus, the disciples interpreted a figurative saying of Christ in a literal way, and then asked Him about it. Whenever this occurred, He always would explain the intended figurative meaning to them. This takes place in John chapter 3. Nicodemus takes Christ's words about the new birth literally, and thus asks, "How can a man be born when he is old? He cannot enter a second time into his mother's womb and be born, can he?" (v. 4). The Savior then explains His words in such a manner that Nicodemus can see those words are to be interpreted figuratively (v. 5). Other such examples of this can be found in Matthew 16:6, 11; 19:24; Luke 12:1; John 11:11; 8:21, 32, 40, 44.

However, when someone correctly understood Christ's words literally, and objected, then Jesus always repeated them; He never explained them. Matthew 9:2 illustrates this point. Jesus had just declared that a certain paralytic's sins were forgiven. Then, after this was interpreted literally by the scribes, as it should have been, they objected to it by charging Jesus with blasphemy. Here our Lord does not explain Himself, but stands His ground by repeating His words and by confirming them through a miracle (verses 5-7; see also John 8:56). As Wiseman expresses it, "The two rules, then, are sufficiently clear; when His hearers, misunderstanding His words, raise objections, Jesus explains them; when understanding them right, they find fault, He repeats them."[20]

With these two rules in mind, the Catholic holds that Christ never accused His audience of misunderstanding His

---

20. Wiseman, p. 99.

words in John 6; He merely repeated them in still stronger terms.

g. Finally, the Catholic refutes the Protestant view of John 6:51-65, and especially verse 63. Most Protestants believe John 6:63, "the flesh profits nothing," proves that Jesus wants us to interpret verses 53-56 figuratively. To them, this verse means that if someone ate Christ's flesh and blood literally and physically in the Supper, it would not benefit the soul at all.

The Catholic responds to this position by making a negative and then a positive answer. First, in a negative way, the Catholic maintains that verse 63 could not possibly mean what the non-Catholic thinks it means. For the multitude certainly never interpreted verse 63 in this manner. Also, Jesus never said, "My flesh profits nothing," which is what the Protestant view would require. He said, "The flesh profits nothing."[21] He was not talking about His own flesh in verse 63.

Second, in a more positive manner, the Catholic interpretation follows either one of three possible avenues: 1) Following some early Christian writers, the Catholic Church maintains that in John 6:63 "the true Flesh of Jesus is not to be understood as separated from His Divinity, and hence not in a cannibalistic sense. . . ."[22] According to this view, Jesus teaches the people of Capernaum that He is not to be eaten in a merely physical way. Transubstantiation, according to this isn't cannibalism; besides that, they believe their doctrine of concomitance protects them from being vulnerable to this charge, for it maintains that the entire

---

21. Pohle, p. 574; Dewan, p. 603.
22. Pohle, p. 574.

Christ is eaten—body, soul, and divinity. Cannibalism ("sarcophagy"), so we are told, is when you eat only Christ's flesh—and not His soul and divinity. 2) Another "more scientific explanation" holds that "flesh" in John 6:63 refers to the carnal-minded attitude of the sinner.[23] Through the indwelling presence of the Holy Spirit, the Church will be enabled to have true communion with Christ, since the flesh profits nothing but the Spirit gives life. Mere external eating of Christ's flesh and blood is not enough— one must also have faith while participating in the Eucharist. The explanation follows the Pauline theme of "flesh" verses "Spirit." 3) John 6:63 teaches that Christ's flesh and blood edify and feed the spirit of man—not man's body or "flesh." Although the doctrine of the Real Presence is still in this third view, the main thrust of the argument is that Christ's flesh and blood nourish the spirit of man.[24]

Whichever of the three explanations of John 6:63 is accepted as the best, the Roman Catholic view of this text forbids watering down Christ's realistic words in John 6:51-65.

2. Besides John 6, the Catholic Church believes that evidence for transubstantiation appears in the "Words of Institution," the very words used by our Lord when He originally instituted the Lord's Supper (see Matthew 26:26-28; Mark 14:22-24; Luke 22:19-20; and 1 Corinthians 11:23-28).

---

23. Pohle, p. 574.; Jean Giblet, "The Eucharist in St. John's Gospel (John 6)," *The Breaking of the Bread,* edited by Pierre Benoit and others, translated by John Drury, volume 40 of *Concilium: Theology in the Age of Renewal* (New York: Paulist Press, 1969), p. 669; Dewan, p. 603.

24. Nicolas, p. 21.

The Catholic interprets these words literally. "This is My body" means exactly that. When Jesus spoke these words, He performed a miracle of turning the bread into His literal flesh. And so with the wine. He transformed it into His very blood. In the words of Wiseman,

> We believe that the body and blood of Jesus Christ are truly and really present in the adorable Eucharist, because, taking bread and wine, He who was Omnipotent, said, "This is My body, this is My blood." Here is our argument; and what can we advance to prove a strict accordance between our doctrine and that of our Savior, stronger and clearer than the bare enunciation of our dogma beside the words which He used in delivering it? "This is My body," says our Lord: "I believe it to be Thy body," replies the Catholic.[25]

They will defend the literal interpretation of these Words of Institution by using the following seven arguments.

a. The literal interpretation is required by the fact that no explanatory words are given that might suggest a figurative view. Never do Matthew, Mark, Luke, or Paul add some such phrase as "Jesus really meant that this symbolized His body" to explain Christ's words of institution. In fact, they all record that Jesus said, "This is My body"—not "This bread is My body," which would destroy the Catholic argument here. Whenever two material objects (such as "bread" and "body") are said to be identical, the text must be interpreted figuratively. However, the Catholic affirms, in the Words of Institution Christ does not say there are two material objects present; He says there is only one, "This is My body." He does not mention the bread.

This point is further strengthened by the fact that the Greek word for "this" *touto* cannot refer to "bread" *artos*, since the gender of both is different; "this" is in the neuter

---

25. Wiseman, pp. 155-156.

gender, while "bread" is in the masculine. Since in Greek a pronoun ("this") must agree with its noun ("bread") in gender and number, therefore "this" cannot possibly refer to the "bread." So Christ did not mean that the bread is His body.[26]

b. The literal interpretation is required by what Paul says in 1 Corinthians 11:27. "Therefore whoever eats the bread or drinks the cup of the Lord in an unworthy manner, shall be guilty of the body and the blood of the Lord." When the Apostle penned those words, he must have believed in the Real Presence. For how can you offend or insult someone who is physically absent? The only way you can be guilty of Christ's body and blood is if He is physically present already when you partake of the Eucharist. Only a belief in the Real Presence of Jesus in the Lord's Supper could do full justice to such a text.[27]

c. The literal interpretation is required by the fact that even Martin Luther himself was compelled by the Bible to interpret the Words of Institution literally. He fully aceepted the Real Presence of Jesus in the "Sacrament of the Altar." The Catholics will quote him to give credibility to their own dogma, even though Luther condemned the theory of transubstantiation frequently.

---

26. Wiseman, pp. 155-156; Bellarmine, *On the Eucharist,* 1:10, whose words are quoted in John Harrison, *An Answer to Dr. Pusey's Challenge Respecting the Doctrine of the Real Presence in Which Greek Catholics, Ritualists and High Anglo-Catholics, Are Examined and Shown to Be Contrary to the Holy Scriptures, and to the Teaching of the Fathers of the First Eight Centuries, with the Testimony of an Ample Catena Patrum of the Same Period* (London: Longmans, Green and Company, 1871), 2:319-320.

27. Victor Warnack, "Symbol and Reality in the Eucharist," *The Breaking of the Bread,* edited by Pierre Benoit and others, translated by Clement Dunne, Volume 40 of *Concilium: Theology in the Age of Renewal* (New York: Paulist Press, 1969), p. 85; Nicolas, pp. 17-18.

d. The literal interpretation is required by the rules for figurative language. The Catholic will contend that there are three rules governing the use of figurative language in literature. These are: 1) Figures of speech are used only when a figurative meaning is made clear from the nature of the subject under discussion. For instance, when someone points to a statue of Abraham Lincoln and then says, "This is Lincoln," it is fairly obvious that the person is speaking figuratively. 2) Figures of speech are used only when a figurative meaning is made clear by means of colloquial expressions. For instance, when someone says, "This glass is water," you know they are using the figure of speech called "synecdoche" (naming the container but meaning that which is contained); the glass container really is not water, but what is contained in the glass is water. 3) Figures of speech are used only when a figurative meaning is made clear by simply declaring that one is using figurative language. For instance, when someone declares, "I am only speaking figuratively," you can tell they must not be taken literally.

The Catholic maintains, however, that none of these three rules for figurative language applies to the Words of Institution. In fact, the weight of this argument is so strong that many Catholic scholars use it alone as the all-sufficient proof of transubstantiation.

To make this argument even stronger, the Catholic refers to the additional ideas that our Lord attached to His Words of Institution. Christ says that this is His body "which is given for you" (Luke 22:19) or "which is for you" (1 Corinthians 11:24), and this is His blood "which is to be shed on behalf of many for forgiveness of sins" (Matthew 26:28; Mark 14:24). That is to say, the same physical body of

79

Jesus that would be nailed to the cross was given to the Apostles in the Upper Room.[28]

e. The literal interpretation is required by the reactions of the Apostles as they heard the Words of Institution. Since the Apostles were simple, unlearned men who were unskilled in the art of language-interpretation ("hermeneutics") and philosophy, they needed a clear word from their Master. They needed a literal word, a word free from the uncertainties of figurative language. It is only reasonable to assume here that Christ met their need by speaking in literal terms—without any figurative meanings hidden under the surface. If, instead, He spoke to them in figurative terms, why didn't He reveal clearly what He meant? Surely, claims the Catholic, Jesus knew by divine foreknowledge that His Church (the Catholic Church) would interpret His words literally to teach the Real Presence by transubstantiation. Why did He not make His meaning plain by telling the Apostles that He spoke figuratively?

f. The literal interpretation is required by the rules for interpreting last wills and testaments. Part of the standard practice of judges and lawyers in the interpretation of disputed passages in all last wills and testaments is to take the said passage in its literal sense. This rule of interpretation is founded upon the maxim that most men, when they are dying or fast approaching death, wish to speak in the clearest, most unambiguous words, so as not to confuse anyone. And at the Last Supper, Christ was quickly approaching death; the Supper was part of the New Covenant in His blood (Matthew 26:28). And therefore the Catholic confidently maintains that Christ must have spoken in literal

---

28. Pohle, p. 575; Anthony J. Maas, *The Gospel According to St. Matthew with an Explanatory and Critical Commentary* (second edition; St. Louis: B. Herder, 1916), p. 271.

language—not figurative—when He introduced the Lord's Supper.

g. The literal interpretation is required by the fact that all figurative attempts end in utter failure. The Catholic shows this by citing more than two hundred different views that come out of a figurative interpretation of the Words of Institution.[29] All of them contradict each other hopelessly. The only way out of such confusion is to adopt the literal view of these words; take the Catholic view as your own and all will be clear and unconfusing. There is comfort in transubstantiation.

Through these seven arguments, the Roman Catholic Church has defended its literal view of the Words of Institution. For these reasons, it maintains transubstantiation.

The final proof of transubstantiation is Tradition, the ancient witness of the early Christian writers and councils.

The Evidence from Tradition

The second major source of evidence for proving the doctrine of transubstantiation is Tradition. They affirm boldly that all the Church Fathers and Ecumenical Councils of the first eight centuries of Christianity maintained the Real Presence dogma. The position of the Catholic Church on this point is quite clear. In the words of Wilfred Dewan, "The early writers were absolutely convinced of the Real Presence of Christ in the Eucharist."[30] In a similar vein, after discussing the witness of the Fathers to the Eucharist, Cardinal Franzelin concludes by saying:

---

29. Pohle, p. 575; cites the book written by Christopher Rasperger entitled *Ducentae verborum "Hoc est corpus meum" interpretationes* (1577), where these two hundred views appear. Bishop Purcell claimed that the number was more like 2,000; see the *Campbell-Purcell Debate*, p. 363.

30. Dewan, p. 604.

I think it sufficiently proved from all which has been said that the faith whereby we profess the change in the substance and the removal of the bread and wine was always in all antiquity as universal as the faith concerning the real presence of the body of Christ, and that this presence was never understood in any other way than that Christ the Lord, in the institution of the most holy Sacrament, by changing the bread and wine themselves made them to be His body and blood in the sense already frequently explained.[31]

Thus Franzelin claims the Fathers from the very beginning proclaimed not only the Real Presence but also transubstantiation.

1. Ignatius of Antioch (110) is the earliest writer cited by the Catholics to believe in the Real Presence of Christ in the Lord's Supper. In condemning the heretics known as the "Docetists," who denied that Christ possessed a true flesh and blood human body, he writes: "They abstain from eucharist (thanksgiving) and prayer, because they allow not that the eucharist is the flesh of our Savior Jesus Christ, which flesh suffered for our sins . . . ."[32] Here he seems to use his belief in Christ's Real Presence in the Eucharist as an argument to prove that He had a human body. If Ignatius did not believe in the Real Presence dogma, his argument would be worthless. We know that Jesus had a human body made of natural flesh and bone, because the Church partakes of this flesh in the Lord's Supper.

---

31. Franzelin, *Tractatus de SS. Eucharistiae Sacramento et Sacrificio,* p. 233, cited by Darwell Stone, *The Holy Communion. The Oxford Library of Practical Theology* (London: Longmans, Green and Company, 1904), p. 46, n. 1.

32. Ignatius, *To the Smyrneans,* 6:3, translated and edited by Joseph Barber Lightfoot, *The Apostolic Fathers* (Grand Rapids: Baker Book House, 1967 reprinted), p. 84; see also *Patrologiae Cursus Completus . . . Series Graeca Prior,* edited by Jacques Paul Migne (Paris, France: Garnier Brothers, 1894), 5:847-848. All future citations from Migne will appear as *PG* (for the Greek series) or *PL* (for the Latin series).

2. Justin Martyr (140) is usually cited as an early witness of the change that occurs in the elements of bread and wine. They are converted into the flesh and blood of Jesus. He says,

> This food amongst us is called Eucharist . . . for we do not receive it as common bread or as common drink, but in that way Jesus Christ our Savior, being through the Word of God incarnate, had both flesh and blood for our salvation, so also have we been taught that the food, over which thanksgiving has been made by the prayer of the word which is from Him, (from which food our blood and flesh are by transmutation nourished), is the flesh and blood of Him, the Incarnate Jesus.[33]

Here he shows, according to the Catholic interpretation of his words, that just as Christ had a true flesh and blood body which expired on the cross for the sins of the world, even so Jesus has a real physical presence in the Eucharist. After the consecration of the elements, they are the flesh and blood of Jesus. A true conversion has occurred in them. This is nothing less than transubstantiation.

3. Irenaeus of Lyon (in France or Gaul; 167) was the pupil of the renowned Polycarp. Dewan holds that Irenaeus "took for granted the reality of Christ's sacramental presence" and from there argued that the gift of resurrection is given to the body through the Eucharist.[34] The Catholics claim that the clearest proof of such a belief appears in that grand work that Irenaeus wrote against both the Docetists and the Gnostics, called *Against Heresies*. He used the same argument that Ignatius did, namely, that Christ's real

---

33. Justin Martyr, *First Apology*, 66:2, in *The Ante-Nicene Fathers. Translations of the Writings of the Fathers Down to A. D. 325,* edited by Alexander Roberts and James Donaldson, revised by A. C. Coxe (American reprint of the Edinburgh edition; Buffalo: Christian Literature Company, 1886), 1:185; All future citations from this work will appear as *ANF. See* also Migne, *PG*, 6:427-430.

34. Dewan, p. 604.

body is present in the Lord's Supper. Therefore, the Lord has a mortal body.[35]

Also, Irenaeus appears to believe in a change of the bread and the fruit of the vine so that they become the flesh and blood of Christ. He declares,

> For as the bread, which is produced from the earth, when it receives the invocation of God, is no longer common bread, by the Eucharist, consisting of two realities, earthly and heavenly, so also our bodies, when they receive the Eucharist, are no longer corruptible, having the hope of the resurrection to eternity.[36]

Transubstantiation provides us with the life-giving flesh and blood of Christ; the Supper will give us a new body.

4. Cyprian of Carthage in Northern Africa (248) declares the Real Presence dogma more than any of his predecessors. He proclaims his views while the problem of backsliding Christians (due to severe persecution) is in the background. Therefore, he declares that if lapsed Christians do not repent but still partake of the Holy Eucharist, then "violence is done to His body and blood, and they sin now against their Lord more with their hand and mouth than when they denied their Lord."[37]

Afterwards he lists the many tragic punishments that would befall those who had profaned the Eucharist, and the stories he tells show that he believed completely in the Real Presence of Christ.[38] Commenting on the Lord's Prayer,

---

35. Irenaeus, *Against Heresies*, 4:17.5, in *ANF*, 1:484; see also Migne, *PG*, 7:1023-1024.

36. Irenaeus, *Against Heresies*, 4:18.5, in *ANF*, 1:486; see also Migne, *PG* 7:1027-1029; cf. *Against Heresies*, 5:2.2-3, in *ANF*, 1:528; see also Migne, *PG* 7:1124-1128.

37. Cyprian, *On the Lapsed*, 16, in *ANF*, 5:441; see also Migne, *PL*, 4:493-494. *Epistle*, 15:1, in *ANF*, 5:295; see also Migne, *PL*, 4:271-272.

38. Cyprian, *On the Lapsed*, 25, in *ANF*, 5:444; see also Migne, *PL*, 4:499-500.

Cyprian says that Jesus is the Church's bread because "He is the bread of us who touch His body."[39]

5. Athanasius of Alexandria (330), the reputed "Pillar of the Church" (according to Gregory of Nazianzus), also talked of Christ's physical presence in the Supper. He affirmed that a true change takes place in the elements of bread and wine; they are converted into Christ's flesh and blood. In a fragment said to have been written by him, he says:

> You will see the Levites bringing loaves and a cup of wine, and placing them on the table. So long as the prayers and invocations have not yet been made, it is mere bread and a mere cup. But when the great and wondrous prayers have been recited, then the bread becomes the body and the cup the blood of our Lord Jesus Christ . . . . when the great prayers and holy supplications are sent up, the Word descends on the bread and the cup, and it becomes His body.[40]

6. Cyril of Jerusalem (350), more than all the others before him, specifically taught the Real Presence, as claimed by the Catholic. After he referred to 1 Corinthians 11:23-25, Cyril writes:

> For you have just heard him say distinctly, that our Lord Jesus Christ in the night in which He was betrayed, took bread, and when He had given thanks He brake it, and gave to His disciples, saying, Take, eat, this is My body; and having taken the cup and given thanks, He said, Take, drink, this is My blood. Since then He Himself declared and said of the bread, This is My body, who shall dare to doubt any longer? And since He has Himself affirmed and said, This is My blood, who shall ever hesitate, saying, that it is not His blood?

---

39. Cyprian, *On the Lord's Prayer*, 18, in *ANF*, 5:452; see also Migne, *PL*, 4:548.

40. Athanasius, *Sermon to the Baptized*, cited by J. N. D. Kelly, *Early Christian Doctrines* (second edition: New York: Harper and Row, 1960), p. 442.

He once in Cana of Galilee turned the water into wine, akin to blood, and is it incredible that He should have turned wine into blood? When called to a bodily marriage, He miraculously wrought that wonderful work; and on the children of the bride-chamber, shall He not much rather be acknowledged to have bestowed the fruition of His body and blood?

Wherefore with full assurance let us partake as of the body and blood of Christ: for in the figure of bread is given to thee His body, and in the figure of wine His blood; that thou by partaking of the body and blood of Christ, mayest be made of the same body and the same blood with Him. For thus we come to bear Christ in us, because His body and blood are distributed through our members; thus it is that, according to the blessed Peter, we become partakers of the divine nature.[41]

Cyril claimed that the Real Presence came upon the elements and produced a changing or converting of them. Thus most Catholic scholars hail him as the first to explain the transformation as a "transubstantiation" (*metaballesthai*).[42] Just as Jesus turned water into wine at the wedding feast in Cana of Galilee (John 2:1-13), so "shall we not believe Him when He changes (*metabalon*) wine into blood?" Catholics have often employed this analogy; for instance John Purcell used it in the Campbell-Purcell debate in 1837.

7. Ambrose of Milan in Italy (374) in the West stressed a change of the elements to become the physical flesh and blood of Christ in the Eucharist. He remarks that "through the mystery of the sacred prayer they are transformed into flesh and blood."[43] The term translated as "transformed"

---

41. Cyril, *Catechetical Lectures*, 22:1-3, in *A Select Library of Nicene and Pose-Nicene Fathers of the Christian Church*, edited by Philip Schaff and Henry Wace (second series; Grand Rapids: Wm. B. Eerdmans Publishing Company, 1953 reprinted), 7:151-152. All future citations from this work will appear as *PNF*.

42. Johannes Quasten, *Patrology* (Westminster, Maryland: Newman Press, 1953), 3:375.

43. Ambrose, *On the Christian Faith*, 4:125, in *PNF*, second series, 10:278.

here is the Latin word *transfigurantur* which, as Tertullian pointed out almost two centuries before, has to do with the real conversion of a thing into an entirely different mode of existence.[44] Though he may still talk about the Supper as signifying Christ's body (*corpus significatur*) and as portraying a "likeness" (*similituninem*) of His flesh and blood, Ambrose emphasizes the conversion. After the elements are consecrated by the priest, a supernatural event—a holy miracle—occurs, producing an actual conversion of the elements. He says,

> Shall not the word of Christ, which was able to make out of nothing that which was not, be able to change things which already are into what they were not? For it is not less to give a new nature to things than to change them.
>
> But why make use of arguments? Let us use the examples He gives, and by the example of the Incarnation prove the truth of the mystery. Did the course of nature proceed as usual when the Lord Jesus was born of Mary? If we look to the usual course, a woman ordinarily conceives after connection with a man. And this body which we make is that which was born of the Virgin. Why do you seek the order of nature in the Body of Christ, seeing that the Lord Jesus Himself was born of a Virgin, not according to nature? It is the true Flesh of Christ which was crucified and buried, this is then truly the sacrament of His body.
>
> The Lord Jesus Himself proclaims: This is My body. Before the blessing of the heavenly words another nature is spoken of, after the consecration the body is signified. He Himself speaks of His blood. Before the consecration it has another name, after it is called blood. And you say, Amen, that is, It is true.[45]

Ambrose becomes a prominent witness of the dogma of transubstantiation; Catholics quote him frequently.

---

44. Tertullian, *Against Praxeas*, 27:7, in *ANF*, 3:623; see also Migne, *PL*, 2: 214-215.

45. Ambrose, *On the Mysteries*, 9:54, in *PNF*, second series, 10:324-325.

8. Chrysostom (390), often called the "Doctor of the Eucharist," is considered by most Roman Catholic scholars to be the one who uses the strongest language to describe the Real Presence of Christ in the Lord's Supper. In fact, Joseph Pohle groups him, Cyril, and Gregory of Nyssa together as being the three witnesses of transubstantiation who appear to "approach exaggeration."[46]

Chrysostom's view may be seen from the following typical example:

> It is no longer in the manger that the body of Christ is visible to you, but on the altar. He is no longer in the arms of a poor woman. See the priest holds him, and this body you not only see, but you touch. You not only touch it, you eat it and carry it to your homes.[47]

Also he refers to eating Christ, and even speaks of burying the teeth into His flesh and into His blood.[48] The elements of bread and wine have been refashioned or transformed into Christ's body and blood.[49]

9. Augustine of Hippo in Northern Africa (395) presents a problem to all—no matter how they might interpret the Words of Institution. He at times writes as an advocate of the Real Presence of Christ in the Eucharist, but at other times he seems to maintain a more symbolic view.

The Catholics claim that Augustine affirms transubstantiation. They state that it is unfair to neglect or to play down Augustine's many references to the Real Presence.

---

46. Joseph Pohle, p. 577.

47. Chrysostom, *Homily*, 24:8 on 1 Corinthians, in *PNF*, first series, 12:143; see also Migne, *PG*, 61:45.

48. Chrysostom, *Homily on John*, 46:3, in *PNF*, first series, 14:166.

49. Chrysostom, *The Treason of the Jews*, 1:6, found only in Migne, *PL*, 49: 380; cf. also Chrysostom's *Homily on Matthew*, 82:5, cited by Kelly, *early Christian Doctrines*, p. 444; see also Migne, *PG*, 58:744.

These "realistic" expressions include: 1) Augustine commanded that all Christians offer divine worship to the Eucharistic flesh of Christ;[50] 2) Augustine claimed that during the night when Jesus instituted the Lord's Supper He "held and carried Himself in His own hands";[51] 3) in a sermon Augustine said that his hearers should know Whom they were eating.[52] Catholics also declare that his ideas about the Eucharist went through a slow stage of development. In earlier years, he did seem to follow a symbolical interpretation, but in later years, especially when he was battling the heretics associated with Pelagianism and when he was carefully studying the works of Chrysostom, he changed his views of the Supper so much he even announced that the Eucharist was to be given to children for their salvation.[53]

Protestants often like to cite the passage from Augustine's writings which seems to deny any Real Presence belief: "To what purpose doest thou make ready teeth and stomach? Believe, and thou hast eaten."[54] It comes from his sermons on the Gospel of John. Catholic, however, answer that here is speaking only of John 6:32-50 (the first level)— not verses 51-56. Therefore, they insist that in this passage Augustine is not denying his firm belief in transubtantiation.

---

50. Augustine, *Expositions*, 4:8 on Psalm 99:5 (in the Vulgate text it is Psalm 98:5), in *PNF*, first series, 8:485.

51. Augustine, *Expositions*, 1:1 on Psalm 34:8 (in the Vulgate text it is Psalm 33:8), in *PNF*, first series, 8:75.

52. Augustine, *Sermon*, 227, cited by Kelly, *Early Christian Doctrines*, p. 447.

53. Augustine, *On the Merits and Forgiveness of Sins*, 1:26, in *PNF*, first series, 5:25.

54. Augustine, *Homilies on the Gospel of John*, 25:12, in *PNF*, first series, 7:164.

Summary of the Roman Catholic View

The Catholic Church affirms the Real Presence of Christ in the Supper; they call their view transubstantiation. The essence of bread and wine are transformed into Christ's flesh and blood. The outward appearance of bread and wine—even after the priest blesses them—remains the same; only the essence of both is transformed into Christ's flesh and blood. Their doctrine of concomitance affirms that the whole Christ is eaten—His body, soul, and divinity—whether only the bread is eaten or both the bread and wine are consumed. Although the Council of Constance in 1415 decreed that the laity will eat only the bread—not the wine, the present-day Catholic is now permitted to eat both bread and wine at the Mass.

The evidences used by Catholics to prove transubstantiation consist of Scripture and Tradition. From the Bible, they use the "Words of Promise" in John 6:51-65 and the "Words of Institution" in Matthew 26:26-28 (its parallels in Mark and Luke) and Paul's words in 1 Corinthians 11:23-25. From Tradition, they quote the early Church Fathers whose writings are given a place of high honor and authority in Roman Catholicism.

THE LUTHERAN VIEW

The Lutheran view of Christ's presence in the Eucharist resembles the Catholic interpretation. I will now discuss the ways in which the Lutheran view comes close to the Catholic position, and also how it differs.

Some have tried to explain the theological differences between the Catholic and Lutheran churches by saying that the former stresses the Sacraments, while the latter emphasizes the Bible. While some truth exists in this statement,

90

it fails to do justice to either of them. From the Lutheran perspective, this explanation overlooks the extreme importance that this Church gives to the Lord's Supper, called by them the "Sacrament of the Altar." The Lutherans give the Lord's Supper a high place of honor. This fact will become clear as we continue.

Since the contributions of later Lutherans to the doctrine of the Supper have not gone beyond those that Martin Luther first propounded, I will limit my discussion to his views.[55]

The one source for all of Luther's Eucharistic theology was the Word of God. He went to it as the all-sufficient rule of faith and practice. This not only holds true of his Lord's Supper ideas, but of all his teachings. He did not concern himself with Patrology, the study of what the early Christians believed. The Fathers of the Church did not carry much weight with him. And in the Bible, Luther felt that he found the answer to the question of how Christ is present in the Lord's Supper. By studying over and over again the Words of Institution, "This is My body" and "This is My blood," he became convinced that Jesus is physically present in the bread and wine (Lutherans, like the Catholics, do not use grape juice in the sacrament of the Altar). Luther affirmed the Real Presence of Christ in the Eucharist. In this way, the Lutheran interpretation is very close to Catholicism. Luther believed that the Words of Institution were simply too plain and too strong for him to deny the Real Presence of Jesus in the bread and the wine. For the very words themselves compelled him to affirm the Real Presence. As he himself says in his letter to the Christians in Strassburg, December 15, 1524,

---

55. See Herman Sasse, pp. 295-344 to see this fact.

That I admit: if Dr. Carlstadt or someone else had told me five years ago that in the Sacrament there is nothing but mere bread and wine, he would have rendered me a great service. I passed through great inner struggles in that respect and had to fight hard to overcome that temptation. For I was well aware that by these means I could strike the hardest blow against the papacy. Besides, there were two men who wrote to me about this in a far more able way than Dr. Carlstadt, without torturing the words according to their own ideas as he does. But I am captured by the Word of God and cannot find a way out. The words are there, and they are too strong for me. Human words cannot take them out of my soul.[56]

The Real Presence of Christ in the Lord's Supper was the very center of Luther's theology. By the year 1523, only six years after he had nailed the famous 95 theses to the church door at Wittenburg, Luther came to see this doctrine as the heart of the Gospel. The Words of Institution were "the sum total of the whole Gospel."

We will investigate the Lutheran view of the Real Presence by looking at the following two topics: 1) the Real Presence defined, and 2) the Real Presence defended. These two divisions will serve us well as we try to understand the manner of Christ's presence according to Lutheranism.

The Real Presence Defined

The Lutheran Creeds

The Real Presence is clearly spelled out for us in the Lutheran creeds; they are their most authoritative and

---

56. Martin Luther, *Werke. Kritische Gesamtausgabe* (Weimar, 1883-), 15: 394, cited by Sasse, p. 81. The most authoritative edition of Luther's writings in German, the *Weimar Ausgabe,* will be hereafter cited as *WA.* The Catholic scholar, John Purcell, quoted a similar set of words from Luther to refute the figurative interpretation of Alexander Campbell *(A Debate on the Roman Catholic Religion Between Alexander Campbell and John Purcell,* p. 377).

informative sources for the definition of this doctrine. In the Large Catechism, written by Luther in 1529, we see a succinct expression of Luther's thinking. Its fifth part explains the Eucharist. There Luther declares that the Supper is "the true body and blood of our Lord Jesus Christ, in and under the bread and wine which Christians are commanded by the Word of Christ to eat and drink."[57] The Words of Institution accomplish such a miracle. Describing their immense power, Luther here proclaims,

> With this Word you can strengthen your conscience and say: Let a hundred thousand devils, with all the fanatics, come, saying, How can bread and wine be Christ's body and blood? Still I know that all the spirits and learned men together have not wisdom to compare with the smallest degree of that of the Divine majesty. Now, we have here Christ's own words: "Take, eat; this is My body." "Drink ye all of it." "This cup is the New Testament in My blood," etc. To this we will cling, and we will see who will dare to exalt his authority over Christ's, and to alter what He has taught. While it is true that you have nothing but bread and wine if you take away the Word or if you fail to take it into consideration, it is assuredly true, likewise, that you have Christ's body and blood when Word and element remain together, as they shall and must. For as we have it from the mouth of Christ, so it is; He cannot lie nor deceive.[58]

In the Augsburg Confession, written by Philip Melanchthon (1530), the Supper is discussed in Article 10. There it says:

> Of the Supper of the Lord they teach that the (true) body and blood of Christ are truly present (under the form of bread and wine), and are (there) communicated to those that eat in the Lord's Supper (and received). And they disapprove of

---

57. *Luther's Large Catechism*, translated by J. N. Lenker (Minneapolis: Augsburg Publishing House, 1968 reprinted), p. 141.
58. *Luther's Large Catechism*, p. 142.

those that teach otherwise (wherefore also the opposite doctrine is rejected).[59]

In the year 1577, the Formula of Concord was drawn up by such eminent Lutherans as Jacob Andreae, Martin Chemnitz, and Nikolaus Salnecker. In Article 7, the doctrine of the Lord's Supper appears. It teaches that "in the Holy Supper the true body and blood of our Lord Jesus Christ are truly and essentially present, are distributed with the bread and wine . . . ."[60] All who eat it, whether they be "worthy or unworthy, godly or ungodly, believing or unbelieving," receive the physical body and blood of Christ. Furthermore, it says,

> We believe, teach, and confess that the words of the Testament of Christ are not to be otherwise received than as the words themselves literally sound, so that the bread does not signify the absent body of Christ and the wine the absent blood of Christ, but that on account of the sacramental union the bread and wine are truly the body and blood of Christ.[61]

The "almighty power of our Lord Jesus Christ" works through the Words of Institution to produce Christ's physical presence in, with, and under the elements of bread and wine. No human word or work does this.

The Mode of the Real Presence

Now that we have looked at the Lutheran creeds, we next analyze what their Eucharistic doctrine is. What

59. *The Augsburg Confession*, 10, cited by Philip Schaff, *The Creeds of Christendom*, 3:13.

60. *The Formula of Concord*. Epitome 7, in *Concordia or Book of Concord: The Symbols of the Evangelical Lutheran Church* (St. Louis: Concordia Publishing House, 1957), p. 224. All citations from this work in the future will appear as *BC*.

61. *The Formula of Concord*, Epitome, 7:3 of the Affirmations, in the *BC*, p. 224.

terminology is used by them to describe the way Christ is physically present in the Lord's Supper?

First of all, they use three prepositions to describe the manner of Christ's presence in the Supper. After the consecration of the elements, the physical flesh and blood of our Savior becomes present "in, with, and under" (*in, cum, et sub*) the bread and wine. In the Lutheran view, the essence is never changed into something else; the essence and accidents of bread and wine remain the same—both before and after the blessing. Although transubstantiation affirms the conversion of the essence of bread and wine into Christ's flesh and blood, this is rejected by Luther. The bread stays bread; the wine stays wine. The flesh and blood of Jesus are simply added to the elements. What was once bread and wine alone, after the Lutheran minister consecrates them through the Words of Institution, they now are bread-Christ's flesh and wine-Christ's blood. This is the Lutheran view reflected by the three prepositions. These three prepositions are used by Lutherans to teach only one thing: their view is not transubstantiation. Do not think that these three words are intended to express an accurate and precise theological formula. Not at all; Luther used them only for the purpose of teaching the Real Presence to little children. Actually, his only precise formula was this: "The bread is the body and the wine is the blood of Christ."[62] The three prepositions, "in, with, and under," only help the human mind to see generally the mode of Christ's presence at the Table of the Lord.

In one sense, Luther interpreted the Words of Institution literally; but yet in another sense, he interpreted them figuratively. Interpreting them literally, he believed that Christ's

---

62. Luther, *WA* 26:265, cited by Ernst Sommerlath, "Lord's Supper," *The Encyclopedia of the Lutheran Church*, edited by Julius Bodensieck (1965), 2:1339.

body is physically present in the bread and wine. But at the same time, interpreting them figuratively, he claimed that Jesus used the figure of speech called "synecdoche" when He said, "This is My body," "This is My blood." Luther said that the words of Institution are a synecdoche because the container is put for that which is contained. The bread is Christ's body because the bread contains Christ's body. The wine is Christ's blood because the wine contains Christ's blood. Luther illustrated this figure with the homely example of a child in the cradle. Just as a mother can point to a cradle and say, "This (cradle and child) is my child," even so Christ proclaimed, "This (bread and Christ's flesh) is My body."[63] Therefore, Luther technically viewed the Words of Institution figuratively, but this did not alter his firm belief in the Real Presence doctrine.

The Theoretical Details of the Real Presence

Many problems surrounded Luther as he taught his own unique view of the Lord's Supper. He was bombarded by Catholics and Protestants. For instance, how is Christ's physical body present in the Eucharist? What good is there in eating and drinking His corporal body when it is the spiritual nourishment that matters? When and how does Christ's body come into the bread and wine? How long does it remain in the elements?

And Luther's one answer to them all was this: I just do not know. The Bible does not tell us. These theoretical issues are not worthy of our speculation anyway. God's ways are not man's ways; no one can search out the paths of the transcendent God. Therefore, man must not ask

---

63. Hugh Watt, "Eucharist (Reformation and Post-Reformation Period)," *Encyclopedia of Religion and Ethics,* edited by James Hastings and others (1921), 5:565.

God the "how" and the "why" of the Real Presence of Christ in the Eucharist. The Christian simply trusts his Savior's Words of Institution that the flesh and blood of Jesus are in, with, and under the bread and wine. The believer, with a child-like faith, takes Jesus at His Word. To ask God why or how He does His mysteries is to commit the sin of pride. "For he who asks why something which God says and does is necessary surely is trying to elevate himself above God and be wiser and better than God."[64] A questioning faith will soon result in total disbelief, says Luther. Therefore, the Lutheran is never concerned about such theoretical details; he trusts God.

Yes, Luther rejected all speculative theories about the nature of the Real Presence; he also denied transubstantiation. That is certain. We can be very sure of his position there. To him, the very idea that the essence of one thing and the accidents of another thing could be joined together seemed absurd and unnecessary. So Luther taught that the Catholic position just could not be true. But what about other names for his view of the Eucharist? What did Luther and later Lutherans think of the term, "consubstantiation"? Does it accurately express their idea? And if not, what does?

Since he rejected all questions respecting the "how" of Christ's Real Presence in the Lord's Supper, Luther totally denied that any theory was a suitable description of his view. This applies to "consubstantiation" as well as to any other theory. He refused to describe Christ's physical presence in terms of any theory. Consubstantiation, a name that is sometimes used to distinguish the Lutheran view from

---

64. Paul Althaus, *The Theology of Martin Luther,* translated by Robert C. Schultz (Philadelphia: Westminster Press, 1966), p. 389; however Althaus gives no information concerning the location of this quotation in the Weimar edition.

transubstantiation, is rarely employed by Lutherans themselves.[65] Most of them dislike it. They are afraid that it might imply the formation of a third substance or the permanent union and mixture of the bread and wine with Christ's flesh and blood. The Lutheran has no trouble with the prefix "con" in this word. It means "with"; and the Lutheran certainly teaches that Christ's flesh and blood are joined "with" the bread and wine respectively. However, he has difficulty with the "substantiation" part of this name. It seems to teach some distinction between essence and accidents, as in the transubstantiation theory. And that in itself is enough to make Lutherans wary of it. Not all of them, however, reject consubstantiation. Generally speaking, they will not protest the use of this term so long as it is understood to mean the "real co-existence of the two substances, the earthly and the heavenly."[66] But since most Lutherans still have a problem with it, we would do well to drop consubstantiation from our vocabulary. It causes more problems than it solves. It was not invented by the Lutherans, as transubstantiation was by the Catholics. Dean Inge said it so well, "All labels are libels." I think the only rationale for this term is that it is a theological word that ends in "tion"

---

65. Watt, p. 565; Sasse, p. 102; Theodore Engelder, William F. Arndt, Theodore Graebner, and F. E. Mayer, *Popular Symbolics: The Doctrines of the Churches of Christendom and of Other Religions Examined in the Light of Scripture* (St. Louis: Concordia Publishing House, 1934), p. 97. One of the authors of the Formula of Concord, Nikolaus Salnecker, vehemently protested against the idea that Lutherans taught consubstantiation; he declared boldly, "Although our churches use the old expressions 'in the bread,' 'with the bread,' or 'under the bread' . . . they do not teach an '*inclusio*,' '*consubstantiatio*,' or '*delitescentia*' locally hidden . . . ." The Lutherans teach that Jesus, "when giving the bread, gives us His body to eat . . . " *(Vom heiligen Abendmahl des Herrn* [1591] Bl E 2; cited by Sasse, p. 103, n. 53).

66. Watt, p. 565; see also Sommerlath, p. 1339.

and sounds a whole lot like transubstantiation! We can live without it.

The Consecration of the Bread and Wine

In Lutheranism, as in Catholicism, the obvious companion of the Real Presence doctrine is the act of consecrating or blessing the elements. In the Catholic Church, the priest proclaims the Words of Institution, and they believe the elements of bread and wine are converted into Christ's flesh and blood. In the Lutheran Church, the same act of consecration occurs, with an emphasis upon repeating the Words of Institution. However, a different result occurs: Christ's flesh and blood enter into the elements of bread and wine without altering the substance of either. Both churches interpret the words of Institution as the means through which God's power operates upon the elements, producing Christ's flesh and blood; these words must be recited before God will perform this work, however. Thus, the Words of Institution are considered by the Lutheran, as well as by the Catholic, as being primarily words of blessing which affect bread and wine by divine power.

One major difference between the two Churches concerns the powers that reside in the officiating clergyman. In the Catholic system, all seven sacraments (and especially the Eucharist) work automatically, that is, *ex opere operato.* Thus, even an unbeliever will receive some grace and blessing from the Supper. This is because of the tremendous power that resides in the priest from his ordination and the power of the Words of Institution. In the Lutheran Churches, however, this principle is rejected. None of their three sacraments of Baptism, Eucharist, and Confession work in such a mechanical, automatic manner. They deny *ex opere operato.*

99

How Christ Is Eaten in the Eucharist

Christ is eaten physically with the mouth. This involves two kinds of eating that are always emphasized by Lutherans: the eating with the teeth and the eating by the ungodly.

First, Luther maintained that Christ's physical body is literally eaten with the mouth and teeth. This follows from his view of the Words of Institution. Christ is truly eaten with the mouth and chewed with the teeth because He said, "This is My body." Of course, Luther states, all true believers eat Jesus spiritually in the Eucharist; but this is not all. They also receive the physical flesh and blood of the Savior. And not only this, but unless you eat Christ's physical body with the teeth, you cannot receive any spiritual blessings from the Eucharist.[67] Luther felt so strongly about this that he even applauded the action of Pope Nicholas, who forced Berengar—the eleventh century opponent of transubstantiation—to confess that Christ's true body is crushed with the teeth in the Supper.[68] To Luther, this eating with the teeth is the main test of one's orthodoxy concerning the Eucharist. If you confess it, you cannot be a symbolist. This is why the oral eating and crushing of Christ's body with the teeth is such an important part of Lutheranism. It is the "shibboleth" in all debates about the Lord's Supper. To claim Christ is received by the mouth as well as by faith is simply to confess the Lutheran doctrine of the Supper.

---

67. Luther, *WA*, 23:239, cited by Alexander Barclay, *The Protestant Doctrine of the Lord's Supper: A Study in the Eucharistic Teaching of Luther, Zwingli, and Calvin* (Glasgow, Scotland: Jackson, Wylie, and Company, 1927), p. 82.

68. Luther, *WA*, 26:442, cited by Sasse, p. 162; and also by Jaroslav Pelikan, *Luther the Expositor*, the companion volume in *Luther's Works* (St. Louis: Concordia Publishing House, 1959), pp. 143-144.

Second, Lutherans declare that even the wicked partake of the physical flesh and blood of Jesus in the Eucharist.[69] This is but the logical and thoroughly consistent result of the previous doctrine, eating Christ with the teeth. Luther and the other Lutherans taught that the effect of the Real Presence upon the unbeliever is dangerous. During the Marburg Colloquy of 1529, Luther proclaimed with great force: "Christ's body is death, poison, and devil to those who eat unworthily."[70] From 1 Corinthians 10:16 Luther found proof that even the ungodly eat the flesh and blood of Christ; he says, "So this verse of Paul's stands like a rock and forcefully requires the interpretation that all who break this bread, receive, and eat it, receive the body of Christ . . . ."[71] "All," that is, includes the ungodly. Luther also based his view upon 1 Corinthians 11:27-29. This doctrine also appears in the formula of Concord. It states that all believers and unbelievers who partake of the Eucharist truly eat Christ's flesh and blood; but the latter eat "to their judgment and condemnation, if they are not converted and do not repent, 1 Cor. 11:27, 29."[72]

The Real Presence Defended

Why did Luther so steadfastly cling to the Real Presence? What were his arguments, both from Scripture and philosophy, for demanding that his interpretation is the only biblical one? This section will seek to answer these questions.

---

69. Theodore Engelder and others, p. 96; Sasse, p. 244-248.
70. Sasse, pp. 244, 248.
71. Luther, WA, 18:172, cited by Althaus, p. 385, n. 28.
72. The Formula of Concord. Epitome, 7:7 of the Affirmations in BC, p. 225.

The Main Arguments for the Real Presence

Lutherans will use the following four arguments to prove their Real Presence doctrine. These are taken from the Formula of Concord.

> The first is this article of our Christian faith: Jesus Christ is true, essential, natural, perfect God and man in one person, undivided and inseparable.
>
> The second: That God's right hand is everywhere; at which Christ is placed in deed and in truth according to His human nature, and therefore being present, rules, and has in His hands and beneath His feet everything that is in heaven and earth as Scripture says. Eph. 1,22, where no man else, nor angel, but only the Son of Mary is placed; hence He can do this and those things which we have said.
>
> The third: That God's Word is not false, and does not deceive.
>
> The fourth: That God has and knows of various modes of being in any place, and not only the one; is not bound to the one which philosophers call localis (local) or circumscribed.[73]

These four arguments will now be taken, one by one, and studied carefully in the remainder of this section.

The Union of Natures of Jesus Christ

Christians have always believed that in the person of Jesus Christ there exist two natures—the divine and human. These two natures are so perfectly joined together that there are not two Christs, but only one. This is often called the "Hypostatic Union." It is definitely taught in the New Testament itself. Notice these passages:

---

73. *The Formula of Concord.* Epitome, 7:7 of the Affirmations in BC, p. 224. This was also Luther's position: *WA,* 36:326, cited by Sasse, pp. 159-160.

"And the Word became flesh, and dwelt among us" (John 1:14); "for in Him all the fulness of Deity dwells in bodily form" (Colossians 2:9); "what was from the beginning, what we have heard, what we have seen with our eyes, what we beheld and our hands handled, concerning the Word of Life—and the life was manifested, and we have seen and bear witness and proclaim to you the eternal life, which was with the Father and was manifested to us—what we have seen and heard we proclaim to you also, that you also may have fellowship with us" (1 John 1:1-3).

And in the famous words of the fifth century Council of Chalcedon (451), Jesus Christ is

one and the same Christ, Son, Lord, only-begotten, made known in two natures without confusion, without change, without division, without separation, the difference of the natures being by no means removed because of the union, but the property of each nature being preserved and coalescing in one *prosopon* and one *hypostasis*—not parted or divided into two *prosopa*, but one . . . .[74]

Therefore, the two natures in Christ are not mingled into two substances, nor the one changed into the other, but each retains its own essential properties. None of this is new to Christianity. It has been taught by us for centuries. The Lutherans definitely are not the only ones who have ever believed in this doctrine of the Union of the Natures in Christ.

But what is unique about the Lutherans is the way they have used this doctrine to prove the Real Presence of Christ

---

74. *Acta conciliorum oecumenicorum,* edited by E. Schwartz, 2:1, 2, pp. 126-130, cited by J. N. D. Kelly, p. 340; see also Gerrit Cornelius Berkouwer, *The Person of Christ* in his *Studies in Dogmatics* (Grand Rapids: Wm. B. Eerdmans Publishing Company, 1954), pp. 66-71; Henry P. Liddon, *The Divinity of our Lord and Saviour Jesus Christ* (the Bampton Lectures of 1866; the fifteenth edition; London: Longmans, Green and Company, 1891), pp. 259-268.

in the Eucharist. They point out that Christ's body is always with His divine nature, wherever it is, even in the Lord's Supper. Because of the union of natures in Christ, His body is always joined to His divine Spirit. Never is His divinity, according to Luther, outside His humanity. The only Christ we can have is the incarnate Christ, the Christ whose flesh is always with His divine nature. To them, it is nothing short of heresy to deny the Real Presence. For that would mean the Christ is split in two. His human nature with its flesh and blood then becomes separated from His divine Spirit. And that would destroy the Union of Natures in Jesus. Therefore, the Real Presence is required by the Union of Natures in Christ. If you are to believe in the Union of Natures, you must believe in the Real Presence. To deny the Real Presence, is to deny this perfect union. Luther began his view of the Eucharist by looking at it through the glasses of the Incarnation of Christ. And when he did that he saw the Real Presence of Jesus in the Lord's Supper. This is the first proof given by the Lutherans to defend their view of the Eucharist.

The Communication of Natures in Jesus Christ

This is the direct result of the previous argument. The Communication of Natures in Jesus Christ follows logically after the Union of Natures. This is the Lutheran reasoning.

What exactly does the Communication of Natures mean? Due to the union of human and divine natures in Christ, the attributes of divinity (such as omnipresence—God is everywhere, and eternality—God is everlasting) are transferred or communicated to the humanity of Christ, and the attributes of His humanity (locality—His body is in one place, the capacity to suffer and to die) are also transferred or communicated to Christ's divinity.

Although this doctrine did not originate with Luther,[75] he is the one who aplied it to the doctrine of the Real Presence in the Eucharist. Stated generally, in connection with the controversies concerning the Supper, this doctrine was used by Luther to prove that Christ's glorified body shares the attributes of omnipresence with His divine nature. In this way, Christ's glorified flesh and blood could be present in thousands of Lutheran altars everywhere in the world. Some of Luther's opponents tried to refute him by saying that Christ's human nature (His body) is at the right hand of God, in a local place, and so it cannot be everywhere. But Luther responded that the right hand of God is everywhere, as the Formula of Concord also states. It is not a circumscribed spot in heaven, but is everywhere—on the earth, in the skies, throughout the universe.

Luther defended his view of the Communication of the Natures by the following arguments from Scripture: 1) there are texts that ascribe human attributes and activities to the divine nature of Jesus (John 1:14; Galatians 4:4; 1 Corinthians 2:8; Romans 5:10); 2) there are texts that ascribe divine attributes or activities to Christ's human nature (Matthew 16:16; Romans 9:5; John 1:14; 6:62; Matthew 28:18-20). And so, to Luther, such passages teach that the entire Son of God, Jesus Christ, really suffered and died on

---

75. The "Communication of Natures" (*Communicatio Idiomatum*) had been formulated by the Greek Church of the fourth century to explain how Christ's two natures can be united in one person. Gregory of Nazianzus had used the illustration of iron and fire to describe this union. Then Gregory of Nyssa and Leontius of Byzantium produced the doctrine itself, though never applying it in the Eucharist. The full statement of this doctrine appears in the work by John of Damascus entitled *On the Orthodox Faith*, 3:3.4; *PNF*, second series, 9:47-48; see also Migne, *PG*, 94:994-996.

the cross, really hungered and thirsted, really wept and laughed, really moved to different places. These activities are human activities, but the New Testament claims that the whole Christ did them; the divine as well as the human side of Jesus did them. Although suffering and death are not divine activities, still, due to the absolutely perfect union between Christ's divine and human natures, the entire Christ suffered and died; He truly experienced other such human activities as hunger, thirst, and fatigue. Luther contended that these expressions are not figurative; they do not mean that Christ's divine nature only seemed to suffer and die. No, Jesus really suffered and then He died. Concerning the three specific divine qualities of omnipotence (infinite power), omniscience (infinite knowledge and wisdom), and omnipresence (present everywhere at the same time), Luther claimed that the New Testament ascribes these to the humanity of Christ. The omnipotence is referred to His human nature in Hebrews 2:8; 1 Corinthians 15:27; Ephesians 1:22; Matthew 28:18-20; John 3:35; 13:3, all of which declare that the Father has put all things in subjection under Christ's feet. The omniscience is referred to His human nature in John 1:18; 3:13, 31-32, all of which teach that during the time of Christ's Incarnation His humanity was in heaven, receiving full knowledge of all things (this also teaches that His human nature received omnipresence). The omnipresence in His humanity appears in such texts as Ephesians 4:10; 1:23; Matthew 28:18-20, all of which speak of the "filling" which His humanity performs over the universe, and of the abiding presence of the whole Christ (the God-Man, the human and divine natures in Christ) with His Church scattered throughout the earth. In all of this, the Lutheran emphasizes that the context of these passages proves that the humanity of Christ is in view—not merely His divinity.

Since the Bible says that the human nature of Christ receives qualities that only the divine nature possesses, then why cannot the physical flesh and blood of Jesus be omnipresent and so descend into countless altars around the world whenever a Lutheran minister speaks the majestic Words of Institution?

The Words of Institution

This is the third proof given by the Lutheran to defend his Eucharistic view. The Words of Institution are the alpha and omega of Luther's proof for the Real Presence of Christ in the Lord's Supper. Luther invariably kept returning to these words of Christ in all his controversies. He remained a staunch defender of the Real Presence to his dying day because he was so thoroughly convinced this doctrine was found throughout the New Testament.

In studying the New Testament, Luther employed one main rule above all others: a text must always be taken literally unless such an interpretation would teach something contrary to an article of faith, or the text itself explains that the reader must interpret it figuratively. However, Luther saw that the Words of Institution, when taken literally, do not contradict any article of the Christian faith, nor do they show indication that the reader should take them figuratively. Therefore, he concluded that they must stand as they are, without any figurative interpretation (except the synecdoche figure).

In 1 Corinthians 10:16-17, Luther saw the Real Presence clearly. Of all the accounts in the New Testament of the Lord's Supper, this passage most positively expressed that view. Since this text is the inspired Apostle's explanation of

107

Christ's words, Luther felt it was a most important text. In the year 1528, He declared:

> This text I have extolled, and I do still, as my heart's joy and crown, for it not only says, "This is Christ's body," as we read in the Lord's Supper, but mentions the bread which was so broken and says, "The bread is not only the body of Christ but the distributed body of Christ." Here, now, is a text so lucid and clear that the fanatics and the whole world could not desire or demand anything more.[76]

He boldly maintained that this passage stood like a "rock" which "forcefully" compelled any honest reader to see the corporal presence of Christ's very flesh and blood contained in, with, and under the natural elements of bread and wine in the Eucharist.

The Lutherans stress the word translated "communion, fellowship, participation" (*koinonia*) in this text. They claim that it really means the true "communion of the bread with the body, of the wine with the blood of Christ."[77] This text is not talking about a fellowship of persons with persons only, but primarily the joining of the elements of bread and wine with the physical body of Christ.

Just as Luther found the Real Presence in 1 Corinthians 10:16-17, so he also found it in the other texts that record

---

76. Luther, *WA*, 26:487, cited by Althaus, p. 384.

77. W. H. T. Dau, "Lord's Supper (Eucharist): Lutheran Interpretation," *The International Standard Bible Encyclopedia,* edited by James Orr and others (1939), 3:1927. Dau also points out that a distinction exists between the two Greek terms for "fellowship" or "communion": *"koinonia"* refers to a communication of things, while *"metoche"* refers to "a participation, which would refer to the communicants" or persons. Since 1 Corinthians 10:16-17 does not use *"metoche"* but instead uses *"koinonia,"* it must refer to a communication of things; the bread and Christ's flesh are literally joined at the Lord's Supper.

Luther himself viewed the term "communion" in 1 Corinthians 10:16-17 as meaning also "distribution" of Christ's flesh and blood in the bread and wine (Pelikan, p. 152; Engelder and others, p. 96).

the Words of Institution (Matthew 26:26-28; Mark 14:22-25; Luke 22:19-20; 1 Corinthians 11:23-28).

One of the strongest arguments used by the Lutherans is that only a belief in the Real Presence would have led Paul to write these words in 1 Corinthians 11:27: "Therefore whoever eats the bread or drinks the cup of the Lord in an unworthy manner, shall be guilty of the body and the blood of the Lord." Not only this, but when Paul speaks of self-examination (v. 28) and of judging the body (v. 29), he refers to the Christian belief that the physical flesh and blood of Jesus are in, with, and under the elements of bread and wine.

Luther insisted that the Words of Institution are simple enough. No need exists for trying to find a figure of speech either in the copula ("is") or in the word "body". Actually, the Lutheran view maintains that when you study these words, no explanation is necessary; one simply lets the words speak for themselves.

Luther also contended that the words "given" and "shed" cannot be interpreted figuratively; our Savior truly gave His life and shed His blood on the cross. And since these words must be taken literally, so must those that are intimately connected with them, namely, "This is My body" and "This is My blood." For if the one is figurative, so is the other. If "this is My body" is figurative, then so are the words, "given" and "shed." And then the entire death of Jesus becomes merely figurative, and we end up casting it aside.

Luther denied that the sixth chapter of the Gospel of John concerns the Eucharist anyway. Therefore, he felt John 6:63 is irrelevant to any discussion of the Supper. However, he was convinced that John 6 did not contradict the Real Presence view.

109

Luther made almost no use of the early Christian writers in order to defend the Real Presence doctrine. In this way he differed greatly from the position taken by the Roman Catholics. He repeatedly pointed out that if the Words of Institution are true—no matter what Augustine or any Father ever proclaimed, the Real Presence is the only true doctrine of Christ's presence in the Eucharist. His partner, Melanchthon, made much use of the Patristic literature for defending the Real Presence. He cited such Church Fathers as Ignatius, Tertullian, Chrysostom, and Cyril of Jerusalem in much the same way that the Catholics had done.[78]

Summary of the Lutheran View

In some respects the Lutheran interpretation of Christ's presence in the Lord's Supper is quite close to the Catholic position. The Lutherans do hold that Christ's literal flesh and blood are physically present in the Supper, which is just what the Catholic maintains. But one can see clearly that Luther did not teach the dogma of transubstantiation. He believed that Christ's flesh and blood are in, with, and under the material elements of bread and wine. Never did he feel that the essence of bread and wine is changed or transformed into the new substance of divine flesh and blood. Luther believed that it was a heresy to deny the Real Presence of Christ in the Lord's Supper.

THE CALVINISTIC VIEW

What did John Calvin say about the manner of Christ's presence in the Lord's Supper?[79]

---

78. Sasse, pp. 313-361; see also Pelikan, pp. 120-121.

79. For information concerning John Calvin's position on the Lord's Supper, see his *Institutes of the Christian Religion*, volume 21 of *The Library of Christian*

He maintained that both the Catholics and the Lutherans are wrong. The flesh and blood of Christ are not physically present in the loaf and cup. In no uncertain terms, he condemned both views.

But neither did he claim that the Lord's Supper is a mere memorial of Christ's death. Calvin asserted that there is a real objective presence of Jesus in the action of the Eucharist. This sacred meal certainly feeds the soul. He maintained that the Words of Institution must be taken figuratively. The bread represents the body of Christ and the cup represents His blood. The literal interpretation of the Words cannot be true.

The real contribution of Calvin's view lies in the fact that although he denied the omnipresence of Christ's glorified heavenly human body (against the Catholics and Lutherans), he yet affirmed the true (but not physical) presence of Christ in the Lord's Supper. He condemned the Real Presence, but he affirmed the True Presence of Christ in the elements of bread and wine to the earnest believer.

The "Dynamical" View of Calvin

Calvin's view may best be described as the "Dynamical" view. That is, he believed that the "dynamic" or power or energy or life-giving virtue of Christ's glorified flesh and blood in heaven are communicated to the believer in the act of reverently eating the bread and drinking the cup; this heavenly "virtue" of Jesus truly feeds the soul.

Calvin expresses himself by saying,

---

79. (continued) Classics, edited by John T. McNeill (Philadelphia: Westminster Press, 1960), volume 2; Alexander Barclay, pp. 113-284; John W. Nevin, *The Mystical Presence: A Vindication of the Reformed or Calvinistic Doctrine of the Holy Eucharist* (Philadelphia: J. B. Lippincott and Company, 1846).

For the sake of clearness, I say that His body is truly and really, but not naturally offered to us, and this I say, to indicate that it is not the actual body that is given for us, but all the benefits which Christ by His body, has procured for us. This is the presence of the body which the intention of the Sacrament requires.[80]

Again he states,

That which pertains to spiritual things does not require an enclosed presence, either of the body under the bread, or of the blood under the wine, for although Christ having ascended into heaven, has departed from the earth on which we are still pilgrims, no distance can prevent His virtue from being communicated to us. Of this truth, He has given us a clear and certain proof, that we may be assured that Christ with His riches is present to us, not less really than if He were actually before our eyes, to be touched with our hands.[81]

Whenever Calvin speaks of the "substance" of Christ's body in the Lord's Supper, he means it in the deeper sense of the power of Christ's glorified body in heaven. He does not mean the same thing that the Catholics and Lutherans do. For over and over again in his writings, Calvin clearly and plainly denies the physical presence of Christ in the loaf and cup. As Calvin says, ". . . that He feeds us truly with the substance of the Lord's flesh and blood unto immortality, and vivifies us by their participation."[82]

Calvin claims that all this is a sublime and mysterious miracle that Jesus accomplishes by the work of the Holy Spirit.

Calvin also explains how Christ's flesh and blood are related to the bread and cup in the Eucharist. He declares,

---

80. Quoted in Alexander Barclay, p. 119.
81. Quoted in Alexander Barclay, p. 126.
82. Quoted in Alexander Barclay, p. 132.

Bread and wine are the visible signs which represent to us the body and blood. We have a very fair parallel in an analogous case. When the Lord was pleased to manifest His Spirit at Christ's baptism, He represented it under the figure of a dove. John the Baptist, narrating the event, says that he saw the Holy Spirit descending. If we look at it clearly, we will perceive that he saw nothing but the dove, for the essence of the Holy Spirit is invisible. As he knew, however, that the vision has no vain show, but the most sure sign of the presence of the Holy Spirit, he hesitates not to say that he saw it (John 1:32), because it was represented to him, according to his capacity. Thus it is with the communion we have in the body and blood of the Lord Jesus. It is a spiritual mystery which can neither be seen by the eye nor comprehended by the understanding. It is, therefore, figured to us by visible signs, according as our weakness requires, in such manner, nevertheless, that is not a bare figure, but is combined with the reality and substance. It is with good reason that the bread is called body, since it not only represents, but also presents it to us.[83]

He also used the illustration of the sun to describe how the virtue or power of Christ's flesh and blood is communicated to the worshipper who receives the Eucharist. Calvin says:

For if we see that the sun is shining, and sending forth its rays upon the earth to generate, cherish and invigorate its offspring, in a manner transfuses its substance into us and it, why should the radiance of the Spirit be less in conveying to us the communion of His flesh and blood.[84]

The Purpose of the Supper

In Calvin's view, the Lord's Supper exhibits to us the meaning and importance of Christ's death. This sacred feast

---

83. Quoted in Alexander Barclay, p. 144-145.
84. Quoted in Alexander Barclay, p. 152.

assures us that the body of Christ was once sacrificed for us; and when we eat it by faith, we feel within ourselves the efficacy of that one sacrifice—that His blood was once shed for us so as to be our perpetual drink.

He also maintained that the goal of the Supper is the nourishment of our spiritual life.

This is Calvin's view of the Supper. In summarizing it, we see that he denied any physical presence of Christ in the Supper. Yet Jesus is spiritually present to feed our souls.

4

THE BIBLICAL VIEW

At the risk of sounding stuffy, dogmatic, and negative, I must say that none of the previous views is correct. They all have defects about them that are unbiblical—some even anti-Biblical.

In this chapter, the Biblical view of Christ's presence in the Lord's Supper will be explained. First, I will present in a negative way the arguments that refute the Catholic, Lutheran, and Calvinistic interpretations of that presence; then I will give in a positive way the arguments that rightly explain the manner of Christ's presence in the Eucharist.

WHAT THE MANNER OF CHRIST'S PRESENCE IS NOT

The Refutation of the Roman Catholic View

The Roman Catholic view of Christ's Eucharistic presence, called "transubstantiation," is wrong for the following four reasons: 1) it cannot be proved from Scripture; 2) it is repugnant to Scripture; 3) it overthrows the nature of a sacrament; and 4) it causes gross superstitions.

1. Transubstantiation cannot be proved from Scripture. The two texts used by Catholics are John 6 and the Words of Institution. But in reality they do not prove this dogma.

a. Concerning John 6, the Catholic claims that although verses 32-50 describe faith in Christ's death (to eat is to believe), verses 51-58 teach that transubstantiation is true. That is, verses 32-50 are figurative descriptions of trusting in Christ's death, while the rest of the chapter is a literal affirmation of transubstantiation.

However, upon closer examination of this grand chapter, one discovers that even in verses 51-58 to eat is to believe in the saving death of Jesus. There are not two levels here, as if John 6:32-50 referred only to faith in Christ, while John 6:51-65 concerned the Eucharistic eating of His physical body. Not at all. Instead, we find only one level, one subject. And that one subject is believing in Christ's death. Let's see this truth.

In verses 32-50, believing on Christ as the Bread of Life produces "eternal life" (v. 47). And in verses 51-58, eating His flesh and drinking His blood also produces the same effect, "eternal life" (v. 54). When two things produce the very same effect, we may confidently say they are the same. If believing in Christ works the same effect as eating His flesh and blood, we may be sure these two actually are the same thing. To eat Christ's flesh and blood is to believe in His death's power to cleanse us from our sins, for the separation of flesh from blood means that death has occurred.

Therefore, all references in John 6 to eating and drinking Christ's flesh and blood are picturesque descriptions of

116

faith in Christ's saving death.[1] They are not really referring to the Lord's Supper at all.

But why describe the act of faith by such realistic expressions as "eating flesh" and "drinking blood"? Jesus wants us to receive Him in our innermost soul until His will and nature will become a part of ours, and, like food, will strengthen all our faculties. There is nothing in our human body that so closely corresponds to this spiritual "digestion" of Christ into our souls as the actions of eating and drinking. And so it is used here. Christ wants us to make Him, His death, His teachings, His life, and His holiness so much a part of us that it is as if we eat and drink His flesh and blood.

The Greek verb, *trogo* ("munch, crunch with the mouth") is used here by Jesus to describe the act of "eating." The Catholic insists that the use of this word requires a literal and physical eating of Christ through transubstantiation. However, as Westcott pointed out years ago, this verb may only mean that the act of trusting in Christ gives pleasure and joy to the soul just as "munching" physical food gives gladness to the body.[2]

John 6 is not talking about the Lord's Supper. For anyone who reads John 6:51-58 gets the distinct impression that all who eat Christ's flesh and drink His blood will surely receive eternal life and salvation from sin. That is obvious. Whatever the precise meaning of the words, "eat My flesh"

---

1. Huldreich Zwingli, "On the Lord's Supper," in *Zwingli and Bullinger*, volume 24 of *The Library of Christian Classics*, translated by Geoffrey W. Bromiley (Philadelphia: Westminster Press, 1953), p. 203; Charles Hodge, *Systematic Theology* (London: James Clarke and Company, 1960), 3:668; Brooke Foss Westcott, "St. John's Gospel," in *The Bible Commentary*, edited by F. C. Cook (New York: Charles Scribner's Sons, 1887), 2:112-113.

2. Westcott, p. 107.

and "drink My blood," it is clear that such eating gives us eternal life. That is what our Lord affirms throughout verses 51-56. Yet no one—not even the Catholic!—believes this concerning the Eucharist. No church affirms that to inherit eternal life and salvation, all you must do is receive the Lord's Supper. The Catholic Church does promise the forgiveness of sins to all who with faith receive the "Blessed Sacrament." But they also insist that merely taking the consecrated bread and wine every week in the Mass will not grant you salvation. You must also receive several other Sacraments such as Baptism, Extreme Unction, Auricular Confession, and Confirmation. Without these, the Mass is of little value. Therefore, John 6 cannot be about the Lord's Supper. If it were, then salvation would be ours by eating the Supper alone. Baptism would be unnecessary for cleansing us from sin. Scripture nowhere connects forgiveness with the Supper.

Actually, John 6 is not about the Lord's Supper, but the Lord's Supper is about John 6. That chapter specifically refers to the glorious act of believing in Christ's redemptive work for our salvation, and being intimately united to Him. And that involves prayer, Bible study, evangelism, purity of lifestyle, and many other facets of the Christian life, including the Eucharist; but John 6 is not limited to the Supper alone. Whenever we rest in the grace of Jesus the Crucified One, we digest him by faith, which is what John 6 is all about. Of course, that will involve receiving the Eucharist, but it certainly is not limited to that sacred feast.

Because Jesus says "the flesh profits nothing" (John 6:63), He shows that His words in John 6:51-58 must not be taken literally. They do not refer to the literal, physical eating of His flesh and blood. Eating His physical body

118

would offer our souls no blessing, since "the flesh profits nothing." Although the Catholic claims that this verse does not mean that, I think their argument is overruled by the text itself. For what does the term "flesh" refer to in verse 63? It must refer to Christ's own flesh. All throughout verses 51-58, "flesh" has this meaning and nothing else. Therefore, since His own flesh profits nothing, the act of eating Christ's flesh and blood literally and physically—as in transubstantiation—would do our souls no good whatsoever.

Finally, the early Christians did not interpret this chapter to refer to the physical eating of Christ's flesh and blood in the Lord's Supper by transubstantiation. Ignatius said that "the flesh of the Lord is faith, and the blood of the Lord is incorruptible."[3] Clement of Alexandria declared,

> Faith, . . . which being more substantial than hearing, is likened to meat, and assimilates to the soul itself, nourishment of this kind. Elsewhere, the Lord in the Gospel according to St. John, brought this out by symbols when He said, "Eat My flesh, and drink My blood," describing distinctly by metaphor the drinkable properties of faith.[4]

Tertullian proclaimed:

> The sense must be guided from the occasion of the discourse. For because they thought His flesh to be eaten by them . . . . Appointing, therefore, the Word to be the vivifier, because the Word is spirit and life, He calleth the same likewise "His own flesh," for since the "Word was made flesh," it was thence to be sought for the purpose of life, and was to be devoured in the hearing, and was to be ruminated upon in the intellect, and was to be digested by faith. Hence, He had shortly before pronounced His to be heavenly bread.[5]

Numerous other early Christian writers could be quoted, but these examples should suffice to prove that they hardly

3. Ignatius, *Epistle to the Trallians*, 8; see also Migne, *PG*, 5:787-788.
4. Clement of Alexandria, *The Instructor*, 1:6; see also Migne, *PG*, 8:295-296.
5. Tertullian, *On the Resurrection of the Flesh*, 37; see also Migne, *PL*, 2:894.

shared the Catholic interpretation of John 6. Most significant of all, however, is the strange but eloquent silence of the Council of Trent concerning this text. That august assembly knew better than to seek the transubstantiation theory in John 6. The early Fathers were too much against it. Most of them interpreted that chapter, especially verses 51-58, figuratively of faith in Jesus.

Therefore, transubstantiation cannot be proved from Scripture, especially John 6.

b. Concerning the Words of Institution (Matthew 26: 26-28; Mark 14:22-25; Luke 22:19-20; 1 Corinthians 11: 23-28), the Catholics interpret them literally. The reasons for this rest upon several arguments.

First of all, in the words, "This is My body," the Catholic argues that this cannot be figurative, or else Jesus would have said, "This bread is My body." But He didn't. He said, "This is My body." Furthermore, they claim, the word "this" cannot refer at all to bread anyway, since "this" is in the neuter gender (*touto*) and bread is in the masculine (*artos*). But the word "body" (*soma*) is neuter. Therefore, the word "this" refers only to "body"—not bread. They emphasize this a lot. The underlying rule here is that in all Greek grammars the pronoun and its noun must agree in "gender, number, and person."[6] Therefore, the Catholic affirms that the Words of Institution really mean, "This (body) is My body."

However, this argument is by no means infallible. Although this grammatical rule concerning gender is generally followed in ancient literature, sometimes a neuter pronoun

---

6. For instance, Henry Lamar Crosby and John Nevin Schaeffer, *An Introduction to Greek* (Boston: Allyn and Bacon, 1963), p. 40.

will refer to a masculine or feminine antecedent. For instance, in the Septuagint version of Genesis 28:17, a neuter pronoun is used to refer to a masculine noun. The Greek text reads this way:

(line 1) *hos phoberos ho topos houtos;*
(line 2) *Ouk estin touto*
(line 3) *all' e oikos theou, kai haute he pule tou ouranou.*

The translation of the Greek text reads this way:

(line 1) "How fearful is this place;
(line 2) this is nothing else
(line 3) but the house of God, and the gate of heaven itself."

Now notice very carefully in lines 1 and 2 the words "this place" and "this." Jacob, according to the Septuagint version of Genesis 28:17, alludes to "this place" (both words are in the masculine gender) in line 1. Then he identifies this place by using the neuter form of "this" in line 2. "This" in line 1 is masculine, but "this" in line 2 is neuter; yet both pronouns modify the same masculine object ("place" in line 1). They do not agree in gender, but still they refer to the same object. And Jacob's meaning is quite clear, though the pronoun in line 2 does not agree in gender with its noun in line 1. The grammatical structure of this text is unusual and breaks the rules of Greek syntax, but its meaning is obvious. All of this should cause us to exercise caution when the Catholic places so much doctrinal weight upon gender considerations in the Words of Institution. When Jesus used "this" in the neuter gender (*touto*), He must have been referring to the bread that He held in His hands. He surely must have meant, "This bread is My body," and not as the Catholic supposes, "This body is My body."

121

Like Genesis 28:17, the Words of Institution are clear in their meaning, though they might break the rules of Greek grammar.

But how do we know that Jesus referred to the bread? First of all, we know this due to the very nature of the case. He held bread in His hands. All Jews broke bread at the Passover meal, a meal that immediately preceded the institution of the Lord's Supper by our Savior.

A second reason that we know Jesus referred to the bread is because the New Testament actually called the elements "bread" and "fruit of the vine," even after Jesus had blessed them (see 1 Corinthians 10:16-17; 11:26-28; Matthew 26:29; Mark 14:25). Catholicism claims that the New Testament here refers only to the "accidents" (not the essence) of bread and wine. But this just will not work. Can this new element—essence of flesh/accidents of bread, and essence of blood/accidents of wine—really be called "bread" and "fruit of the vine"? How could anyone accurately call it "bread" when all of the reality of essence of bread has been changed into an entirely different substance (flesh)? Why would the New Testament call it "bread" when in all actuality it is Christ's own flesh? The Catholics respond to this evidence by saying that in at least two places the Word of God calls a totally changed substance by its former name.[7] For instance, they point out in Exodus 7:10 that Aaron's rod is changed into a living serpent, but in verse 12 it is still called a "rod." And in John 9:17 a man who had already been healed of his blindness is still called a "blind man." Therefore, so reasons the Catholic, the essence of the bread has been transformed into Christ's physical flesh,

---

7. Anthony J. Maas, *The Gospel According to St. Matthew with an Explanatory and Critical Commentary* (second edition; St. Louis: B. Herder, 1916), p. 270.

but it is still called "bread" in the Bible. However, in answer to this, we need to make clear that such texts form no analogy with the transubstantiation dogma. For the one main ingredient found in Exodus 7:1-12 and John 9:17 is lacking in the Catholic theory of the Eucharist. That one indispensable element is the visibility of the miracle itself. All the people could see that the rod had been changed into a snake and the blind man had been healed. It could be tested by any one of their senses to prove that the miracle occurred. The Catholic Church, however, has yet to prove that one can know with any of the five senses, that a true transubstantiation has occurred at the Mass.

A third reason that we know Jesus referred to the bread when He proclaimed, "This is My body," is because the early Fathers of the Church say so. Clement of Alexandria declares, "The Savior, taking the bread first spake and blessed, then breaking the bread, He presented it."[8] Also Tertullian often alludes to the fact that Jesus, in the Words of Institution, calls His body the "bread."[9] Cyprian says it "was wine which He called His blood."[10] The Catholic might claim that all these writers agree with the Transubstantiation theory because they are referring only to the "accidents" of the bread—not to its essence. This answer, however, is preposterous, since no such philosophical distinction between "essence" and "accidents" was ever heard of among the early Christian writers.

Therefore, since Scripture calls the elements "bread" and "fruit of the vine" even after Jesus consecrated them, "this" must refer to the bread and fruit of the vine—not to Christ's physical flesh and blood. They do not change at all.

---

8. Clement of Alexandria, *The Stromata*, 1:1; see also Migne, *PG*, 8:686-708.

9. Tertullian, *Against Marcion*, 4:40; see also Migne, *PL*, 2:490-493.

10. Cyprian, *Epistle*, 63; see also Migne, *PL*, 4:385-386.

They are bread and fruit of the vine before, during, after the consecration of them occurs. Their essence remains the same throughout the ceremony. There is no transubstantiation at all.

The second reason the Catholic will insist that the Words of Institution are literal is because of the solemnity of the occasion when Jesus instituted the Last Supper.

However, this argument is weak. Who would dare set himself up as judge of our Lord, telling when and where He can speak figuratively? Jesus did speak figuratively all throughout His glorious Upper Room discourse found in John 13-16. He compared Himself to a vine, to a way, to many other such objects that must be interpreted figuratively. And this was spoken during the highly solemn occasion of the Last Supper. Yet it did not keep Him from speaking figuratively in John 13-16. And when He was dying on the cross, our Lord spoke figuratively to both His mother Mary and the Apostle John (John 19:25-27). Jesus said to the Apostle, "Behold, your mother," referring to Mary the mother of our Lord; then He spoke to His mother, "Behold your son." These statements cannot be anything but figurative; for neither was John the son of Mary, nor was she his mother. Who says that men who are face to face with death cannot speak figuratively? Jesus could and He did. So why couldn't He speak just as figuratively in the Upper Room when He gave the Words of Institution, "This is My body" and "This is My blood"?

In the third place, the Catholic claims that only transubstantiation does justice to the Words of Institution. When Jesus says, "This is My body," then it is physically His body. Period!

However, I find no justification in the Words of Institution for any conversion theory like transubstantiation. Jesus never said, "This is transubstantiated into My body." The copula "is" merely connects the subject ("This") with the predicate nominative ("My body"). Of itself, the word "is" does not mean a literal or a figurative idea. But regardless of all that, it never means "to become," "to be changed into."[11] Also, one must at least grant the bare possibility that the copula "is" could mean "to symbolize" in the Words of Institution. For it does carry that figurative meaning in such texts as John 15:1 ("I am the vine"; "you are the branches"), John 10:7 ("I am the good shepherd"), and Matthew 13: 38-39 ("the field is the world"). So why can't the Words of Institution mean, "This represents or symbolizes My body"? This idea is confirmed all the more when we notice the expression, "This cup is the New Covenent in My blood" (Luke 22:20; 1 Corinthians 11:25), which Jesus spoke as part of the Words of Institution. Obviously the copula, "is," cannot be interpreted literally; the cup really was not the New Covenant, of course. To say that a cup is literally a covenant is tantamount to saying that a man and a woman are a marriage. "Cup" is material; a covenant is an immaterial state of agreement between two persons. Therefore, "is" must be taken figuratively here to mean "symbolizes." It seems that Luke and Paul may be interpreting for us the meaning of the Words of Institution in Luke 22:20 and 1 Corinthians 11:25. If so, the Catholic contention that the Words of Institution are never explained figuratively

---

11. William Tyndale, whose fiery martyrdom in 1536 helped to fan the flame of the Reformation Movement, said: "But yet was there never such manner of speaking in the scripture, 'This is that;' that is to say, 'This is converted and transubstantiated into that . . . ' " (William Tyndale, *An Answer to Sir Thomas More's Dialogue, The Supper of the Lord After the True Meaning of John VI. and 1 Cor. XI. and Wm. Tracy's Testament Expounded,* edited by Henry Walter [Cambridge: at the University Press, 1850] , p. 261). See also Gerrit Cornelius Berkouwer, *The Sacraments* in his *Studies in Dogmatics* (Grand Rapids: Wm. B. Eerdmans Publishing Company, 1969), pp. 207-208.

in Scripture is proven false. If this is true of the "cup," why cannot it be true of the "bread" as well? If "is" might mean "It symbolizes" concerning the cup, why can't "is" mean the very same thing concerning the bread? As Brooke Foss Westcott put it,

> "This is" must be taken in the same sense in "This is My body" as in "This cup is the New Covenant." It cannot be used of material identity. Cf. John xv. 1; the Lord is most really and yet not materially the True Vine.[12]

Finally, the Catholic defends transubstantiation by going to 1 Corinthians 11:27-29. Paul talks about taking the Lord's Supper in an unworthy manner, and so being "guilty of the body and blood of the Lord." According to the Catholic interpretation, only a belief in the Real Presence does full justice to those words. For how can you insult an absent object? You offend an object that is present; therefore, the only way you can possibly be guilty of Christ's body and blood is if He is physically present in the bread and wine.

However, this entire line of reasoning is fallacious. Its fallacy lies in the idea that one can insult or offend only an object that is present. This simply is not true. You most certainly can offend an absent object by profaning its symbol.

---

12. Brooke Foss Westcott, *The Life and Letters of Brooke Foss Westcott,* edited by his son Arthur Westcott, 2:352, cited by W. H. Griffith Thomas, *The Principles of Theology: An Introduction to the Thirty-Nine Articles* London: Church Book Room Press, 1945), p. 392, n. 1. Also see Huldreich Zwingli, *De vera et falsa religione* (1525), 3:147, cited by Alexander Barclay, *The Protestant Doctrine of the Lord's Supper: A Study in the Eucharistic Teaching of Luther, Zwingli, and Calvin* (Glasgow, Scotland: Jackson, Wylie and Company, 1927), p. 56; Ezra P. Gould, *A Critical and Exegetical Commentary on the Gospel According to St. Mark* in *The International Critical Commentary* (Edinburgh: T. and T. Clark, 1896), pp. 254, 264; Alfred Plummer, "Lord's Supper," *Dictionary of the Bible,* edited by James Hastings and others (1902), 3:149; H. C. G. Moule, *Outlines of Christian Doctrine* in *The Theological Educator* (London: Hodder and Stoughton, 1892), p. 263.

In every station of life, this rule holds true: "dishonor to the symbols is dishonor to that which they represent."[13] By burning an American flag, one insults the American nation. The flag symbolizes the nation itself. Defacing a person's picture, refusing to wear or to accept a wedding ring, these actions are guaranteed to offend the personal feelings of others, for such symbols represent the person who is absent. Therefore, the Roman Catholic argument is groundless. 1 Corinthians 11:27-29 does not require a belief in the dogma of transubstantiation. It makes perfect sense from a symbolical view.

In conclusion, we have found that from an examination of the "Words of Promise" (John 6:51-65) and the "Words of Institution" (Matthew 26:26-28 and its parallels; 1 Corinthians 11:23-28) the Catholic view of transubstantiation cannot be proved from Holy Scripture.

2. Transubstantiation is repugnant to Scripture. This view is not found in Scripture, and it is diametrically opposed to the clear teachings of the Bible.

It is repugnant to Scripture because of the fact that the Bible always condemns any form of cannibalism. Drinking blood is vehemently spoken against in the following passages: Genesis 9:4; Leviticus 3:17; 7:26-27; 17:12-14; 19:26; Deuteronomy 12:16, 33; 15:23; 1 Samuel 14:32-34; Acts

---

13. Archibald Robertson and Alfred Plummer, *A Critical and Exegetical Commentary on the First Epistle of St. Paul to the Corinthians* in *The International Critical Commentary* (Edinburgh: T. and T. Clark, 1914), p. 251. See also G. G. Findlay, "St. Paul's First Epistle to the Corinthians," *The Expositor's Greek Testament,* edited by W. Robertson Nicoll (London: Hodder and Stoughton, n. d.), 2:882; G. G. Findlay, "Paul the Apostle," *Dictionary of the Bible,* edited by James Hastings and others (1902), 3:727.

15:20, 29; 21:25.[14] If transubstantiation is correct, and the worshipper eats the physical flesh and blood of Christ, then he or she commits the sin of cannibalism. It is as simple as that. The Catholic attempts to rid himself of this difficulty by bringing forth the doctrine of concomitance. He insists that cannibalism would occur in the Mass if they ate only the physical flesh and blood of the Savior. But their doctrine of concomitance maintains that they eat not only His flesh and blood, but also His soul and spirit and divinity; the whole Christ is eaten—not just His fleshly body. This line of argument, however, assumes what must first be proven from Scripture. There is no evidence in the Bible that the worshipper actually eats the soul and spirit and divinity of Christ. To imagine that we actually can do such things seems to border on blasphemy! The Scripture directly and clearly sets forth its case on this point: no cannibalism. All drinking of flesh and/or blood—animal, human, or even divine—is sin.

In the second place, transubstantiation is repugnant to Scripture because of the recorded reactions of the disciples in the Upper Room as our Lord instituted the Eucharist. What did they see? When each disciple took the bread and wine, he could see that those elements possessed all their ordinary physical properties (every Catholic will admit this). Also, each disciple could see that the Christ was still in His flesh-and-blood body, talking with them. What they saw seems to indicate they did not interpret His Words of Institution literally. Next, how did they react? Usually when

---

14. Zwingli, "An Exposition of the Faith," *Zwingli and Bullinger,* Volume 24 of *The Library of Christian Classics,* translated and edited by G. W. Bromiley Philadelphia: Westminster Press, 1953), p. 261; Loraine Boettner, *Roman Catholicism* (Philadelphia: Presbyterian and Reformed Publishing Company, 1964), p. 178; John L. Brandt, *America or Rome, Christ or the Pope* (Toledo, Ohio: The Loyal Publishing Company, 1895), pp. 116-118.

Christ spoke figuratively and His followers took Him literally, He corrected their mistaken views. Also when such things happened, the Twelve would usually become upset or begin asking questions among themselves to find the proper understanding of their Master's words. Now He had just told them to eat His flesh and drink His blood. How did they react? In light of the Jewish aversion to drinking blood, this statement would have caused them tremendous problems, if they had interpreted Him literally. Yet, there is no recorded instance of any such questioning or consternation on the part of the Apostles during the Last Supper. They seem to have calmly accepted it; why? Most likely because they did not interpret the Words of Institution literally. If the disciples had taken those words literally, why did they not question them, since they usually were puzzled over other teachings that were much easier to figure out than the Words of Institution?[15] As Wetstein points out, "They did not ask whether the bread which they saw was bread, or whether some other body being invisible in the interstices of the bread was being hid, but what this action signified . . . ."[16] Since the Gospel narratives do not record any astonishment in the Apostles, it seems most probable that they did not interpret Christ's Words of Institution literally. The idea of eating divine flesh and drinking divine

---

15. Tyndale, p. 262. Oecolampadius, Zwingli's trusted companion, points out two things: the lack of astonishment in the Apostles shows that they did not interpret Christ's Words of Institution literally; and if, during the Last Supper, Peter objected to Christ's washing of his feet, how more strongly would the Apostle have protested if His Lord had actually asked him to eat the very flesh and blood of God's Son! (De genuina verborum Domini expositione, cited by Alexander Barclay, p. 62).

16. Quoted by Heinrich A. W. Meyer, Critical and Exegetical Handbook to the Gospel of Matthew, translated by Peter Christie (New York: Funk and Wagnalls, 1884), p. 463.

blood seemed as repugnant to them as it did to the Bible writers themsleves.

The third reason that transubstantiation is repugnant to Scripture is because of what we find concerning the Corinthian Church's abuses of the Eucharist (1 Corinthians 11: 17-28). What was the nature of those abuses? The record indicates that this church had too low a view of the Lord's Supper. They treated it too lightly, too irreverently. Almost all commentators (both Catholic and Protestant) contend that Paul's reference to the Supper as "the night in which Jesus was betrayed" (verse 23) is motivated by the Apostle's desire to impress upon them the high and holy nature of the Eucharist. It is a sacred feast not to be taken lightly. And it appears that if Paul had taught the Real Presence doctrine of the Eucharist, the Corinthian abuses would more likely have tended to go in the direction of making an idol of worship out of it. However, no record of this can be found. The Corinthian Christians had too low a view of the Lord's Supper—not too high a view. And this type of abuse is not likely to have arisen from a belief in transubstantiation.[17] That the Apostle never taught the Real Presence is confirmed by the kind of abuses committed against the Supper in this Church. The symbolic view of the Eucharist—the bread and the fruit of the vine represent or symbolize the death of Jesus without any Real Presence notion included therein—seems much more compatible with the nature of the Corinthian abuses.

For these three reasons, the dogma of transubstantiation is repugnant to Scripture. It is diametrically opposed to the clear teachings of the Bible.

---

17. W. H. Griffith Thomas, p. 409; Alexander Campbell, *A Debate on the Roman Catholic Religion Between Alexander Campbell and John Purcell* (Nashville: McQuiddy Printing Company, 1914 reprinted), p. 392.

3. Transubstantiation overthrows the nature of a "sacrament." This discussion of a sacrament by no means suggests that the concept is taught in Scripture. I am merely accommodating myself to the Roman Catholic definition of a sacrament. I am merely refuting them by using their own theology.

The Catholic Church follows the definition of a sacrament as given by Augustine: it is a "visible word." It is a material sign that points to or signifies some invisible reality.

Augustine stressed the fact that the sign is not the thing which is signified; both aspects of the sacrament (the sign and the thing it signifies) are to be kept distinct and separate. To confuse them would be disastrous. The sign in the Eucharist is the bread or fruit of the vine, and the thing signified is the body and blood of our Lord Jesus Christ.

The dogma of transubstantiation, however, ruins this clear-cut distinction between sacramental sign and the thing signified. The sign, bread and wine, exists only in its outward appearance ("accidents"); and the thing signified, Christ's flesh and blood, also exists essentially under the forms of bread and wine. Such a conglomeration and confusion of the sign and the thing signified tends to overthrow the very heart of the Eucharist as a Catholic sacrament.[18]

4. Transubstantiation causes gross superstitions. The very nature of this doctrine tends to produce strange and unusual superstitions that are far afield from the sobriety of the New Testament records about the Lord's Supper. The superstitious practices of Roman Catholicism include the Reservation of the Host, the logical result of this practice being the Adoration of it and the Elevation of it. None of these practices can be found in the Word of God; they are the result of the dogma of transubstantiation.

---

18. Campbell, p. 349; W. H. Griffith Thomas, pp. 388-399; Brandt, pp. 109-110.

Some of these gross superstitions even take the form of bizarre miracles which are supposed to have been witnessed by people during the Middle Ages. A few examples will suffice.

When a Roman Catholic priest named Henry was celebrating one day at the altar of St. John the Baptist in Hemmenrode, one of the people in the congregation saw Christ Himself in the form of a man in the hands of the priest (but the priest never witnessed this).

At another time, a certain lady had attempted to grow a luxuriant garden of vegetables by scattering the consecrated host upon them. For punishment, the Lord sent a demon to torment her.

A man wanted the bees in his land to dwell in a bee hive that he had constructed. So he placed portions of the consecrated host in the hives. In this way, so he thought, the bees would produce more honey for him than for anyone else. However, his plan failed. The bees, out of reverence for their creator, built little altars for each of the pieces of bread and encased them in a little church building they had made from wax. Then they sang or buzzed beautiful hymns of praise in their little church structure. Needless to say, they produced absolutely no honey for the wicked man who had chosen to dishonor the host in such a way. [19]

Many more strange tales could be added to this small list. I maintain that the magical nature of transubstantiation provides fertile ground for these bizarre stories to develop and grow.

---

19. These stories are taken from "Monastic Tales of the XIII. Century," in *Translations and Reprints from the Original Sources of European History, Series for 1895* (Philadelphia: University of Pennsylvania, 1899), 2:18-20.

An excellent illustration, which shows how uncertain some priests are in their belief of transubstantiation, can be found in W. H. Book, "The Communion of the Blood and the Body of Christ," *Christian Standard*, 42 (December 15, 1906), p. 1907; it also appears in his *Columbus Tabernacle Sermons* (Cincinnati: Standard Publishing Comany, 1909), 1:183-184.

The Refutation of the Lutheran View

Most of the arguments presented against the Catholic theory also serve to refute the Lutheran view. So in this section, I will give arguments that apply only to the Lutheran theory.

The Lutheran view is based upon three arguments, as we have already seen in the earlier portion of this chapter: 1) the union of natures in Jesus Christ; 2) the communication of natures in Jesus Christ; 3) the Words of Institution. I will take each in turn and refute them by Holy Scripture.

1. The union of natures, as maintained by the Lutherans, stresses that the flesh and blood of Christ are in, with, and under the bread and wine, since the humanity of Christ goes wherever His divine nature goes. Jesus is one; His flesh cannot be separated from His spirit. Jesus must be physically as well as spiritually in the bread and wine.

However, one can consistently affirm this union of Christ's two natures—the divine and the human—without believing in the Real Presence of Christ in the Eucharist. The union of natures in our Lord need not involve the Lord's Supper at all. To me it seems rather forced for the Lutherans to make the union of natures in Jesus apply to His physical presence in the Lord's Supper. At least the Bible has never applied it in this manner.

The Lutheran, by maintaining that Christ's human nature does everything and goes everywhere His divine nature does and goes, seems guilty of deifying the human nature of our Lord. And in this way Lutheranism, instead of affirming the union of Christ's two natures, may actually be obliterating the proper human characteristics of Christ's humanity and turning it into simply divine nature number two. When they claim that His human body shares such distinctly divine attributes as omnipresence so that His flesh and blood can be in Lutheran altars around the world, they are making Christ's humanity take on divine characteristics. His humanity then becomes just another name for His divinity. And this is a serious flaw in their theology of Christ. To deify the humanity of Jesus may be just as grave an error as it is to humanize His deity. Yes, Colossians 2:9 and John 1:14 truly do teach an interpenetration and permeation of Christ's two natures, but this must never be used to teach that the properties of each nature are conglomerated. No wonder John Calvin said that in Luther's view Christ's "body was swallowed up by His divinity," thus leaving "no difference between deity and human nature."[20]

At any rate, the union of Christ's person in no way demands that one believe in the Real Presence doctrine.

A most interesting sidelight appears when we compare the Lutheran doctrine of Baptism with their view of the Lord's Supper. True, the Lutherans stress that both acts take away sins: Baptism cleanses from both original sin and personal transgression, and the Eucharist gives to the believing communicant the forgiveness of sins. However, the way these two function to cleanse from sin is different in Lutheranism. For the Eucharist to cleanse from sin, the Lutheran maintains that one must believe in the Real Presence of Christ. The union of natures in Christ requires such a belief. Unless you believe that the physical flesh and blood of Christ are "in, with, and under" the bread and wine, you receive no blessings from it. But for Baptism to cleanse from sin, you should not believe that Christ's physical blood is "in, with, and under" the water, even though the Lutheran believes that the blood of Jesus is applied to the sinner at

---

20. John Calvin, *The Institutes of the Christian Religion*, Volume 21 of *The Library of Christian Classics*, edited by John T. McNeill (Philadelphia: Westminster Press, 1960), 2:1398-1399.

Baptism. For the Eucharist to work the physical flesh and blood of Jesus must be there. But for Baptism to work, no part of Christ's physical nature is required. This seems odd, especially in light of the Lutheran's emphasis upon the union of natures in Jesus. If the humanity of Christ goes wherever His divinity does, and the blood of Jesus is intimately connected with the waters of Baptism (just as His flesh and blood are intimately connected with the bread and wine of the Eucharist), then why doesn't the Lutheran claim that the physical blood of the Savior is "in, with, and under" the Baptismal waters as it is in the Eucharist? Is not the Lutheran interpretation of Baptism the splitting up of Christ's union of natures? I think so. The point I am getting at is simply this: to deny the Real Presence of Christ in the Supper does not denote a splitting of Christ's union of natures any more than it does when a Lutheran denies the Real Presence of Christ in Baptism.

2. The communication of natures in Jesus Christ, as maintained by the Lutherans, stresses that the humanity of Christ shares such attributes as omnipresence. In this way, the Lutheran can show that Christ's physical body is "in, with, and under" the bread and wine of countless worship services all around the world. Catholics also have asserted this.

This view's main weakness is that the Bible leaves no room for such a theory. Luther repeatedly proclaimed that you must not be guided by the vain philosophies of men, but only the pure Word of God. That meant one should throw out all notions that a finite body (such as Christ's human nature) cannot participate in the attributes of an infinite body (such as Christ's divine nature). However, the Bible itself declares that the body of Christ (His human nature) is not omnipresent; it does not share the attributes

135

of His divine nature. In His human nature, Jesus is absent from the earth; His body does not descend into countless Lutheran worship services. People do not eat the physical flesh and blood of Jesus when they receive Communion.

The Bible teaches that Jesus' heavenly body is not omnipresent in the following texts: 1) Hebrews 2:17 tells us that Christ was "made like His brethren in all things." This means that Christ's human nature is the same as every man's nature. Therefore, since no man's body is omnipresent or omnipotent, then neither is Christ's. Of course, we need to point out that Christ's human nature is unlike ours because His is sinless (Hebrews 4:15) and incorruptible (1 Corinthians 15:51ff.; Philippians 3:20-21). 2) Acts 3:21 is probably the strongest text to prove that Christ's human nature is not omnipresent. It declares that the heavens must receive Christ's body until the restoration of all things at His Second Coming. That is, Christ in His human nature—in His human body—is absent from the earth. In His divine nature, He is with us, of course. But His humanity is not here on earth. This is what the Bible says; this is not human philosophy talking here. 3) 1 Corinthians 16:22 contains an ancient Christian prayer ("Maranatha") that means, "Our Lord, come." It is a request for Jesus to return in glory on the clouds of heaven. To pray for Him to come to earth again means that He is absent from the earth in His humanity right now. 4) Matthew 26:11 points out that the poor will always be here with us; but, Jesus says, "you do not always have Me." If this is so, then He is not here among us in His human body. 5) Matthew 24:23 tells us not to believe false Christs and false prophets who come saying, "Behold, here is the Christ, or There He is." If anyone tells us that there Christ is, in the bread and wine of the Eucharist, we are not to believe him. In fact, anyone who maintains the Real Presence view of the Supper is actually saying, "Behold,

136

here is the Christ, in, with, and under the bread and wine of the Lord's Supper." And we are not to believe him. This is what the text commands us. 6) John 17:11 indicates that at Christ's Ascension, He will be "no more in the world." Does not this plainly teach that He is absent, according to His human nature? 7) John 16:28 indicates that Jesus at His Ascension will be "leaving the world again, and going to the Father." He is not here in His bodily nature. He has left. 8) John 16:7 states that unless Jesus leaves us, the Holy Spirit, here called the "Helper" or Comforter," cannot come down to us. The text evidently teaches that Jesus will leave His disciples, and the Holy Spirit will come to earth to carry on the work of Christ in the world. Jesus comes to the world at His Incarnation; then He leaves it; He sends the Holy Spirit to the world to take Christ's place. The text leaves no room for any Real Presence or communication of natures.

These texts are easy to interpret; they do not bear mysterious meanings. They destroy the Lutheran view of Christ's communication of natures. For they teach that the human nature of Jesus, His body, is not omnipresent; it is in one place: the right hand of the Father, which is not everywhere, but in one locality. Christ is evidently absent from the world, according to His humanity. His body is not in the Eucharist.

God certainly can make it possible for one body to be in different places at the same time. But is there any Biblical proof that He does this with Christ's human body?

Therefore, the Word of God leaves no room for such a philosophical theory as the Lutheran view of Christ's communication of natures. His human body is in the heavens, and it will stay there until He wills to return at the Second Coming. He does not come in a physical way to the earth in the Lord's Supper. That would contradict what he has already told us in His Word. And that is the only reason we condemn this Lutheran belief. It is not based upon the infallible Word of God.

3. The Words of Institution, as interpreted by the Lutherans, teach the Real Presence of Christ in the Eucharist. But their main proof is found in 1 Corinthians 10:16-17. They claim that the Greek term translated "communion" or "fellowship" or "participation" (koinonia) really means "communication"; that is, the bread communicates with the flesh of Jesus, and the wine communicates with His blood. It is not about the fellowship of persons with persons, but things with things. It shows that the physical flesh and blood of Jesus are "in, with, and under" the consecrated bread and wine.

However, the unanimous testimony of all reputable Greek-English lexicons and dictionaries proclaims that this term denotes a sharing or fellowship of persons with persons—not things with things. It has nothing to do with the Real Presence idea. Even the Missouri-Synod Lutherans, Arndt and Gingrich and Danker in their excellent lexicon, agree with this point.

Also Paul's comparison of the Lord's Supper with both the Israelite and pagan sacrifices in 1 Corinthians 10:16-22 proves that he did not accept the Real Presence theory. He claims that both the Jews and the pagans ate sacred meals which were similar to the Eucharist. Now, did the Jews believe that in their sacrificial meals they ate the physical flesh and blood of Yahweh God? No, they did not. Did the pagans believe that they ate the physical bodies of their deities? No, they did not. Even the Lutherans and Catholics must admit this. Therefore, when Paul says that those sacrificial meals were similar to the Eucharist, he shows that this Christian feast does not have the physical flesh and blood of

Jesus in it. On the other hand, if Paul shows that these sacrificial meals were a spiritual communion or fellowship (*koinonia*) with Yahweh or with pagan deities (called "demons" in verses 20-21), it must logically follow that in the Lord's Supper a similar spiritual fellowship occurs. But no Real Presence is implied in this text. The physical flesh and blood of Jesus need not be in the bread and wine in order to have fellowship with Christ's body any more than the physical presence of demons must be in the pagan sacrifices to have fellowship with them.

1 Corinthians 10:16-17 simply means that "the bread and wine after their benediction or consecration . . . are not indeed changed in their nature but become in their use and in their effects the very body and blood of Christ."[21] The Christian fellowships with the person of Christ and with other disciples. The believer has precious communion with the blessed effects of Christ's death. The idea of "flesh and blood" in 1 Corinthians 10:16-17 is that the blood is separated from the body, thus indicating the death of Christ. This is also true of all the Words of Institution.[22]

1 Corinthians 10:16-17 was considered by Luther to be the strongest passage that proves his view of the Real Presence. However, as we examine this text, we find that it does nothing of the sort. Rather it teaches the spiritual fellowship of Christ with Christians as they eat the loaf and drink the cup.

---

21. T. S. Evans, "1 Corinthians," in *The Bible Commentary,* edited by F. C. Cook (New York: Charles Scribner's Sons, 1887), p. 311. See also Plummer, "Lord's Supper," *Dictionary of the Bible,* edited by James Hastings and others (1902), 3:149.

22. Plummer, "Lord's Supper," 3:149; Moule, pp. 262-263; James S. Candlish, *The Christian Sacraments* in *Handbooks for Bible Classes and Private Students* (Edinburgh: T. and T. Clark, n. d.), pp. 115-116.

The Refutation of the Calvinistic View

Much of what Calvin proclaimed concerning the Lord's Supper was biblical and uplifting. His Eucharistic view has many advantages that merit our closest attention. For instance, he denied the Real Presence, which as we have already seen is not supported in the Bible. He strongly stressed the memorial character of the Supper. He emphasized the covenant relationship that exists in the Eucharist. He also makes much of the eschatological aspect of the Lord's Supper.[23]

However, the main problem with the Calvinistic view, as with the Catholic and the Lutheran views, is that he believes "the body and the blood" of the Holy Supper is Christ's body and blood glorified in heaven.

But the Words of Institution on the contrary fix our whole thought upon Christ's body as sacrificed and His blood as shed in the past event of His death at Calvary.[24]

Also, does Jesus now in His glorified state in heaven have "flesh" and "blood" at all?

For these reasons the Calvinistic view is less than Biblical. The Lord's Supper directs us not to the glorified Christ, but to the death of Christ for our sins.

So far we have studied the manner of Christ's presence in the Lord's Supper from the Catholic, the Lutheran, and the Calvinistic view points. We refuted them from Scripture. In the final section of this chapter, we will offer the Biblical view of that presence.

---

23. Alexander Barclay, pp. 260-268, where these points are fully explained.
24. H. C. G. Moule, *The Supper of the Lord. Present Day Papers on Romanism* (London: The Religious Tract Society, n. d.), pp. 42-46.

WHAT THE MANNER OF CHRIST'S PRESENCE IS

The Different Kinds of "Presence"

A physical object is present when it operates upon the physical senses; a spiritual object is present when it is perceived by the spiritual mind of mankind. Yet, and this needs to be stressed, the one kind of presence is just as real as the other. It is just as important as the other. It is just as true as the other. To say that only the Real Presence—that is the physical presence of our Lord in the Eucharist—can bless the soul, is just not true. A spiritual presence can bless the soul just as well (if not far better).

Notice the different ways that Christ is present to His people. He is present in the Lord's Supper. But one must always remember that Christ is also present in other ways and at other times. He is present where two or three are gathered together in His name (Matthew 18:20). He is present in the individual Christian through the Holy Spirit (Ephesians 3:17; John 17:23). Christ is also present everywhere, even where the wicked live. Besides the fact that Christ is present in these different ways, He is present at different times in a sharper degree than at other times. "Certainly, in hours of worship, reading the Holy Scriptures, and prayer God is present in a way that He is not present in the kitchen, field, or factory."[25] However, this does not mean He is "more real" during the hours of prayer. Instead, it means that when one is engaged in some activity that stimulates him to think more clearly of God's presence, then God becomes present in a sharper way to the worshipper.

---

25. Joseph Shultz, *The Soul of the Symbols: A Theological Study of Holy Communion* (Grand Rapids: Wm. B. Eerdmans Publishing Company, 1966), p. 129.

If the foregoing refutations are correct, then Christ actually has only two modes of presence: His physical presence during His earthly ministry which ended in A. D. 30 and His spiritual presence through the Holy Spirit which began at Christ's Ascension and continues still today. The important point here is that Jesus has no third mode which is called by Catholics and Lutherans the "sacramental presence."

What kind of presence does the Christian need the most? A physical presence or a spiritual presence? Do we need Christ's physical presence in the bread and fruit of the vine in order to receive blessings from the Eucharist? And the answer to this is, "No." One can gain much benefit from the sun, from property, and from money without having them physically present before him. Christ's death has given eternal and manifold blessings to thousands of people for many centuries. Yet that event did not have to be physically present to each generation before they could benefit from the cross of Christ. Is it not logical to conclude from all of this that we have spiritual needs and the only way they can be satisfied is by spiritual food—not physical food? Christ's physical body cannot help our souls.

We need to keep this discussion in mind as we study what the New Testament says about the presence of Christ in the Lord's Supper. For the Scriptures are our only and all-sufficient rule of faith and practice; they are our infallible guide. So let us go to them now for the answers to our questions.

The Words of Institution
What Do the Words of Institution Really Mean?

1. Whatever they mean, it is clear that they reveal a close and intimate connection between the Passover meal

142

and the Lord's Supper. We saw this already in chapter one.[26] What implications does the Passover-Lord's Supper relationship have for discerning the manner of Christ's presence?

First of all, the wording in the Words of Institution is extremely similar to that in the Passover. In Exodus 12:11, the little phrase, "It is the Lord's Passover," sounds a whole lot like the phrase used by our Lord, "This is My body." And the Exodus text means, "This Feast represents or symbolizes the event when the Lord 'passed over' the Israelite houses and killed all the Egyptian first-born sons."[27] The copula "is" must mean "symbolizes or represents." No other view fits. The only way the meal became known as the "Passover" was due to this interpretation of Exodus 12:11. It is called the "Passover" because it symbolized the time in Old Testament history when Yahweh "passed over" His people and delivered them from Egyptian slavery. And since the Lord's Supper is the New Passover for the New Israel of God—the Church of Jesus—and it follows much the very same wording that the old Passover did (Exodus 12:11), we may safely conclude that the phrase "This is My body" means, "This Lord's Supper

---

26. Angus J. B. Higgins, *The Lord's Supper in the New Testament. Studies in Biblical Theology no. 6. First Series* (London: SCM Press, 1972), pp. 13-23, 45-47; Candlish, p. 88; Joachim Jeremias, *The Eucharistic Words of Jesus* (London: SCM Press, 1966), pp. 15-88; Wm. F. Skene, *The Lord's Supper and the Passover Ritual* (Edinburgh: T. and T. Clark, 1891).

27. Huldreich Zwingli, "On the Lord's Supper," pp. 226-229; Brandt, p. 112; Higgins, pp. 52-54; Robert B. Girdlestone, "Brief Notes on Some Texts Which Are Frequently Misinterpreted or Misapplied: VII.," in *English Church Teaching on Faith Life and Order* (London: Charles Murray, 1898), p. 237, n. 1; George A. Chadwick, *The Gospel According to St. Mark* in *The Expositor's Bible* (London: Hodder and Stoughton, n. d.), p. 376; John M. Gibson, *The Gospel According to St. Matthew* in *The Expositor's Bible* (London: Hodder and Stoughton, n. d.), pp. 392-393.

feast symbolizes or represents My body." "Is" meant "to represent" or "to symbolize" in Exodus 12:11, and therefore it must mean the same idea in the Words of Institution. Exodus 12:11 provides an important key for the proper interpretation of the Words of Institution. This is the first result of seeing the close relationship between the Passover and the Eucharist.

Secondly, the Passover feast contained much dramatic symbolism throughout. We saw this already in chapter one, but it needs to be stressed now. According to Ralph P. Martin,

> At the annual feast the Israelite is linked, in a realistic and dynamic way, with his forefathers whom the Lord redeemed from Egypt. The bread on the table is to be regarded as though it were "the bread of affliction" which the Jews of old ate (Dt. xvi.3 as interpreted in the Passover Haggadah); he is to account himself as though he personally was set free from Egyptian tyranny in that first generation of his nation long ago (Mishnah, Pesahim x.5).[28]

As he celebrated the Passover feast with his companions, the Jew transported himself in a sort of "time-machine" back into the past to the very time when his forefathers were set free from Egypt by God. The participant in this meal believed he was really there in Egypt in the fifteenth century B. C. The Passover is replete with dramatic symbolism or I should say symbolic drama. And when we apply this dramatic symbolism to the Words of Institution in the Lord's Supper, we see that this is also a dramatic meal, intended to stimulate our minds to go back to the Good Friday when our glorious Savior died on the cross. The elements of bread and fruit of the vine are designed to cause us to remember how our Lord redeemed us from the slavery of sin. Christ

---

28. Ralph P. Martin, "The Lord's Supper," *The New Bible Dictionary*, edited by J. D. Douglas and others (1973), p. 750.

is not present in the bread and cup, but He most certainly can be present to the believer in the use of those elements. Jesus is not present in them, but He is present in the use of them. It "was not so much the bread as the breaking, not so much the elements as the actions, that were symbolical."[29] The entire Lord's Supper meal contains one grand symbolic drama. It takes us back to A. D. 30 at the hill called Mount Calvary. There we see our Savior dying for our own sins. It becomes so real to us that we can even run our fingers across the wood of the cross and get a splinter in our hand. For we are there through the dramatic symbolism of the Eucharist. The church "relives that experience by which it came out of the Egypt of sin and was ransomed to God by the precious death of God's paschal victim."[30]

The Passover-Eucharist relationship helps us to see these two all-important themes: the figurative nature of the copula ("is") in the Words of Institution, and the dramatic symbolism portrayed at the Lord's Supper.

2. In the Words of Institution, that little word "is" means "to symbolize" or "to represent." We know this first of all because of what we have already seen of Exodus 12:11. We know this also because we have seen the failure of Catholic and Lutheran attempts to interpret this little word literally.

Hans Lietzmann is surely correct when he said that the figurative use of "is" in the Words of Institution "ought never to have been disputed."[31]

---

29. Peter T. Forsyth, *The Church and the Sacraments* (1953), cited by Donald M. Baillie, *The Theology of the Sacraments and Other Papers* (New York: Charles Scribner's Sons, 1957), pp. 93-94

30. Martin, p. 750.

31. Hans Lietzmann, *Mass and Lord's Supper* (Leiden: E. J. Brill, 1953 reprinted), cited by Martin, p. 750. See also Zwingli, "On the Lord's Supper," pp. 225-236.

The word "is" often bears such a figurative meaning. As G. A. Chadwick says,

> Even in the Gospel they (Christ's disciples) could discover that seed was teaching, and fowls were Satan, and that they were themselves His mother and His brethren. Further knowledge of Scripture would not impair this natural freedom of interpretation. For they would discover that if animated language were to be frozen to such literalism, the partakers of the Supper themselves, though many, were one body and one loaf, that Onesimus was St. Paul's very heart, that leaven is hypocrisy, that Hagar is Mount Sinai, and that the veil of the temple is the flesh of Christ (1 Cor. x.17; Philem. ver. 12; Luke xii. 1; Gal. iv. 25; Heb. x. 20).[32]

— 3. The Words of Institution represent before our very minds the death of Jesus Christ for our sins.[33] Nothing more, and nothing less than that grand event. They do not speak to us primarily or directly about His resurrection, ascension, or present session at the Father's right hand. No; rather they take us back in time to the cross and how Jesus died upon its accursed wood for our salvation by God's grace. They tell us what we are to remember as we break the loaf and drink from the cup. Jesus told us, "Do this in remembrance of Me" (Luke 22:19; 1 Corinthians 11:24). And in obedience to His dying words, we take the Eucharist to remember His glorious death on the cross.

James Hastings expressed this theme so well,

> It is "the Lord's death"—His death, not His life, though that was lustrous with a holiness without the shadow of a stain;

---

32. Chadwick, p. 376.

33. H. C. G. Moule, "The Holy Communion," in *English Church Teaching on Faith Life and Order* (London: Charles Murray, 1898), pp. 122-123; Moule, *The Supper of the Lord*, pp. 42-46; Zwingli, "On the Lord's Supper," p. 228; Alexander Barclay, pp. 224-225; Hodge, 3:641, 645-647, 666-667.

His death, not His teaching, though that embodied the fulness of a wisdom that was Divine; His death, not His miracles, though His course was a march of mercy, and in His track of blessing the world rejoiced and was glad. His death! His body, not glorious but broken; His blood, not coursing through the veins of a conqueror, but shed, poured out for man.[34]

4. In 1 Corinthians 11:26, we find that we are to take the Lord's Supper "until He comes." This shows us that in His human body and human nature Jesus is absent from the world. He is not here. His flesh and blood do not come down into the elements of bread and fruit of the vine.[35]

Anyway, the glorious Return of Christ makes His physical presence in the Eucharist unnecessary.

These four facts help us understand the Biblical meaning of Christ's presence in the Lord's Supper. It is a spiritual presence, yet a true presence. The Words of Institution are to be interpreted figuratively; "This is" means "This symbolizes," just as it meant in Exodus 12:11. And it is a dramatic symbolism reminding us of the death of Christ for our redemption, just as the Passover meal dramatically symbolized God's miraculous deliverance of Israel from Egyptian slavery.

---

34. James Hastings, *The Great Texts of the Bible; 1 Corinthians* (New York: Charles Scribner's Sons, 1912), p. 325.

35. Zwingli, "On the Lord's Supper," p. 230; Hodge, 3:630-631, 633, 636; Tyndale, pp. 251, 268; John Calvin, *The Institutes of the Christian Religion,* Volume 21 of *The Library of Christian Classics,* edited by John T. McNeill (Philadelphia: Westminster Press, 1960), 2:1373, 1393-1403; Herman Sasse, *This Is My Body: Luther's Contention for the Real Presence in the Sacrament of the Altar* (Minneapolis: Augsburg Publishing House, 1959), pp. 228, 251-252, 254-256, 261 note 103.

PART III

THE
MEANING
OF
THE LORD'S SUPPER

5

THE SIGNS: THE BREAD AND CUP

What is the meaning of the Lord's Supper to the Christian? How can we enrich our Communion experiences so that we gain all the devotional blessings we can? What should we be meditating upon as we eat the bread and drink the fruit of the vine?

This section, Part Three, will answer these questions. It is probably the most important portion of the whole book. All that has gone before is but preparatory to this. For here we view the devotional values of the Feast. Since it is a memorial designed to remind us of our Savior's grand redemptive work on the cross, the meaning of the Lord's Supper is essential for our Christian growth.

In this chapter, we will study how the signs of bread and fruit of the vine are related to the meaning of the Communion. We will see their nature, their suitability, their simplicity and finally their universality. This may seem a short chapter, but it is a vital one.

The signs of the Lord's Supper are bread and the fruit of the vine. As signs, they are pointers, directing our attention to the death of the Redeemer. They represent before our very eyes the grandeur of divine grace. In a simple but yet profound way, they are the divinely-ordained means of grace that feed our souls. To understand them is to grasp the meaning of the Lord's Supper in all its richness.

But also as signs, they do not contain the physical flesh and blood of Jesus. They are not the Christ, but they truly do point to the Christ; they direct us to Him. They rivet our attention, our hopes, our faith, and our love upon Jesus and Him crucified. Though they be signs, they are not mere memorials; but they truly bless and feed these souls of ours as we receive them in faith and holy reverence.

THEIR NATURE

What is the nature of the bread and the cup? Is any kind of bread suitable? What kind of liquid do we drink?

The Nature of the Bread

The nature of the bread is two-fold: it must be unleavened and it must be broken in full sight of the ones who are about to receive it.

The bread should be unleavened because of the following two reasons: 1) When Jesus instituted the Lord's Supper, He probably used unleavened bread. We believe this because that was the only type of bread at the Passover feast. No leaven was allowed in a Jewish home during Passover week (Exodus 12:8, 15, 18-20; 13:3; 34:18; Deuteronomy 16:3-4). Since Christ celebrated the Eucharist right after He ate the Passover, the bread used at both feasts must have been unleavened. We use unleavened bread because Jesus did. 2) In Scripture, leaven is often a symbol of sin and the corruption it produces (1 Corinthians 5:6-8). At the Lord's Supper, the unleavened bread reminds us of purity—our Lord's holiness and our own. He is light and in Him is no darkness at all (1 John 1:5). The unleavened bread reminds us that Jesus died as the spotless Lamb of God who takes away the sins of the world (John 1:29, 36; 1 Peter 1:18-21). And we as His children are to walk in the light, even as He is in the light (1 John 1:6-7). The unleavened bread reminds us that we are to be pure and righteous (1 Corinthians 5:7-8). This comes forth loudly and clearly as we eat the unleavened bread. For these two reasons, we ought to use unleavened bread.

The bread should be broken in full sight of all who are about to receive it. I alluded briefly to this point in chapter two when the "Breaking of the Bread" name was discussed. But I need to stress it now. There are four reasons that the bread ought to be broken by those who partake of it. 1) The name of the Feast demands it. It is called the "Breaking of the Bread." That majestic name suggests we ought to break the bread when it is passed to us at Communion services. Is it a vain, empty name or does it reveal the action to be done? 2) The Lord Jesus Himself broke the bread and distributed it to His disciples when He instituted the Eucharist (Matthew 26:26; Mark 14:22; Luke 22:19; 1 Corinthians 11:24). It was broken in full sight of all who would eat it. Thus, at the very first time the Lord's Supper was ever offered, the bread was broken. 3) The early Church followed the blessed example of their Lord (1 Corinthians 10:16-17). 4) Breaking the bread fits the purpose for which bread is given to us at Communion. Why was the bread broken? What is its purpose? It portrays vividly to us the broken body of our Lord on the cross. Remember that Christ is present not in the bread, but in the action of breaking the bread. That action represents how our Lord's body was broken by cruel hands as they nailed Him to the tree. For this reason, we see the grand importance of breaking the bread in the sight of all who will partake of it. When the worshipper does not see this action, much of the beautiful and edifying symbolism of the bread is ruined or at least diminished.

For these four reasons, we ought to break the bread. To do any less is to diminish the meaning of the Eucharist. And therefore I am opposed to the modern practice in some churches of distributing the Lord's Supper in the form of tiny "chiclets." This error keeps the bread from being broken in the full sight of all who will partake of the Eucharist. Since there is no breaking of the bread, there is nothing to remind the worshipper that Christ's precious body was broken on the cross for our sins. We cannot see Jesus Christ openly crucified before our eyes (Galatians 3:1). And this tends to ruin the purpose of the bread. But, we are told, the "chiclets" bread has already been broken bread. Yes, I know all of that. I did not say the bread is never broken, but it is never broken in the sight of all who intend to partake of Holy Communion. That is the issue here. In the "chiclets" method, no one gets to see the bread broken. It has already been broken in some factory somewhere—miles away from my sight. And that to me is a travesty. And it seems that the only reason we have the "chiclets" method in the first place is because of convenience. It is easy to eat and cheap to buy. Yet we are striving to be "Restoration Movement" churches, doing things the very same way that the original Christians did them in the first century. If we really meant that, we would end the "chiclets" system forever. Let us return to the original plan that our Savior laid down centuries ago and that the early Christians followed diligently. Let us truly break the bread in full sight of all who will partake. I think that this is an important matter for our most serious consideration. Most of us have not even taken the time to think about it. I do pray that you will. You may not agree with me here, but at least consider diligently what is presented.

The Nature of the Fruit of the Vine

What kind of drink is suggested by the phrase, "the fruit of the vine?" What do the Synoptics mean when they all say that Jesus and His disciples drank the fruit of the vine at the Last Supper? Was it grape juice or fermented wine? This question has been hotly debated for centuries.

I believe that this phrase means grape juice—not fermented wine—for the following reasons:

1. The unfermented juice of the grape was used at the Jewish Passover. The Jews were clearly forbidden to use anything that had fermented at that time. All leaven was to be rejected, and therefore so were all fermented drinks. This prohibition applied to liquids as much as it did to solids, because "ferment" is the same in one as the other. Even Gesenius, the venerable Hebraist, says that leaven applied to the wine as really as to the bread. it was just as inconsistent and improper to use "the symbol of corruption" in drink as food. For fermentation is nothing else but the putrefaction of a substance containing no nitrogen; ferment, or yeast, is a substance in a state of putrefaction. For this reason all ferment was excluded from Israelite homes during the Passover week.

The practice of the Jews confirms this position. Rabbi Manasseh Ben Israel (1656) says, "Here, at this feast (the Passover), every confection ought to be so pure as not to admit of any ferment, or anything that may fermentate." Judge Noah, a leading Jew of New York during the latter part of the nineteenth century, said that the use of wine, prepared from steeped raisins, in order to avoid fermented wine, was general among American Jews at the Passover. Dr. Cunningham, a learned Hebraist, says:

> What is now chiefly used by the Jews at the Passover for wine is a drink made of an infusion of raisins in water, which is either boiled at once or simmered during several days . . . . No Jew with whom I have conversed, of whatever class or nation, ever used any other kind.

Thomas Horne declares,

> The modern Jews, being forbidden to drink any fermented liquor at the Passover, drink either pure water or a wine prepared by themselves from raisins. It is not known when the Jewish custom began of excluding fermented wine from the Passover feast. It is, however, very ancient, and is now almost universal among the modern Jews.

Moses Stuart declares,

> I can not doubt that khahmatz (fermented substance), in its widest sense, was excluded from the Jewish Passover when the Lord's Supper was first instituted . . . . That this custom is very ancient; that it is even now almost universal; and that it has been so from time whereof the memory of man runneth not to the contrary, I take to be facts that cannot be fairly controverted.

That some of the Jews, ancient and modern, have departed from this custom, does not refute our view of the general practice among them as a whole. As a religious group, per se, the Jews in all ages have abstained from fermented wine during the Passover.

156

And since the Savior instituted the Lord's Supper by using one of the four cups of the Passover, at the very first Eucharist they used grape juice—not fermented wine.

2. The Savior's language implies that He continued the practice of using the unfermented juice of the grape. At the institution of the Eucharist, He did not use the word "wine" (*oinos*)—the word in general use among the people. But He employed a phrase which has been translated, "fruit of the vine." We see this recorded three times (Matthew 26: 27-29; Mark 14:23-25; Luke 22:19-20). Every time it is called "fruit of the vine." As if He would distinguish the wine which was used on that occasion from that which the people were taught not to "look upon," and which "at the last bites like a serpent and stings like a viper" (Proverbs 23:31-32). As if he meant that no man should ever point to His example on that holy night to defend the use of intoxicating wine on a secular occasion. It has the appearance of a studied, consistent, Christian arrangement to discard the fermented wine entirely. If the Savior used fermented wine (*oinos*) at the Last Supper, it is amazing that He avoided the name by which it was known, and instead called it the "fruit of the vine."

3. Also, grape juice itself is surely "the fruit of the vine" in a truer sense than fermented wine can be. For all chemists agree that fermentation destroys the nutritive element of grape juice, while the unfermented juice is highly nutritious. Actually the chemical properties of both liquids is different. While grape juice is definitely the fruit of the vine, fermented wine is not; it is a different substance. How could fermented wine be called the fruit of the vine?

4. In its appearance, the unfermented grape juice more fitly represents the blood of Jesus than fermented wine does. Jacob called the juice of the grape, "the blood of grapes" (Genesis 49:11). And again, in Deuteronomy 32:14, we

157

read of "the blood of the grape." There may be here the foreshadowing in a certain sense of that blood of which Christ spoke when He instituted the Lord's Supper. "This is My blood of the New Covenant which is shed for many" (Mark 14:24). Now, the unfermented grape juice resembles blood, in its consistency, more than fermented wine. It is thicker, and therefore more like blood. Fermentation not only destroys the nutritive element, but it thins the blood of the grape. So I maintain that they who rely upon the fitness of the symbol should insist upon the unfermented juice.

5. There is a fitness in the selection of symbols made by the Master. The unleavened loaf and the fruit of the vine appropriately represent the body and blood by which sin is to be removed and the world is to be redeemed. But it is inconsistent with the character and teachings of Jesus to suppose that He would use to symbolize His shed blood a liquor that had done more toward the corruption and sorrow and poverty and wretchedness and degradation of humanity than all other causes combined.

Therefore, since there is no evidence that Christ instituted His Feast with the use of alcoholic wine, for He did not use the word "wine" at all but "the fruit of the vine," and since we know that as wine ferments, the fruit of the vine disappears, the probabilities are, at least, that He used innocent grape juice for the Communion with His disciples in the Upper Room. He did not use fermented wine for that occasion. And neither should we. There is no sufficient reason to forbid using grape juice at the Table of the Lord. It is appropriate, while fermented wine is not. There may be persons sitting in our churches who might be endangered by the taste of fermented wine. They have become addicted to drink until it has turned into a disease. The taste of alcohol unbalances them; they lose control of themselves, and plunge again into drunkenness because of the poison in the cup that was supposed to contain a blessing. We may laugh at this, but many among us have been rescued from the prison-house of alcoholism by the grace of Christ. To them this is no laughing matter. We should never place a stumbling block in the path of those for whom Christ died (Romans 14). For these reasons we ought to use only unfermented grape juice at our Communion services.

THEIR SUITABILITY

A memorial feast should be suited to that for which it is intended to be a memorial. At the Table of the Lord, the signs of bread and fruit of the vine are well suited to represent the death of our Redeemer.

The Suitability of the Loaf

The loaf is solid. Therefore, it suitably represents the solid portion of the human frame—the flesh of Christ.

The loaf is unleavened, not subject to decay from yeast. It lacks those elements that would cause it to spoil. So the body of our Lord was in no way defiled or corrupted. He had lived a sinless life, and thus the body that was suspended on the cross was an undefiled body. That was true of Jesus alone.

The loaf is broken. The breaking of the loaf tenderly and beautifully symbolizes the mangling of the precious body of our blessed Lord. First, there was the breaking of the skin and flesh when the crown of thorns was jammed into His skull; then the terrible scourging which always lacerated the flesh; next, the cruel tearing of the flesh when the heavy nails were driven through His hands and His feet; and, finally, the piercing of His flesh when the soldier

159

thrust his spear into Christ's side. All these facts come to our minds as we quietly, deliberately, reverently and solemnly break the loaf.

The Suitability of the Cup

The fruit of the vine is a liquid. It is, therefore, at least partially fitted to represent the blood of our Savior.

The fruit of the vine is unfermented. This symbolizes the same spiritual lesson that the unleavened nature of the bread does: the undefiled and sinless character of Jesus.

The fruit of the vine is the result of crushing and bruising. The grape must be crushed before it will yield its juice. We have already seen how the body of Christ was bruised, broken, and wounded. It was this crushed body that yielded the blood for the salvation of all believers.

The fruit of the vine is poured out. Into the cups the juice is quietly, reverently and tenderly poured and our minds and hearts instinctively turn to that scene where the blood of our loving Savior oozed and flowed from the cruel wounds and made the unmerited cross crimson with its stain. How beautifully does the cup represent His blood!

The Suitability of Sequence

The order chosen by our Savior is fitting—first the loaf, then the cup. His body was bruised before the blood came forth.

THEIR SIMPLICITY

When you examine the Jewish religion, you are impressed with its complexity. There were five offerings, each one requiring a variety of ceremonies; the three feasts, each with its respective rites and ceremonies; the Day of

Atonement with its many details; the apparel of the High Priest with its many pieces and colors; the manifold civil laws; the Sabbath ceremonies. And the 613 laws found in the Old Testament.

A diligent study of pagan religions in the ancient world will reveal this same complexity. Some of them are complex unto weariness. Much hair-splitting abounds in the legalities and liturgies of modern heathen religions, such as Buddhism, Hinduism, and other Eastern movements.

How different—how refreshing—is Christianity! While there are many deep things in it, there is little or nothing that does not bear the mark of simplicity. The plan of pardon is simple—four steps, all of which are easily understood. They are faith in Jesus as Savior and Lord, repentance from sin, confession of one's faith in Christ as Lord, and immersion in water for the forgiveness of sins. One might philosophize much about them, yet even an unlearned man may grasp their practical significance and render acceptable obedience. As a Christian, one's duties are plain. There is duty toward God, involving worship, obedience and service; to one's fellow man, involving honor, helpfulness, kindness, forgiveness, and love.

The New Testament organization of the church is simple. It is made up of elders, deacons, and evangelists.

The purpose of the church is simple—to make known to all men the grace of God in Christ and to make disciples of all the world.

Christianity rests on three simple facts—the death of Jesus, the burial of Jesus and the resurrection of Jesus. Each of these grand facts has its own memorial. The memorial of His death is the Eucharist. Let us notice its beautiful simplicity.

The emblems are few in number—only two.

161

They are easily made. The loaf is a simple cake without leaven; the cup, the unfermented juice of the grape.

They are easily eaten.

The time required to observe this Supper—to observe it properly and solemnly—is brief. Many of the ceremonies of non-Christian religions require a great deal of time—even days—and are difficult to observe properly, but here we have something beautifully simple.

In the glorious simplicity of the Lord's Supper, we see the marvelous evidences of divine wisdom and a love that embraces all mankind. Truly the Supper is a simple but profound testimonial of Christ's love for His church.

THEIR UNIVERSALITY

Our Lord intended His Gospel to become universal. He commissioned His Apostles to go into all the world and preach the Gospel to every creature.

If the Gospel is to become universal, its essential elements must be of universal application. Let us notice some of these aspects:

The terms of pardon can be complied with by all humans. They are faith, repentance, confession and Christian baptism for the forgiveness of sins. The pragmatic test has been applied to these, and it has been found that men of all races can experience these things. As to Christian baptism, man cannot live on the earth where sufficient water cannot be found for immersion.

The conditions of the Christian life are equally of universal application; namely, honor, purity, prayer, service, forgiveness, patience, worship, giving, fellowship and love.

There is no one place on earth to which Christians are expected to gather regularly. Judaism had its Jerusalem,

Mohammedanism has its Mecca, but the Author of Christianity declared that one may worship Him acceptably anywhere on the globe (John 4:21-24).

Jesus Himself is a universal character. Though living almost wholly in Palestine, he was not provincial. Though a Jew, He was not Jewish. "Jesus was not Jew-wide, but man-wide."

Since this is true, we would expect to find the Lord's Supper an ordinance of universal application. For it is not only an essential element of the Gospel, but the very center of Christian worship. Let us notice the following universal characteristics of the Holy Eucharist:

1. Unleavened bread can be made anywhere on the globe where people now live.

2. The grape will grow wherever man can live.

3. None of the constituents of either emblem will do the human body any harm. Indeed, grape juice is healthful.

4. They are taken in such small quantities that even the sick may take them without injury.

5. These emblems can be preserved for a reasonable length of time in any climate.

6. Perhaps neither one tastes bad to any human being. Throughout the world, bread and the fruit of the vine have been enjoyed by all people. The emblems are delicious to the taste and beneficial to the body.

6

THE THINGS SIGNIFIED – COMMEMORATION

We have studied the meaning of the bread and cup. They serve as holy signs, pointing us to spiritual realities. We noted their nature, suitability, simplicity, and universality.

These signs signify something; but what? This brings us face-to-face with the meaning of the Lord's Supper. Answering this question will cause us to see the glory of the Eucharist.

The signs of bread and fruit of the vine signify or symbolize these four realities: 1) commemoration; 2) confession; 3) communion; and 4) covenant. These are the things signified in the loaf and cup. In chapters six through nine, we will study them in order to understand the full meaning of the Lord's Supper. In the present chapter, we look at the commemoration aspect of it.

165

Luke 22:19 forms the blessed motto for the Feast: "Do this in remembrance of Me." This banquet commemorates our Lord and all that He means to us. It reminds us of Him in a special way that nothing else can.

We celebrate the Lord's Supper to remember Christ's death. Through His blood, we have been freed from the pollution, the power, and the punishment of sin. And out of loving gratitude for Him, we observe this banquet. It reminds us that we have been washed in the blood of the Crucified One. It is for His honor. And He who instituted the Feast engraved, as it were, this motto upon its Table:

"When this you see,
Remember Me."

Remember Him! Is there any danger of our forgetting Him? If we were not so taken up with the world and the flesh and the devil, we could not forget Him. But, due to the treacherous forgetfulness of these souls of ours, the Supper of Christ has been appointed to remind us of His death for us. The center of it is His cross. In it we are to know Christ and Him crucified.

We take the Lord's Supper to remember His death in our own hearts. This Feast is admirably designed to stir up our pure minds by way of remembrance, that, giving such earnest attention to the things that belong to the great salvation, we may not at any time let them slip. The Supper protrays the crucifixion of Jesus in a manner that greatly impresses us as we partake of its heavenly food. He is openly set forth before us suffering and dying and saving us from our sins (Galatians 3:1).

How does the Breaking of the Bread do this for us? In these three ways: 1) by instilling in us an adequate knowledge of Christ crucified; 2) by presenting before our very

eyes the glories of Calvary; and 3) by stimulating holy meditation concerning Jesus and His dying love for us. In these
three ways, the Lord's Supper causes us to remember our
Lord at Calvary and to praise Him for His wondrous love.
Let us study how the Feast is a commemoration.

REMEMBERING HIS DEATH
TO UNDERSTAND HIS CROSS

The Lord's Supper as a commemorating feast causes
us to preserve the memory of His death in our hearts by
instilling in us an adequate knowledge of Christ crucified.
The very nature of the Eucharist stimulates us to know the
doctrine of the cross. It compels us to understand His death.
The Supper creates in our souls a deep desire, an earnest
cry, a hungering and thirsting after the knowledge of Calvary and all that Jesus did there. It motivates us to labor
after a clearer insight into the grand mystery of our salvation by the death of Jesus.

And these two work hand in hand. The more earnestly
we desire to receive the Supper reverently, the more we
will want to know about the cross. And the more we learn
of Calvary, the more we will want to partake of the Lord's
Table.

Therefore, let us come to the Feast with minds and
hearts filled with the theology of the cross. May we let the
Holy Communion draw us like a magnet to the Holy Scriptures. There we will study at the Master's feet, learning all
we can about "the old rugged cross . . . where the dearest
and best for a world of lost sinners was slain." The Word
of God and the Supper of God are thus seen to be the
siamese twins of the Gospel of God. The Lord's Supper
will effectively cause us to remember Christ's glorious work

on the cross only in so far as we have diligently studied all about it in Holy Writ.

Yes, the Lord's Supper as a commemorating banquet stimulates us to learn more and more about God's grace for us.

REMEMBERING HIS DEATH TO SEE
CHRIST CRUCIFIED

The Lord's Supper as a commemorating feast causes us to preserve the memory of His death by showing us the glories of Calvary. The Eucharist brings clearly before the eyes of faith the death of Jesus in all its radiant splendor. The Feast is one grand symbolic drama of Christ dying for us. It is one tremendous object lesson or visual aid that reveals to our minds the grandeur of grace in all its manifold beauty. In the Supper, we see Jesus Christ lifted up before us. He is dying there on the accursed tree for our sins. He is enduring the horrific wrath of God in our place so that we may be saved by faith at the time of water baptism. He is suffering for sinners such as we.

And we are to meditate solemnly, reverently, and seriously upon that which is represented and set before us at the Supper. David of old desired only one thing: to dwell in the house of the Lord all the days of his life, that he might behold the beauty (literally, "delightfulness") of the Lord and to see His power and His glory (Psalms 23:6; 27:4; 63:2). And so it is with us at the Table of the Lord. We come together to behold the beauty of the Christ, to see the "delightfulness" of His love and grace and mercy, to bask in the Sonlight of His cross, and to realize the power and glory of Calvary. The Communion reveals these sights to our eyes as we meditate on things signified by the signs of bread and fruit of the vine. We truly see Jesus crucified through the elements. He is not in the elements, but they direct our thoughts to His cross. This is commemoration.

The Holy Eucharist beckons us on to see great sights, the glories of Calvary. And what should we see with the eyes of faith?

We See the Lamb of God Slain from the Foundation of the World

As we partake of the Communion, we behold the Lamb of God slain from the foundation of the world. This is the most basic scene given for our eyes to see in the Lord's Supper.

In the Supper we see Jesus the Perfect Sin-Sacrifice, as if He had been slain (Revelation 5:6). In the last book of the Bible, the Book of Revelation, the Apostle John is given the marvelous privilege of seeing visions of heaven and writing them down. But of all the sights he records, none to me is so thrilling as the vision of the Throne-Room in chapter 4. In the center is the Father, the Almighty and Sovereign Lord of the universe, seated high and lifted up in radiant splendor on His majestic throne; surrounding Him are the four living beings, the twenty-four elders, and countless thousands of other angels. But between the throne and the twenty-four elders, there stands "a Lamb, as if slain" (Revelation 5:6). He forms the very center of attention throughout this chapter (not to mention the entire book of Revelation!). Even in heaven, Jesus is always remembered and honored as the Lamb of God who takes away the sin of the world, whose death redeems sinners, whose blood cleanses our filthy souls. He stands forth in matchless beauty and holiness as if He had just been sacrificed for us, bleeding afresh, and yet alive, constantly presenting His blood within the veil—the blood of the Lamb always available to save sinners to the uttermost, that it may still be sprinkled on our consciences, to purify and comfort them, and may still speak in heaven for us, in that prevailing intercession which the Lord Jesus ever lives to make there in virtue of His death on the cross.

In the Lord's Supper, the Lord's death is shown forth; it is shown forth to us, that it may be shown forth by us. We meet together at the Table of the Lord, awed by the tremendous privilege given to us, "before whose eyes Jesus Christ was publicly portrayed as crucified" (Galatians 3:1), that we may "all with unveiled face beholding as in a mirror the glory of the Lord" (2 Corinthians 3:18) see "the light of the knowledge of the glory of God in the face of Christ" (2 Corinthians 4:6). Still He is seen through the Eucharist as the Lamb that had been slain; for this sacrifice does not, like the Old Testament offerings, decay and wear out.

This is the sight, the great sight, that God grants us as we partake of Communion. The wounds of this Lamb are here open before us. Come, let us see in Christ's hands the very print of the nails, see in His side the very mark of the spear. Behold Him in His agony in the Garden of Gethsemane, "praying very fervently; and His sweat became like drops of blood, falling down upon the ground" (Luke 22:44). Behold Him before the judgment bar of Caiaphas, Annas, Pontius Pilate, and Herod Antipas, being prosecuted and condemned as a common criminal, because He was made sin for us, and had undertaken to answer for our guilt. Behold Him upon the cross, enduring the pain and despising the shame of the accursed tree. Here is His body broken, His blood shed, His soul poured out in death; all His sufferings with all their agonies are revealed to us at the Supper. And we see them and are impressed by them.

We See the Horrific Evil of All Sin

Sin never appeared uglier than at Calvary. For there we see the horrific evil of sin. This we are concerned to see, that we may be truly humbled for our past sins and resolved to conquer sin in the future. To hate sin, we direct our eyes to Calvary; to direct our eyes to Calvary, we receive the Eucharist. It was for our transgressions that Christ was so wounded, for our iniquities that He was so crushed and bruised (Isaiah 53:5).

Here sin appears as sin, and by the cross of Christ, as well as by the command of God, it becomes "utterly sinful" (Romans 7:13). The Lord's Supper reveals to us how much God hates our sins but loves our souls. The malignant nature of all iniquity, even the smallest, comes forth in bold array at the cross. And we behold this through the Breaking of the Bread.

Here sin appears as death, and in the cross of Christ shows itself utterly hurtful. Behold and see what evil and trouble and harm sin produces, by observing how much it cost the Redeemer, when he undertook to save us from its punishment. Notice how He sweated and groaned, bled and died, when the "Lord caused the iniquity of us all to fall upon Him" (Isaiah 53:6). See the ugly wretchedness of all sin here. Nothing can be more so. The wages of sin is death: physical, spiritual, and eternal (Romans 5:12-21; 6:23; Ephesians 2:1, 5; Revelation 20:14-15). The fatal consequences of sin are seen more in the sufferings of Christ, than in all the calamities that it has brought upon the world of mankind. Oh, what a painful, what a shameful thing is sin, which put our Lord Jesus to so much pain, to so much shame, when He bore our "sins in His own body upon the tree" (1 Peter 2:24)!

171

In the Lord's Supper, I bring all of this home to my own heart, applying it to me, as if my sins and my sins alone had nailed the blessed Savior to the cursed cross. There I forget about everyone else. I do not think of their sins for the time being. Instead, I think of my own. I remember how much pain and woe that I caused Jesus. He died for my sins. And now I behold the horrific nature of my sins through observing the Lord's Supper.

Let me illustrate what I mean here. Isaiah 53:5 declares, "But He was pierced through for our transgressions, He was crushed for our iniquities; the chastening for our well-being fell upon Him, and by His scourging we are healed." To make the Supper all the more personal to me and me alone, I find it most helpful to read it like this: "But He was pierced through for my transgressions, He was crushed for my iniquities; the chastening for my well-being fell upon Him, and by His scourging I am healed." That is, every time "our" occurs in the text, I insert the word "my." My sins nailed Him to that cross.

Notice something else about this text in Isaiah 53:5. The Hebrew word that is translated "crushed" in the phrase, "he was crushed for our iniquities," occurs also in Psalms 51:17 where David says the only sacrifice well-pleasing to God is a heart that is "contrite." A contrite heart is a crushed heart, crushed as fine and small as Jesus was at the cross. When we partake of Communion and see the crushed and broken body of our Lord dying on the cross, our only response can be a crushed and broken heart. The Supper destroys our pride. "When I survey the wondrous cross," I must "pour contempt on all my pride."

You see, it was your sin, your own iniquity, that lay so heavily upon the Lord Jesus, when He cried out, "My soul is deeply grieved, to the point of death" (Matthew 26:38).

It was your pride and lust, your worldliness and uncleanness, the fleshly mind in you, the sin-loving heart in you,
which is hostility against God, that crowned Him with
thorns, and nailed Him to the cross, and caused the Father
to turn His back on His only begotten Son. If this is true,
never again will we treat sin so lightly. Never again will we
make a light matter of that which Christ made so great a
matter. The pleasures of sin for a season, the worldly profit
that sin can promise, will never balance the pain and shame
they caused my dear Redeemer.

When the Feast brings before our eyes the horrific evil
of our sins, we must do nothing else but take holy revenge
upon ourselves. That is, our attitude will be: if sin was the
death of my Savior, why should not I be the death of all my
sin? Such an attitude is one of the fruits of godly sorrow. As
we eat the bread and drink the fruit of the vine, we see that
our own sin caused His cruel death. It was our fault that
He had to die. We feel deep sorrow in our hearts for doing
that to Him. This godly sorrow ought to lead us inevitably
to hate our sin and to meditate holy revenge against it. Did
sin, did my sin, nail Jesus to the awful cross? And shall not
I nail sin to a cross also? Shall not I crucify it? If it be asked
"Why, what evil has it done?" I respond, "It cost the blood
of the Son of God to cleanse it; and therefore, I cry out so
much the more, 'Crucify it, crucify it!'" As Christ died for
sin, so we must die to sin (Romans 6:3-14). This attitude of
holy vengeance comes forth brilliantly in Luke 18:13,
where the penitent tax-collector in the Temple beats against
his chest, crying out: "God, be merciful to me the sinner."
Or in 1 Timothy 1:15, "Jesus Christ came into the world
to save sinners, among whom I am foremost of all." But
especially it appears in 2 Corinthians 7:9-11. The Corinthian Christians had fallen into grave error and loose living.

173

Their lifestyle was fleshly, their orthodoxy was shaky, and their unity was a travesty. In his first epistle to them, the Apostle to the Gentiles had castigated them severely by the authority of Christ. They had read his letter and grieved over their wrongs, repenting of their sins and reforming their lives. In the text before us, he praises them for their transformed attitudes. In verse 11, Paul describes how their godly sorrow had led them to take holy revenge against their sins: "For behold what earnestness this very thing, this godly sorrow, has produced in you: . . . what avenging of wrong! In everything you demonstrated yourselves to be innocent in the matter." Obviously, Paul approved of their actions. He applauded this holy vengeance. It is from the Holy Spirit. And we ought to do a lot more of it, especially as we partake of Communion.

When we think of the Supper, we think of the Christ; when we think of the Christ, we think of His cross; when we think of His cross, we think of our sins that put Him there; and when we think of our sins, we must meditate holy revenge against them, hating them, despising them, vowing never to commit them again as long as we live. In this manner, the Lord's Supper brings to our attention the horrific evil of all our sins.

We See the Justice of God

At the cross of Christ, God the Judge appears in all His justice and righteous wrath against sin. It is true, as 1 John 4:8 points out, "God is love"; but He is also holy and righteous and totally opposed to all sin (see Hebrews 10:30-31; 12:29; Romans 1:18ff.; Habakkuk 1:13; Psalm 94:23; John 3:36; Revelation 6:16). One of the most common errors in Christian thought today is for us to make one divine attribute more important than any other. God's love is great, but so is His justice. In sending His Son into the world to die on the cross, God has done everything possible to demonstrate His forgiving love and grace for all mankind (John 3:16; Romans 5:6-8). But His righteous wrath will execute justice upon all who spurn His mercy. From the second chapter of Genesis to the last verse of Revelation, the Word of God declares in unmistakable language that the soul that sins will die. In many remarkable punishments of sin, even in this life, it is written as with a sunbeam, so he that runs may read, "The Lord is righteous."

In many ways God has made it crystal clear that He hates sin. And, both by the judgments of His mouth in the written Word, and the judgments of His hand in the course of His providence, He has revealed "His wrath from heaven against all ungodliness and unrighteousness of men" (Romans 1:18).

But never did the justice and wrath of God appear so clearly as in the death and sufferings of Jesus Christ set before our eyes in the Lord's Supper. Come and see the holy God, showing His displeasure against sin in the death of Christ, more than in the ruin of angels, the drowning of the old world, the burning of Sodom, and the destruction of Jerusalem—yes, even more than in the eternal torments of hell.

To see the justice of God in the death of Jesus, we need to study the nature of the atonement. What do we mean by that term "atonement"? We mean first of all that our sins have separated us from God's fellowship (Isaiah 59:1-2). We are at enmity against Him, hostile to Him; and His wrath hangs over our heads like the proverbial sword of Damocles. We mean secondly that His love sent Jesus into the world to bring us back into harmony with Him. Jesus

175

accomplished this reconciling act by dying on the cross, producing the "at-one-ment," or atonement. But why did he have to die? What was there about the nature of God and the nature of sin that necessitated such an act?

The answer is found in the term "propitiation." Christ's death is a propitiatory sacrifice. To understand it, we need to see the nature of God: First, God is absolutely righteous, holy, and just; He despises all sin, and has decreed that it be punished in hell. Therefore, His wrath requires man's condemnation in hell. Second, God is absolutely loving, gracious, and compassionate, never willing that any should perish in hell. He loves mankind, His creation. Therefore, His love desires our salvation in heaven. But, thirdly, this presents a problem: since His wrath requires the punishment of the sinner and His love desires the salvation of the sinner, how can God do both at the very same time? How can the sin be punished so that the righteous demands of God's law and justice are satisfied, but how can the sinner be forgiven so that the loving desires of God's mercy are satisfied? It has rightly been called "a problem fit for God."

And God answers it by "propitiation." Although the term itself does not occur often in Scripture (Romans 3:25; 1 John 2:2; 4:10; with the verb appearing in Hebrews 2:17), the idea fills the pages of the Word of God. The word itself means "to turn away God's wrath from sinners by placing it upon Jesus at the cross." The *New International Version* calls it an "atoning sacrifice," with a footnote, "The One who turns aside God's wrath." God sends Jesus into the world to die on the cross. As Jesus is dying there, God places all the hellish torments of eternal punishment upon His Son. Thus, Jesus endures God's full wrath in our place, as our Sin-Substitute, so that we do not have to be punished. As a propitiation, the death of Christ removes the wrath

176

of God from us. This is clearly taught in the following texts of the Bible: "He made Him who knew no sin to be sin on our behalf, that we might become the righteousness of God in Him" (2 Corinthians 5:21); "Christ redeemed us from the curse of the Law, having become a curse for us" (Galatians 3:13); "but the Lord has caused the iniquity of us all to fall on Him" (Isaiah 53:6). This is "propitiation." It satisfies both the justice of God, which is the main point we are discussing here, as well as the love of God. Since all sin is thoroughly punished in Jesus on the cross, God's justice and wrath are satisfied. Since sinners do not have to suffer the wrath of God because their sins have already been punished at Calvary, God's love is satisfied. (And they will appropriate this salvation to their own personal souls through faith in Christ and baptism for the forgiveness of sin). The problem has been answered.

But the vital point here is that God's justice is fully satisfied at the cross of Jesus. There on Mount Calvary the price for sin was paid in full. His wrath was revealed, but it was also pacified. For sinners to go to heaven, Jesus had to suffer hell at the cross. There was no other way. By His wounds we are healed; the well-being of our souls is possible only because He was severely punished (Isaiah 53:5).

Part of the propitiatory nature of the cross is the fact that Christ's death was a substitutionary sacrifice. That is, He took the sinner's place. We deserved to go to hell, but He endured its awful punishment in our place at Calvary; He never actually went to hell itself, but what He suffered at Calvary was the fullest equivalent of eternal torment in hell. The doctrine of Christ as our glorious Substitute is found in such passages of Scripture as, "Christ redeemed us from the curse of the Law, having become a curse for us"

(Galatians 3:13); "the Son of Man did not come to be served, but to serve, and to give His life a ransom for many" (Matthew 20:28; see Mark 10:45). In all three texts, the preposition "for" means "in the place of," "instead of." It is the Greek word *anti*.

At the Lord's Supper, we see the justice of God. At the cross sin is fully dealt with. The Eucharist causes us to behold his sight fully and impressively. We take the broken bread and the cup and we think, "What was done to Him, shows what should have been done to us, if Jesus had not been our Substitute—our Propitiation, and what will be done to us if we reject Him." It reveals to us that our salvation may be free as far as we are concerned, but it cost God everything He had. It was certainly not inexpensive or free to Him; it cost Him His only Son; it cost His Son the very life He had. What a price they paid for me! "Jesus paid it all; all to Him I owe; sin had left a crimson stain; He washed me white as snow." At the Table of the Lord, we see the justice of God making possible our salvation in Christ.

We See the Love of Christ

At the cross of Christ, the love of God shines forth with a dazzling brilliance. This is what we behold as we eat the broken bread and drink the fruit of the vine. The dying love of our Savior fills us with joy. This is the blessed result of the Eucharist. Where we see Christ and Him crucified, we cannot but see the love of Christ, which surpasses all understanding. When He did but drop a tear over the grave of Lazarus (John 11:35), the Jews there exclaimed, "Behold, how He loved him!" (John 11:36). Much more reason have we to say, when we commemorate the shedding of His

178

blood for us, "See how He loves us!" "Greater love has no man than this, that one lay down His life for His friends" (John 15:13). Thus Jesus has loved us; but wait, He laid down His life for us when we were enemies (Romans 5: 6-8). His is a divine love, a supernatural compassion, a miraculous grace. It is unlike any other kind of love witnessed by mortals. Here is real love without parallel.

See in the Eucharist that Christ's love was free. He gave Himself for us, freely, voluntarily, without being forced. It was a free gift. His love was free because it was unmerited: there was nothing desirable in us, nothing promising; the relation in which we stood to God as creatures did but underline our guilt still more and make us appear all the more obnoxious. Since God does not need our happiness, so He cannot be damaged by our misery. Yet He loved us anyway. Also, His love was free because it was unforced. He willingly offered His very own self. He showed forth the "here am I—send Me" attitude in every step of His earthly ministry, and especially at the cross. His sacrifice was bound to the horns of the altar, only with the cords of His own love.

See in the Eucharist the distinguishing love of Christ. It was good-will to fallen man, and not to fallen angels (Hebrews 2:16). He did not lay hold on a world of sinking angels, to lift them up and rescue them from their demonic sins. No, as their tree fell, so it lies, and so it will lie forever. The demons who sinned cannot be saved. They are lost. But on the seed of Abraham Jesus takes hold to save. Although angels—even demons—are a higher form of creation than man, yet God chose to send His Son to die for the lost humanity alone. Christ's love was a distinguishing love; He came to redeem mankind alone—not the fallen angels.

179

See in the Eucharist the condescending love of Christ. Never did love humble itself and stoop so low as the love of Christ did. It was great condescension that He should fix His love upon creatures so sinful, so low, "man who is a worm and the son of man who is a worm." Mankind, due to sin, had fallen so low that they were closer to the brutes of the field. One would think we should rather be the scorn than the love of the heavenly beings. Yet we are the reason He suffered and died. Oh! what infinite condescending love this is! Oh! the mighty gulf that God did span when He sent His Son to save us from sin!

But the glory of His condescending love is seen also in His death, that He should humble Himself as He did. He humbled Himself at His Incarnation when He came into the world, taking on full human nature (yet without sin— Hebrews 4:15); but He humbled Himself in the fullest possible degree when He suffered and died on the cross. He became obedient to death, even the death of a cross (Philippians 2:8). That was the lowest humiliation He could ever endure; and He endured it for you and for me. His condescending love is truly an impressive sight to behold, and we behold it at the Lord's Supper.

See in the Eucharist that Christ's love was expensive. It cost Him all He had. His washing the feet of His disciples is spoken of as an act of love to them; and that was truly condescending love, but not costly like His death was. He loved us, and bought us, and paid dearly for us, that we might be to Him a purchased people, a people belonging to the Lord (1 Peter 2:9; Titus 2:11-15). Because He loved us, He gave Himself for us, even His own blood for the ransom of our sinful souls.

See in the Eucharist the strong love of Christ. It is strong as death. Many waters cannot quench it. This is the greatness of His strength, in which the Redeemer travelled, who is mighty to save. That love conquered all the many difficulties that got in its way. When Jesus had this baptism of blood to be baptized with, it was His mighty love that exclaimed: "But I have a baptism to undergo, and how distressed I am until it is accomplished!" (Luke 12:50). He came into the world for only one purpose; and that was to die for our sins. His love constrained Him to set His face steadfastly toward Jerusalem (Luke 9:51). And He let nothing keep Him from that awesome appointment with death and sin. In this manner, His love underwent great distress until His death was accomplished. When Jesus was suffering in the Garden, He prayed that His heavenly Father would make this cup pass from Him so that He would not need to die. But it was His divine love—so strong to save—that caused our Lord to change the petition to be, "Yet not as I will but as Thou wilt" (Matthew 26:39).

And finally, we see in the Eucharist that Christ's love was everlasting. It was from everlasting in its counsels and will be to everlasting in its results. It is not like our love, which comes up in a night and perishes in a night. He loved to the end, and went on loving even while He said from the cross, "It is finished!" (John 19:30).

Yes, as we partake of the Holy Supper, the love of our Lord is portrayed in all its radiance.

We See the Defeat of the Devil

This is a most pleasing sight to all those who have been transferred out of the domain of darkness into the kingdom of the Son of His love (Colossians 1:13). Christ has delivered us from the devil's strangle-hold. Come to the

Supper of the Lord and see that at the cross our Lord rendered the devil powerless (Hebrews 2:14), and He "destroyed the works of the devil" (1 John 3:8). Christ our Joshua has conquered the Amalekites, our David has beaten the Philistine giant—Goliath. See Jesus disarming "the rulers and authorities, making a public display of them, having triumphed over them" through the cross (Colossians 2:15). These "rulers and authorities" are nothing less than the demons and evil spirits who follow their leader, Satan (see Ephesians 6:11-12). And Jesus robbed them of their property, their goods, and their control over the lives of men. And He did all of this through His glorious death and resurrection. Though, when He was in the most painful stage of His sufferings, there was darkness over all the land, which gave the powers of darkness all the advantage they could possibly wish for, yet Christ Himself beat the enemy upon his own ground—at Calvary.

Christ, by dying, made atonement for sin, and therefore conquered Satan. By the merit of His death, Jesus satisfied God's justice for the sins of all that should believe in Him; and if the judge cancels the sentence, the executioner has nothing to do with the prisoner. The accuser of our brethren has been cast down (Revelation 12:10-11). Who shall accuse God's people (Romans 8:33-34)? No one, especially not Satan, for Christ's blood has covered our sins and God cannot see them. If we cannot be condemned by the Judge, then we are saved from coming into the execution-chamber of hell.

Christ, by dying, guaranteed the Gospel of grace, and purchased the Spirit of grace; and so conquered Satan. The Gospel, acting as the tool of the Holy Spirit, and the Holy Spirit, acting as the Agent of the Gospel, are both "divinely powerful for the destruction of fortresses" and strongholds owned and operated by Satan (2 Corinthians 10:4). Thus a foundation is laid for a believer's victory over the temptations and terrors of the wicked one. Christ's victory over Satan is our victory, and we overcome him "by the blood of the Lamb" (Revelation 12:11). Christ, having thus trampled the devil under our feet (Genesis 3:15; Romans 16:20), calls to us, as Joshua to the captains of Israel, "Come near, put your feet on the necks of these kings" (Joshua 10:24). "Resist the devil, and he will flee from you" (James 4:8), for he is a conquered foe. His forces cannot harm us. We are more than conquerors through Him who loved us and died for us. We remember that death at the Eucharist. There we see the conquest of Satan.

We See the Infinite Worth of a Human Soul

Our souls—all human souls—become extremely valuable and precious when viewed from the perspective of Christ's cross. For we judge the value of something by the price which a wise person who understands it gives for it. He who made our souls, and understood them perfectly, offered for their redemption, not "perishable things like silver or gold" but the "precious blood . . . of Christ" (1 Peter 1:18-19). It was not a purchase made quickly and hastily, for it was the plan of infinite wisdom from eternity; it was not made out of necessity—it was not forced upon Him, for God neither needed us nor could be helped by our feeble efforts, but He taught us what value we ought to place on our own souls, and how much He was willing to give for their salvation. Christ's incarnation honored our human nature. But the death and sufferings of Christ add much more to its value, for He laid down His own life to be a ransom for ours, when nothing else was sufficient to answer the price.

We need to see this grand truth and learn how to put a value upon our own souls. And the result of this will not be the inflation of our pride. Hardly so, for nothing will be more humbling and humiliating than to see our lives sold by our own foolishness and sin, and then redeemed by the merit of another. And that is what the Gospel does. It humbles us. It declares that if we are to be saved, Christ must do it all. We cannot redeem ourselves. So we learn to put a value upon our souls not to increase our arrogance, but rather to increase our concern for ourselves and our own spiritual interests. Shall the souls, the precious souls, the beloved souls, upon whom Jesus placed such a value and for whom He paid such a price, debase and under-value themselves so far as to become slaves to Satan? That is the reason we ought to learn to value our souls correctly. We have been bought with a price, the very blood of Jesus (1 Corinthians 6:19-20). And therefore we not only injure the buyer's right to us, but we also insult His wisdom in paying such a price, when we leave Him and join ourselves to Satan and sin. Since Christ has paid for our souls at such a great cost, His own blood, we do spit on our own souls when we sell them to the world at such a cheap price. We are worth more than that! Jesus says so through His cross. And we behold the great price we are worth when we partake of the Communion.

We need to see this grand truth and learn how to put a value upon the souls of others. This forbids us from doing anything that may cause them to stumble or sin. The Apostle Paul stresses this argument when he pleads with the stronger brother: "Do not destroy with your food him for whom Christ died" (Romans 14:15b). That is, we ought to deny ourselves any conveniences rather than cause guilt or grief to someone for whom Christ humbles Himself, even to the point of death on a cross. Shall we slight those upon whom Christ put such a high value? Shall we think ill of those whom Jesus purchased with His own blood? Since Jesus died for others, should we not strive to love them, aid them, and meet their needs? To see the value of souls through the mirror of the cross, motivates us to love them with His love. And we see this grand sight when we partake of the Communion. It portrays how much Jesus loves us all.

And finally, when we see the high value Christ puts upon the human soul, we will realize that evangelism is the Spirit-led fruit of rightly receiving the Lord's Supper. What we see at the Table of the Lord leads us to do all we can for the spiritual welfare and salvation of others. Did Christ think them worth His blood? And shall not we think them worth our care and pains? Shall not we willingly do our utmost to save a soul from death, and thereby cover a multitude of sins (James 5:19-20), when Jesus our Savior did so much and suffered so much to make it possible? Shall not we pour out our prayers for those for whom Christ poured out His very soul unto death?

In the Lord's Supper, we behold how much the human soul is truly worth; we are worth the very blood of the Son of God. We see this and meditate upon it as we break the bread and drink the cup. It motivates us to live only for Jesus who thought so much of us and was willing to suffer so much for us. This teaches us never to devalue our precious and expensive souls by living for the flesh, the world, and the devil.

REMEMBERING HIS DEATH TO MEDITATE UPON HIS LOVE

So far in our discussion of the Lord's Supper as a commemorating feast, we have seen that it preserves the memory

of Christ's death by instilling in us an adequate knowledge of the cross and by presenting before our very eyes
the glories of Calvary.

Now we consider the third way it makes us commemorate Christ's death: by stimulating holy meditation concerning Jesus and His dying love for us as it was demonstrated
at the cross. Here we receive the Lord's Supper and learn
the art of holy meditation.

Meditation and prayer are the daily exercise and delight
of a devout and pious soul. In meditation we converse with
ourselves; in prayer we converse with God. The power of
godliness withers and declines if secret devotion is either
neglected or negligently performed.

Now what do we mean by holy meditation? It is two
things: thought engaged and thought enflamed. First, it is
thought engaged. The heart fastens itself to a select subject
with a desire to dwell and enlarge upon it. We discipline our
minds to concentrate intently upon one blessed thought or
theme and meditate upon it for as long as we wish. It is
actually not prayer, though the two are not far apart. Meditation is the private act of thinking about themes that enrich
the soul and strengthen the heart. Second, meditation is
also thought enflamed. To meditate is not only to think
seriously of divine things, but to think of them with care and
deep affection. When the heart meditates, the spirit will
burn within us; we will feel deeply about the themes we are
considering. It will influence us to be on fire for Jesus. The
whole purpose of meditation is to make us feel deeply about
those things we are acquainted with, so that the impressions
they bring to our souls may be deep and long-lasting.

Meditation forms the center of the Eucharist; the two are
Siamese twins. To get any blessing from the Supper, we

186

must meditate as we partake. This sacred banquet enflames our hearts to love the Christ of Calvary all the more.

Serious meditation before we partake of the Communion will be of great benefit to us. It will make the things of the cross very familiar to us, and our spirits will already be prepared for a profitable time of communing with our Redeemer. We cannot come to the Lord's Table with cold hearts and numb minds and expect to see Jesus. If we would gain blessings from this Feast, we must spend some time in earnest holy meditation before we ever arrive at the church-house.

But on what should we meditate? Permit me to mention a few ideas that are fit themes for our meditations around the Table of the Lord. Use them not only for your private devotional thoughts, but also for public Communion meditations on Sunday.

Let Us Meditate on the Sinfulness and Misery of Mankind

Most of us are prone to think how good we are; few of us enjoy meditating upon our own sinfulness. Yet that is one of the most important themes we should be considering as we eat the broken bread and drink the cup. Until we see the enormity of our sin, we will never appreciate the excellence of His grace.

Think of the original Fall of Mankind in the Garden of Eden. There Adam and Eve fell from their state of innocence into one of guilt and weakness. There mankind fell into sin. There death passed on to all mankind (Romans 5:12; 1 Corinthians 15:21-22). Never was beauty so deformed, never was strength so weakened, never was honor so laid in the dust. See how miserable fallen mankind has become: see them excluded from God's favor, expelled

187

from the Garden of the Lord, and forbidden to eat from the Tree of Life. See what curses the sin of Adam brought upon all mankind; behold how man is surrounded with what armies of diseases, disasters and deaths, in the most horrid and frightful shapes.

See mankind attacked on every side throughout human history by the malignant powers of darkness that seek to destroy his soul. See mankind sentenced for sin to utter darkness, to the fires of everlasting burning. Oh what a pit of iniquity has man fallen into! His condition in himself is helpless and hopeless. A deplorable case! And shall not all of this beget in me a hatred—a holy hatred—for sin? May I never be friends of sin again, of that which has caused so much mischief and trouble to the whole race. Shall I not be revived and stimulated to flee to Christ, in whom alone help and salvation is to be found? Is this my condition? Then I will pray that God will give me grace to overcome all sin. I solemnly promise to repent and change and deny ungodliness and worldly lusts.

Here we are talking about serious self-examination of one's own sins. Am I cuddling some pet sin or sins that I have hidden from Christ? At the Supper confess them. Am I stubbornly indulging in a sinful habit that I should have given up long ago? Then at the Supper get rid of it. This is the time for us to think seriously and soberly about the lies, the gossiping, the lusts, the dirty thoughts, the critical tongue, and the impatient spirit that we from time to time reveal in our daily walk.

Speaking of self-examination and taking a long hard look at our own failings, most of us know what happened the first time Jesus observed the Eucharist with His disciples. But have you ever thought what the second observance of the Lord's Supper was like? Since the Bible does

188

not tell us, we cannot be sure. But Edwin Errett, former editor of the *Christian Standard,* says that it might have been something like this (his piece appeared in the November 9, 1929 issue of the *Christian Standard*). When the disciples met together for the second observance of the Lord's Supper, their thoughts went back to that first Eucharist. Oh how they had boldly and proudly promised never to leave Christ's side; they would stick with Him until the death; they would be His loyal followers no matter what. And this, even though He had predicted one of their number would deny Him three times! Thoughts of sin and self-examination were the farthest things from their minds on that first Eucharistic night. All they cared about was how great they were, and how they would do such great things for Jesus. But now their minds return to this second observance of the Lord's Supper. It is painfully evident to them how much they had failed their precious Lord. They had not kept even one of those rash promises. They had denied their Lord; they had forsaken their Lord; they had sinned. How differently they partake of the communion at this second observance! Deep remorse, sorrow for sin, earnest repentance are all they can think about. Now they are not quite so proud. Their thoughts are centered upon self-examination, confessing their sins, and seeking Christ's forgiveness. And this is the way we ought to take the Lord's Supper. Let us never forget that as we partake of the Eucharist, we are sinners saved by the blood of the Lamb.

Let Us Meditate on the Attributes of God in Our Redemption

As we take the Lord's Supper, we see the divine attributes shining forth in the marvelous work of our redemption. Here is a bright and noble subject, the contemplation and wonder of the heavenly angels and blessed spirits above.

At the Lord's Supper, we come and see the kindness and love of God our Savior, His good-will and grace to man, who designed our redemption, the Author and Finisher of our faith. Herein is love. Though God was happy from eternity before man had a being, and would have been happy to eternity if man had never been; though man's nature was sinful; though his crimes were heinous and detestable; though by his disobedience he had forfeited the protection of a prince; though by his ingratitude he had forfeited the kindness of a friend; and though by his fickle nature he had forfeited the benefits of a covenant; yet the tender mercies of our God moved for his relief.

Come and see God's patience and longsuffering towards man. Think how much He bears, and how long, with the world, with us, with me, though we are most provoking and obnoxious at times. This patience left room for salvation (Romans 11:33-36). Think of the measures God has taken, the means that He has devised, that the banished might not forever be expelled from Him. Think with wonder how all the divine attributes are by this plan secured from damage and reproach, so that no attribute is glorified by lessening the luster of the other. This is especially true of the way propitiation glorifies both God's wrath and His love. Oh the depths both of the wisdom and the knowledge of God! This is truly astounding and astonishing to think about during the Supper. At the Table we meditate upon such things and glorify the God of all grace.

Let Us Meditate on the Cross of Our Lord Jesus Christ

Think of the dishonors done to Him and the honors done to us through the cross of Jesus. At the Table of the

Lord, we meditate upon the Person and Work of Christ. Come and think of Him who first thought of you and died on the cross to save you. Think of Him as the eternal Son of God, the brightness of His Father's glory, and the very image of His nature; who sat at the Father's right hand from all eternity, and had an infinite joy and glory with Him before the worlds were; and in whom dwells all the fulness of deity in bodily form. He is the eternal wisdom, the eternal Word; who has life in Himself, and is one with the Father; and who did not think that being on an equality with God was a thing to be grasped and held at all costs, but humbly and unselfishly emptied Himself by taking the form of a servant, and being found in fashion as a man He humbled Himself, becoming obedient to death, even death on a cross. He is your Lord; worship Him at the Feast of bread and fruit of the vine.

Think of Him as Creator and Governor and Sustainer of the universe, without whom was not any thing made that was made.

Think of Him as Immanuel, the Incarnate Word, clothed with our lowly nature, taking part in flesh and blood, that for us in our nature He might satisfy the justice of God whom we ourselves had offended, to break the power of Satan by whom we were enslaved.

Think of Him as the Captain of our salvation, the redemption of our souls. When sacrifice and offering would not do, since the blood of bulls and goats cannot remove sin, then He said, "Behold, I have come to do Thy will"; and "we have been sanctified through the offering of the body of Jesus Christ once for all" (Hebrews 10:4, 9). See how willingly He offered Himself to do that service of salvation.

191

But also think of the dishonors done to this glorious One. Meditate upon the particulars of our Christ's sufferings, all the humiliations of His life; and especially the pains, agonies, and anguish of His death. Here is a wide field in which our minds can roam. Nor can I determine to know any thing more proper and profitable to prepare me for the Lord's Supper than Jesus Christ and Him crucified.

Come and behold the specifics of Christ's agonies on the cross. Review the story; you will still find something in it surprising and very impressive; it may even bring tears to your eyes. Take notice of all the circumstances of His sufferings. Open your Bible to Matthew 26-27; Mark 14-15; Luke 22-23; John 18-19. Read these sections prayerfully, reverently, devotionally. Pay attention to the disgrace and reproach done to Him, the shame He was burdened with. And now you can thank God for His glorious grace. Who says there just is not enough for me to think about before the bread and cup are given to me? Why, there is more than enough to meditate upon! Even if we had as much as two whole hours of meditation time before the bread came to us, it would still not be enough time.

At the Lord's Supper, we see the purchases of the cross. The blood shed at Calvary is the ransom with which we are delivered from hell; the price with which heaven is bought for us. This death of Jesus, His blood, is a price of inestimable value. We have been redeemed not with perishable things—not even the gold of Ophir or the topaz of Ethiopia—but with the precious blood of Jesus Christ, a lamb without blemish or spot. The pardon for sin, the favor of God, the fruit of the Holy Spirit, the blessings of the New Covenant, and the eternal life could not be purchased by anything less than the blood of the Lamb.

192

At the Lord's Supper, we see the victories of the cross. We behold the Lord Jesus even then a conqueror as He dies on the accursed tree. See Him disarming the rulers and authorities when He seemed totally defeated and ruined by them. Watch Christ upon the cross breaking the power of Satan, crushing the serpent's head, triumphing over death and the tomb, leading captivity captive, and going forth in that chariot of war, conquering and to conquer.

In all of this meditation, may we ever be mindful of what we owe our dear Jesus: the privileges of the Christian Way, and the glories of the heavenly home; all we have, all we hope for that is valuable, they are all precious fruits gathered from this tree of life we call the cross of Christ. Christ's wounds are for our healing, His agonies for our rest, His conflicts for our conquests, His groans for our songs, His pains for our ease, His shame for our glory, and His sufferings for our salvation.

Let Us Meditate on the Unsearchable Riches of the New Covenant

Jesus has entered into an eternal covenant with us. And it is sealed or confirmed to us in the Breaking of the Bread. Study this covenant in the inerrant pages of the New Testament. Read over the several articles of it, and see how well ordered it is in all things, so well that it could never be improved. Review its promises, which are precious and many, very many, very precious, and sure to all who believe in Jesus. Search into the hidden wealth that is treasured up in them. Dig into these mines. Bring your bucket and draw with joy out of these wells of salvation.

Meditate as you partake of this Feast. Stir up yourself to think of the privileges of being in Christ, of being justified or "declared righteous by God the Judge," of being sanctified or "made righteous by God the Surgeon." Oh the blessedness of the one whose sins are forgiven and whose iniquities are covered (Psalm 32:1; Romans 4:7-8)!

Meditate on the comforts of being a Christian, a child of God. If now I am adopted and born from above, and have received the Holy Spirit of adoption (Romans 8:15-17; Galatians 4:5-7), I possess freedom of access to the throne of God's grace, I have precious fellowship with the Holy Trinity. I have meat to eat that the world does not know about. Let such thoughts work their way into your mind and do their wondrous work upon your life as you meditate on the unsearchable riches of Christ's New Covenant.

Throughout this chapter, we have studied the commemoration aspect of the Lord's Supper. Since this feast is a memorial, it stresses the remembrance theme.

We saw that it reminds us of Christ's death in three ways: 1) by instilling in us an adequate knowledge of Christ crucified; 2) by presenting before our very eyes the glories of Calvary; and 3) by stimulating holy meditation concerning Jesus and His dying love for us.

May we let this sacred feast do its work in these hearts of ours to motivate us to remember our Lord's death, for its whole purpose is wrapped up in these words: "Do this in remembrance of Me" (Luke 22:19).

7

THE THINGS SIGNIFIED: CONFESSION

The Lord's Supper not only means commemoration, but also confession. Here the Christian openly confesses something that is of utmost importance. "For as often as you eat this bread and drink the cup, you proclaim the Lord's death until He comes" (1 Corinthians 11:26). We confess or proclaim to all around us that Jesus has saved us from all our sins, and we are eagerly awaiting His Return.

The Lord's Supper distinguishes us from all other religions. Circumcision in the Old Testament was a lasting badge of distinction. It distinguished the Jews from all other nations and religions of the ancient world. The Lord's Supper is a solemn rite by which we constantly avow the Christian name, and declare that we are not ashamed of the banner of the cross under which we were enlisted. It is a token or badge of our profession. It means that we publicly announce our loyalty and allegiance to Jesus and His cause alone. It proclaims to the world that we resolve to remain faithful servants and soldiers of the cross until death (Revelation 2:10).

In the Breaking of the Bread, we are showing forth or proclaiming the Lord's death (1 Corinthians 11:26). What does that involve? This chapter answers that all-important question to enrich our time of communion with Christ.

WE CONFESS AND PRAISE CHRIST CRUCIFIED

At the Table of the Lord, we openly praise the Christ who died for us. We glory in the cross (Galatians 6:14). We are never ashamed of it. We hold it in high esteem as the mark of our redemption.

The cross of Christ was to the Jews a stumbling-block, because they expected a Messiah who would commandeer an earthly Jewish army to conquer Rome. The cross of Christ was foolishness to the Greeks, because the doctrine of man's salvation by it was not agreeable to their own pagan philosophy. The wisdom of this world ridiculed the cross. It was absurd to them. How could anyone who had died the ignominious death of a slave and a criminal on a cross outside the gates of Jerusalem be the Savior of the world? The civil authorities of Rome and of the Jews did everything in their power to keep people from owning Jesus as their Lord. They wanted everyone to denounce Him.

However, in spite of all these ungodly efforts to ridicule the cross, the wisdom of God so ordered things that it became that which above anything else Christians have cause to glory in and to boast about. Such are the fruits, the blessings, the purchases, the victories, the triumphs of the cross, why we call it our crown of glory and diadem of beauty. The authorities of Rome thought the Church would have wanted to forget about the humiliating manner in which their God had died. But no! The Church remembers that death of their Savior-Lord upon the cross every Sunday in the Eucharist. They are proud of that tree; they honor it; they praise the Christ who died on it. As Galatians 6:14 so eloquently expresses it: "But may it never be that I should boast, except in the cross of our Lord Jesus Christ, through which the world has been crucified to me, and I to the world."

And this is what we mean when the Lord's Supper is observed. We thereby solemnly declare that we do not believe the cross of Christ is any reproach or insult or absurdity to Christianity. Rather it is our only reason for living at all in Christ. We are so far from being ashamed of it, that, whatever an unbelieving world may think of it, to us it is the wisdom of God and the power of God (1 Corinthians 1:18). It is our salvation and our only desire. We do not praise the cross, of course, but the Christ who died upon it. In the cross we see God glorified in it, and man saved by it; then is its reproach rolled away.

And we confess this grand fact for the sake of the next generation of Christians. Jesus has graciously delivered into our hands the memory of His death. This is a sacred trust to be kept and faithfully given to the next generation, to the children yet to be born, that the remembrance of it may be ever fresh and not die in our hands. This is why we confess it at the Supper.

The last verse of Psalm 22 teaches this. In that passage, David, the "sweet psalmist of Israel," sees in graphic details the agonies Christ would endure on the cross. When our Lord was dying, He applied this text to Himself as He cried out, "My God, my God, why hast Thou forsaken Me"?

(Psalm 22:1; Matthew 27:46). In verses 1-21, we behold Christ's sufferings at Calvary; then in the rest of the Psalm we see His triumphant resurrection and majestic reign at the right hand of the Father.

In the last verse, Psalm 22:31, David calls us to proclaim the good news of Christ's death to the next generation: "They will come and will declare His righteousness to a people who will be born, that He has performed it." Performed what? That Christ has performed His grand work of redemption at Calvary for the sins of the world. Through His death and resurrection, sin has been decisively dealt with; it has been fully punished; its awful price has been paid. The law of God has been satisfied and justice is pleased. The work of salvation is completed. The very last words our Savior spoke before He died reveal this grand truth: "It is finished!" (John 19:30).

We declare to the next generation, to the children yet to be born, that "the blood of Jesus His Son cleanses us from all sin" (1 John 1:7), that Jesus is the "Lamb of God who takes away the sin of the world" (John 1:29), that "He loved me and delivered Himself up for me" (Galatians 2:20), "who gave Himself up for our sins, that He might deliver us out of this present evil age" (Galatians 1:4), that "in Him we have redemption through His blood, the forgiveness of our trespasses, according to the riches of His grace" (Ephesians 1:7), "who became to us wisdom from God, and righteousness and sanctification, and redemption" (1 Corinthians 1:30).

And we do this by celebrating the Eucharist. Through it, we show them that we firmly believe and frequently think of Christ's dying for our sins. We desire that those who should come after us may do so too.

WE CONFESS OUR CONFIDENCE IN AND DEPENDENCE ON CHRIST CRUCIFIED

To confess the Lord's death until He comes is not merely to announce our belief that Jesus died upon the cross some two thousand years ago. For any atheist could do that. Any non-Christian might do that. Anyone who is a mere world-ling, someone who is completely careless about living the Christ-like life of faith in the Son of God, would probably be able to announce that. All these individuals might accept the fact of Christ's dying as an historical event. And they might even confess that the one who so died on that tree was no ordinary man. But such a confession would not be Christian confession. It would not be what the Apostle Paul is getting at in 1 Corinthians 11:26.

No. What he means by the phrase, "you proclaim the Lord's death until He comes," is simply this: we proclaim that death as a fact upon which all our hopes of access to God and all our hopes of life, salvation, and of blessedness depend. Then—and only then—do we truly confess His death at the Lord's Supper. We announce our confidence in and dependence on Christ's blood as the only means of salvation from sin. "All other ground is sinking sand. All other ground is sinking sand."

Jesus alone is Lord. As we are not ashamed to own Him, so we are not afraid to commit our souls and their eternal salvation to Him, believing that He is able to save to the uttermost all who come to God through Him (Hebrews 7:25).

And by partaking of the broken loaf and fruit of the vine, we deliberately put ourselves under the protection of His righteousness, the influence of His grace, and the conduct and the operation of the Holy Spirit. We give ourselves totally to Him. "I am not ashamed; for I know whom I have believed and I am convinced that He is able to guard what I have entrusted to Him until that day" (2 Timothy 1:12). This is what we confess through the celebration of the Lord's Supper. We confess that He is our Lord. We are His willing and obedient servants. We put ourselves under His authority, doing whatever He tells us. We confess that He is a skillful surgeon, and that we are His patients. We will obey the infallible prescriptions of our Great Physician.

In short, at the Lord's Table we profess and confess that we are not ashamed of the Gospel of Christ, nor of the cross of Christ which is the power of God for salvation to all believers.

WE CONFESS THAT JESUS IS
COMING AGAIN FOR US

The belief in Christ's return on the clouds of heaven is a glorious by-product of the Lord's Supper. By observing this Feast, we not only declare that Jesus cleanses us from all sin, but also that He will return again to take us to heaven with Him. Through it, we confess not only the Gospel of Christ's death, but also that great Gospel which is the center and basis of all Christian hope: the Gospel of the second coming of Jesus Christ our Lord. This "blessed hope" (Titus 2:13) is what we confess at the Table of the Lord. As we eat the broken bread and drink the fruit of the vine, we look backward to the past and forward to the future. We look back at Christ's first coming and confess its redemptive power; then at the same time we look forward to His second coming and confess it as being the one grand act in which that redemptive work on Calvary will reach its full and its glorious climax. And in between these two tremendous events stands the Supper of the Lord as a majestic bridge, linking the past with the future.

In the original Words of Institution spoken by our Lord, we see a clear reference to the future: "but I say to you, I will not drink of this fruit of the vine from now on until that day when I drink it new with you in My Father's kingdom" (Matthew 26:29; see also Mark 14:25; Luke 22:18). God's Kingdom comes in two phases: 1) the Kingdom militant has been on the earth ever since the Day of Pentecost in A. D. 30 (see Acts 2:22-36; Colossians 1:12-14; Hebrews 12:22-29). 2) When Jesus returns on the clouds of heaven in splendor and glory, He will inaugurate the second phase of that Kingdom—the Kingdom triumphant, victorious over all evil and opposition. That is heaven, and it is what Jesus is referring to at the Last Supper.

In 1 Corinthians 11:26, Paul also clearly refers to the future: we proclaim the Lord's death "until He comes."

At the Supper we remember His death which implies His Return. His cross and throne are thus linked by an eternal bond. Being what it is, if He has once been offered to bear the sins of many, so He must come the second time for salvation without reference to sin, to those who eagerly await Him (Hebrews 9:27-28). So as we eat the bread and drink the cup, we confess that Jesus is returning for us. His Ascension is not the end of things. He will one day split open the skies and descend in full power and glory to redeem us from all sin and its mortifying effects. He will raise us from death, giving us new glorified bodies that will never decay or die or suffer. He will take us home with Him to the New Jerusalem. We will see His face and serve Him always. This we proclaim at the Breaking of the Bread. That sacred meal is a glorious prophecy of future blessings that will certainly come to us.

Of all earthly signs and tokens, there is none which seems so wonderfully ordained to prepare us for the last Day and keep us in mind of it, as the . . . holy Communion of the Body and Blood of Christ. Holy Scripture expressly connects the one with the other; the Communion with the Day of Judgment. . . . this mode of remembering our Lord's Death, and setting it forth before God and man, should never cease, while the world should stand. One generation after another will perish from the face of the earth; cities and empires will fade away; the wisdom of the wise, and the understanding of the prudent will be forgotten; customs, manners, languages may change, and the outward face of things be ever so different: but still this holy memorial of God made Man and crucified for us will go on being . . . [remembered], and the holy Feast will go on to be received, from time to time, in all Churches of all lands, until that last morning break upon the earth, and the very meaning and substance of . . . the body of our Lord Jesus Christ, shall appear openly in the eyes of men.[1]

Yes, in the Supper of the Lord we confess our hope in the second coming of Christ. This simple feast stimulates us to look forward to that glorious time. But how does it do this? What is there about this meal that excites us to hope in His Return? Precisely how is the Supper of Christ connected to the Appearing of our great God and Savior Jesus Christ? It is connected in the following three ways: 1) as the Banquet of Christian Assurance, 2) as the Banquet of Christian Conformity, and 3) as the Banquet of Christian Perseverance.

The Banquet of Christian Assurance

The Lord's Supper confirms our hope that Jesus shall come. The Feast assures us that He is coming again for His People—the Church. Truly the Lord's Supper is the banquet of assurance.

---

1. John Keble, *Sermons for the Christian Year* (Oxford: James Parker, 1876), 2:469.

The Bible never uses the word "hope" to mean a doubtful wish, something that we are not sure will come true. We might use it in that way, but Scripture never does. Instead, the Word of God uses this glorious term to mean the confident expectation of future good to men from God. It is something we can bank on for sure; it will certainly come to us from God. It is packed with blessings from the Father of mercies. But it comes in the future. This is true Biblical "hope."

And the Lord's Supper gives us that kind of confident hope in the return of Jesus Christ. It provides us with that assurance by which we know He is returning for us; it is sure. The more we celebrate it, the more the certainty of His coming rests in our hearts.

The Supper provides this certainty by showing us that we are at peace with Christ. "Therefore, beloved, since you look for these things, be diligent to be found by Him in peace, spotless and blameless" (2 Peter 3:14). If we ever are to have a strong hope in the return of Jesus, we must be sure that when He comes back we will be found by Him in peace.

And this peace can come only by the assurance that we are now the friends of God. Formerly we were His enemies, but now we have become His children. He is our Friend; we are His own.

And in this sacred meal, we are fully assured that we have become His friends. How? Because the Eucharist shows us that Christ's death has fully reconciled us with the Father. "And although you were formerly alienated and hostile in mind, engaged in evil deeds, yet He has now reconciled you in His fleshly body through death, in order to present you before Him holy and blameless and beyond reproach" (Colossians 1:21-22). His death has united us

203

with Him. At the Table of the Lord, this death is preached to us through powerful symbolism and dramatic actions. Christ is openly set forth before our eyes as crucified for our sins. In graphic and picturesque realism, the Supper portrays the reconciling death of our Redeemer. And in this manner, it confirms our conviction that we are at peace with God through the marvelous work of Christ on the cross.

Therefore, the Holy Eucharist is the banquet of Christian Assurance, testifying to us that God loves us, He has saved us, and Jesus is coming again for us. We can anticipate His return without fear, for we will be found by Him in peace.

This is the first way that the Lord's Supper is connected with the second coming of Christ.

The Banquet of Christian Conformity

If we are to be fully prepared for the return of our Lord, we must be conformed to His holy image (Romans 8:29). All who are seriously awaiting the return of their Savior on the clouds of heaven will also be conforming their lives to His. "And everyone who has this hope fixed on Him purifies himself, just as He is pure" (1 John 3:3). To be ready for the second coming is to be conformed to Christ's likeness.

As we endeavor to walk the Christian way, God in His abundant mercy has provided many means of grace by which He molds us and makes us after the image of His own Son. But one of the most important of these is the Eucharist. For there we confess Christ's return; we think forward to that time when He returns for His Church. And this stimulates us to be conformed to His holy image. The Feast is a banquet of Christian conformity.

This is the second way that the Lord's Supper is connected with the second coming of Christ.

The Banquet of Christian Perseverance

The Lord's Supper provides us with the grace needed to live the Christian life to the very end. It strengthens us so that we never give up or despair. We persistently continue on the Christian way and we gain blessed perseverance by communing with the Christ in the Breaking of the Bread.

And is not this the one thing needful as we live in the present, between the first and second coming of our Lord? We must have perseverance, the ability to keep on keeping on in the life Christ calls us to live, day by day acting more and more firmly. If we are to be prepared for His return, we do need this grace of perseverance to await His coming with all patience by doing good for others. And it somes to us in many different ways from God's bounty, but especially in and through the Supper of the Lord.

In the days of old, God told His prophet Elijah to arise and eat; and after the man of God did so, he went in the strength of that food for forty days and forty nights to Mt. Horeb—the mountain of God (1 Kings 19:7-8). And so it is with us in the Lord's Supper. God says to us: "You who are wearied and burdened with life's toils and difficulties and woes, come and sit at My Table; here is the bread and the cup. Take and eat." And through His love we find strength in weakness and refreshment in weariness. We persevere through the Eucharist.

In these three ways the Supper of the Lord is intimately connected with the second coming of Christ. It confirms our hope, it conforms our lives to His, and it bolsters our perseverance. We need all three if we are to wait patiently for His return on the clouds of heaven with His holy ones.

205

So in the Eucharist, we truly confess our hope in the second coming of our Lord. We proclaim His death until He comes. This prophetic confession stimulates us to lift our eyes to the heavens for our redemption is drawing near (Luke 21:28).

WE CONFESS OUR SINS TO GOD

Finally, at the Table of the Lord we confess to God that we are sinners saved by His divine love and grace. We confess our sins to Him, knowing that they have already been forgiven through the death of His only begotten Son (1 John 1:8-10).

Self-Examination

To do this properly, we must devote ourselves to self-examination. At the Lord's Table we pray with the Psalmist of old:

Search me, O God, and know my heart;
Try me and know my anxious thoughts;
And see if there be any hurtful way in me,
And lead me in the everlasting way
(Psalm 139:23-24).

The beloved Apostle to the Gentiles declared: "But let a man examine himself, and so let him eat of the bread and drink of the cup" (1 Corinthians 11:28). Self-examination, retiring into our own hearts, forgetting the world, confessing our sins, these acts from the very center of the Lord's Supper. Without such self-examination, we "shall be guilty of the body and the blood of the Lord" (1 Corinthians 11:27).

To examine ourselves is to put serious questions to ourselves, and to our own hearts; and to think about them until
we give a full and true answer. This is how we confess our
sins at the Eucharist. As we prepare to receive the symbols
of bread and cup, we ask ourselves these six questions: 1)
What am I? 2) What have I done? 3) What am I doing? 4)
What progress do I make? 5) What do I want? 6) What shall
I resolve to do?

What Am I?

This question requires no deep thought, but it calls for
serious consideration, that I am a reasonable creature,
lower than the angels, higher than the brutes, capable of
knowing, serving, and glorifying God in this world, and of
seeing and enjoying Him in the age to come, I am made for
my Creator and am accountable to Him. Have I so lived
that all of this glorious privilege has been in vain? Have I
been made in the holy image and likeness of God, only to
live as the child of the devil?

But here this question has another meaning. All the
children of men are either sinners or saints, ungodly or
godly, non-Christians or Christians, unbelievers or believers.
Some remain in a state of sin, while others become converted,
transferred out of the domain of darkness into the kingdom
of the Son of God. Some are the saved and others are
the lost. This distinction divides all of mankind. Now when
I ask, "What am I?" the meaning is, "To which of these
two do I belong? Am I in the favor of God, or under His
wrath and curse? Am I a servant of God, or a slave to the
world and the flesh?" At the Lord's Supper we ask ourselves, "Where am I going to? To heaven or to hell? If I
should die this very night, (and I am not sure that I will be

alive on this earth tomorrow) would I go where there is the weeping and gnashing of teeth? Am I in the narrow way that leads to life, or in the broad way that leads to destruction? I am called a Christian, but am I a Christian—really? Do I have a godly nature that fits such an exalted name?"

And we must ask ourselves these questions and also answer them honestly and strictly. What good will it do us if we try to deceive ourselves? We cannot fool God; He knows all. We deceive only ourselves.

Therefore, to discover what my spiritual health really is, we inquire further.

1. What choice have I made? Have I chosen God's favor above all other things in this life? Is that my only desire? Is it the only thing that truly satisfies me and fills me with joy? Have I chosen God for my portion and inheritance, Christ for my Master, the Scripture for my rule, holiness for my way, and heaven for my home and eternal resting place?

2. What change have I experienced? At one time in my life I was a child of divine wrath, a sinner, lost and bound for a Christless eternity in hell, separated from the fellowship of God. I once was blind, but now I see. I have become a Christian. Though I still sin, I do not sin as much and now I am forgiven of all those sins. There was a time when I minded nothing but sin and the pleasures of sin for a season, but now I care for nothing but pleasing God. There was a time when my sinful nature had no desire to celebrate the Lord's Supper. But now I earnestly crave to meet together with the saints of like precious faith and partake of the blessed bread and cup, remembering Christ's death for my sins. Now I love to be alone with God in Bible study and prayer. I enjoy the ministry of serving others, evangelizing the lost, strengthening the saved.

But the question is this: have I truly experienced such a change? Or am I the same sin-loving person that I was years ago? In what specific areas of my life do I still need to be transformed into Christ's holy image?

3. What is the bent of my affections and desires? The affections and desires are the very pulse—the heart-beat—of the soul. If we wish to know its state, we must observe how that pulse beats. How do I stand affected to sin? Do I dread it as most dangerous, loathe it as most obnoxious, and complain of it as most grievous? Or do I make a light matter of it as if it were not all that important? Which lies heavier upon me—the burden of sin or the burden of affliction? What do I hate more —the sin itself or the punishment due to the sin?

What do I think of Jesus Christ? How do I stand affected to Him? Do I love Him, and prize Him as the fairest of ten thousand to my soul? Or has He in my eyes no form or comeliness that I should desire Him? Is He the only love in my life, or just another beloved? Have I crowned Him king in my heart?

How do I stand affected to the Word of God and the Church of Jesus Christ? Can we say with Timothy Dwight, "I love Thy kingdom, Lord; the house of Thine abode, The Church our blest Redeemer saved with His own precious blood"? When I am in the service of God, am I in my own element, as one who calls it a delight? Or am I forced to serve Him, as if it were a drudgery to me? How do I stand affected to good people? Do I love the image of Christ wherever I see it, regardless of race or color or neighborhood? Do I honor those who fear the Lord, and choose His people for my people, in all conditions?

How do I stand affected to this present world? Is it under my feet, where it should be; or in my heart, where Christ should be? Do I value it and love it and seek it with a prevailing concern and obsession? Are television and VCR's my only reason for living? Do I horde up possessions like the fabled King Midas of old? Which things have the greater command and control over my life: those riches, honors, and pleasures that are worldly, or those that are spiritual and divine?

How do I stand affected to the next world—to heaven? Do I desire eternal happiness there more than all this present world can offer me? Or are the things of heaven, though sure and near, looked upon as doubtful and distant, and consequently of little value? Do I have "heaven on my mind" throughout the day?

4. What is the course of my life? What kind of lifestyle do I lead? The tree is known by its fruits. Do I work the works of the flesh (Galatians 5:19-21) or the fruit of the Holy Spirit (Galatians 5:22-23)?

What "pet sins" do I cherish close to my heart, cuddling them and coddling them and indulging in them daily? Do I cuss or swear or curse or use my Lord's name in vain when provoked? Do I gossip and speak evil of others, even my fellow Christians? Do I defile my physical body, the temple of the Holy Spirit (1 Corinthians 6:18-20) by indulging in such polluting activities as adultery, fornication, uncleanness, lusting after sinful sexual pleasures? Do I tell lies for my gain or reputation? Do I oppress others by shady business deals and dishonest dealing? Do I deny relief to the poor when I have it in my hand to help them? Do I hold grudges against others, and do I study how to take vengeance upon those who have wronged me?

If this be the life I live, I am certainly a stranger to the life of Christ. I need to confess these iniquities to God when I eat the Eucharist. But if, upon self-examination, my own heart tells me that I keep myself pure from these pollutions, and "I also do my best to maintain always a blameless conscience both before God and before men" (Acts 24:16), so that I heartily repent of any defects and shortcomings in my life, then I may be reasonably sure that I am walking the Christ-like way.

5. What can I do about it? After I have examined my own life, what should I do?

If we find cause to fear that our spiritual state is bad, and that we are yet immature Christians, indulging in some of the sins already mentioned, we must quickly correct that problem. Let the Eucharist become the time of revival and improvement in your lifestyle. Diligently mend your ways. Pray more seriously than ever for the sanctifying grace of God. Work more earnestly and vigorously to improve that grace; resolve more firmly than ever to live a holy life, and depend more closely than ever upon the merits and strength of Jesus Christ.

If we find cause to hope that our spiritual state is good, then let the Eucharist be the occasion for glorifying God in this. It is only by His loving grace and power that you could do any good in the first place (Hebrews 13:20-21; Philippians 2:13). Though we must always humble ourselves, yet we must not dishonor God's grace by denying its work in us. May God preserve all of us from both deceiving ourselves with groundless hopes and from disquieting ourselves with groundless fears!

What Have I Done?

This is the second question that we ask as we come to the Table of the Lord to examine ourselves.

Here we are most concerned to confess our sins to God. We ask ourselves, "What have I done?" And may our hearts give the true and honest answer to that all-important question. If we do this, the Scripture promises that "God is faithful and righteous to forgive us our sins and to cleanse us from all unrighteousness" (1 John 1:9). But if we try to cover them up, we will lose. Not that we can by our confession inform God of anything He did not already know; but through confessing our sins to Him we give glory to God, and take shame to ourselves, and strengthen our guard against sin for the future.

In this matter of confessing our sins, we must be specific and particular. We cannot be content with saying some such general drivel as, "God, forgive me of all my sins. Amen." No! That will never do. The High Priest of Israel in the Old Testament, on the Day of Atonement, must confess over the scape-goat "all the iniquities of the sons of Israel, and all their transgressions in regard to all their sins" (Leviticus 16:21). It is simply not enough to say as King Saul, "I have sinned" (1 Samuel 15:30). We must follow the holy example of David, "For I know my transgressions, and my sin is ever before me" (Psalm 51:3). In this manner, a broken heart will become more broken and better prepared to be bound up as we observe the Breaking of the Bread. Usually, the more particular and specific we are in confessing our sins to God, the more comfort we have in the pardon we receive from God. Deceit inhabits general confessions.

Therefore, in order to offer specific confessions of sin to God, we must search and try our ways, examine our consciences, look over their records, examine the actions of our past life, and seriously call to mind where we have offended God in any thing. At the close of each day and each week, we should set aside some special time to review what sins we have recently committed. Then as we take Communion, we bring these to mind and confess them to our forgiving Father. In this way, we prepare for the Eucharist every day—not just in the few minutes before the emblems are distributed to us. We might ask ourselves these questions:

1. How have I employed my thoughts? Has God been in all my thoughts? Has He been in many of them? When I awake in the morning, am I still with Him? When I should have been contemplating the glory and majesty of God, the love and grace of Jesus, and the great things of the Holy Spirit, has my heart been following after "lying vanities"? How often (or seldom) has my heart thought seriously and with any degree of constancy on spiritual and divine matters?

2. How have I governed my passions and desires? Have they been kept under the dominion of the Holy Spirit's will? Or have they not grown out of control and transgressed the righteous bounds of my Savior's will? How well have I controlled my temper? Has the godly virtue of patience been my motto throughout the days? Have malice and ill-will and a "Rambo-like" revenge set up their demonic abode in my heart?

3. How have I preserved my purity? Have I tried to keep my heart pure and clean and holy? Have I kept my soul and spirit from the defilements of the sinful age around me? Have I made a covenant with my eyes not to look and lust, and have I been faithful to it? Have I endeavored to be true to my promise that "I will set no worthless thing before my eyes" (Psalm 101:3)? Have I controlled my television set or has it controlled me? Have I sold my soul for the VCR idol? Do I really understand what Jesus meant when He declared, "Beware, and be on guard against every form of greed; for not even when one has an abundance does his life consist of his possessions" (Luke 12:15)?

213

4. How have I used my tongue? It was designed by God to be my glory, but has it been my shame? Has any unwholesome (literally, "rotten") word proceeded from my mouth (Ephesians 4:29)? Do I enjoy gossiping and backbiting my fellow Christians? Have I been guilty of being silent when I should have spoken forth for my Master? Is my "guilty silence" convicting me of an unevangelistic spirit? Have I sometimes spoken unadvisedly and in haste that which later on I wished had never been said?

5. How have I spent my time? God commands me to make the most of my time, because the days are evil (Ephesians 5:16). How well have I obeyed that? Do I waste time? Do I realize that time is one of the most precious possessions God has ever given me? So long as I have lived in this age, to what purpose have I lived? What improvement have I made of my days for doing or receiving good?

6. How have I managed my calling? I am employed; I make a living in some job. Have I used that occupation to glorify God? Have I been just and fair in all my business dealings and spoken the truth from my heart? Or have I not sometimes dealt deceitfully in bargaining and said that which bordered on a lie? Has fleshly wisdom governed me more than holy sincerity which befits a child of the King?

7. How have I received my daily food? Have I never transgressed the law of self-control and moderation in eating and drinking? Am I a glutton? Have I not eaten merely to please and satisfy myself, when I should have eaten for God's glory?

8. How have I lived towards my family? The Bible teaches me my duty as a husband, wife, father, mother, son, daughter, brother or sister. In what specific areas have I failed to perform my Scriptural duty? Have I been a comfort

or a grief to those in my family? Have I given that which is right and fair to each member of my household? Have I been patient with them?

9. How have I worshipped in private? Have I been faithful at the morning watch, rising early and spending the quiet of the morning in devotional Bible reading and prayers? Has prayer been for me the key of the morning and the lock of the evening? Do I open each day with it and close each evening with it? Or is devotional time a hit-or-miss, haphazard, non-systematic part of my life? Have I sometimes just omitted it altogether with some lame excuse? Do I spend time alone with God because I love Him and His Word, or because it is a mere habit, a cold formality? As I read my Bible, do I apply the text to my heart and life? Or does my mind wander so much as I read it that it is almost a waste of time for me even to open that sacred Volume?

10. How have I taken care of what God has given? Have I been a faithful and trustworthy steward of the money God has first given me? Have I honored Him with my money, not content with merely a tithe but going well beyond that tenth of my monthly income? Or have I wasted and misapplied my Lord's goods? That which should have been given to charity or to the Lord's work, has it not been either sinfully spared or sinfully spent? Am I stingy and selfish, or generous and charitable?

I could go on and on, suggesting other questions that will stimulate us to confess our sins as we meditate at the Table of the Lord. But these ten will suffice.

Now, after asking ourselves these questions, may we answer them with contrite hearts, confessing our sins and repenting of them with a devoted spirit.

What Am I Doing?

When we have diligently considered what our way has been, we ought to consider what it now is.

215

1. What am I doing in the general course of my living? Am I doing anything for God, for my soul, for eternity, for my fellow man? Or am I just standing idle all the day long?

2. What am I doing in approaching the Lord's Supper? I know what it is that I ought to be doing at the Lord's Table, but am I doing it? Do I apply myself to this holy banquet in sincerity and with singleness of spirit, in the right manner and for the right aim? Am I partaking of the bread and fruit of the vine in a worthy manner?

What Progress Do I Make?

We are commanded in 2 Peter 3:18 to grow in the grace and the knowlege of our Lord and Savior Jesus Christ. Am I doing that? Am I progressing upward in the Christian way?

What Do I Want?

Only the hungry are filled with good things. Before we can be filled, we first must discern what we need. Since the Lord's Supper is a feast to fill the soul with blessings, we ought to discover our deepest spiritual needs before ever coming to that sacred meal.

1. What grace do I need the most? In what areas of the Christian life am I the weakest and most exposed to the enemy? The grace that is opposite to that is what I need the most. Just what is my problem? Is it pride or sinful passions? Then humility and meekness are the graces that I desire. Do I have a problem with fear and distrust? Faith and hope, then, are the graces that I must have. With what temptations am I most often assaulted by the devil? Then I need heaven's strength to overcome them. Do circumstances cause me at times to be impatient, deceitful, or fretful? Then self-control, justice, and confidence are the things most

216

necessary for my Christian life. What is the nature of my duties? Do they require me to stoop to that which is lowly? Then self-denial is what I need. Do they cause me to struggle with difficulties and discouragements? Then I need the graces of courage and wisdom. Whatever we need, the New Covenant in Jesus will provide. His supplies are infinite. These magnificent and extremely precious promises will truly strengthen us when we need divine help the most. For His grace is sufficient for us (2 Corinthians 12:9).

In the Lord's Supper, we receive those blessings that will equip us to meet every need that arises.

2. What comfort do I most want? What is the burden that lies most heavily upon my heart? What is the specific grief that grieves me the most? In the New Covenant of Christ, there is a cure for every heart-ache, a remedy for every sorrow, and comforts suited to every distress. But to receive such comforts, we must first know what the problem is, and then spread it before the Lord. In this way, we may receive from Christ's fulness "grace upon grace," help for all occasions (John 1:16). Let every care be cast upon the Lord, for He cares for you (1 Peter 5:7). And especially leave those cares with the God of all comfort. Do not try to carry them around. You have given them all to the Lord; now let Him have them; let Him take care of them; but let our own spirits be eased and relieved of those troubles.

What is the concern that burdens me the most, relating to myself, my family, or my friends? Let that be committed to the Lord, and to His wise and gracious disposal; and then let my thoughts about it be freed from all worry and concern. Rest in the Lord.

What is the complaint I make the most? Is it a puny and sickly body, bad relations between my employees at work or fellow brethren at the Church, or the death of a loved one? Whatever it is, spread it before the Lord, just as holy Hezekiah did with the evil letter of the Assyrian Rabshakeh (see 2 Kings 19:14). God comforted the King of Jerusalem then, and He will do likewise with us when we come to Him with our complaints and problems.

And at the Supper of the Lord, we bring these burdens and complaints before Christ. We ask ourselves, "What Do I Want the Most?" We list the problems we are enduring as we meditate on Christ's death. We give them all to Him, and He comforts and strengthens our weary, burdened souls. By confessing our difficulties to Jesus, His Supper will revive and bless us.

What Shall I Resolve to Do?

When he was travelling on the road to Damascus and saw the risen Christ appear in glory, Saul of Tarsus asked: "What shall I do, Lord? (Acts 22:10). And at the Table of the Lord, we ask the same question. We come to this Feast solemnly to dedicate ourselves against all sin and to all duty. Therefore it is good to consider what that sin is which we should particularly deny, and what that duty is to which we should devote ourselves.

We ought to be specific here. It is good to be specific and particular in our pious resolutions as well as in our penitent reflections. We saw earlier that confessing sin in general is not half as good as confessing sins in particular. And the same principle follows here. We resolve to rid ourselves of these particular sins, and to commit ourselves to these specific duties. We ought to mention those sins and duties by name. In this way, we realize more completely our task as Christians in the world.

So at the Table of the Lord, we resolve to live a better Christian life than we have ever lived before—to pray more,

218

to study God's Word more, to win more souls for Jesus, to speak more encouraging words than ever before.

The Grace Robbers: The Supper and Forgiveness

The Lord's Supper is the time when we confess our sins to God. By emphasizing the theme of "Self-Examination," we have seen this in a positive way. This is what the Supper is.

But now we need to see in a negative way what the Supper is not. It is not primarily designed to give us the forgiveness of sins. Yes, there is confession of sin at the Lord's Table. But we do not take the loaf and cup to receive forgiveness, but to remember that we have already been forgiven by Christ's death. And there is a big difference between these two. Always remember this: at the Lord's Supper we confess our sins to God, knowing they have already been forgiven through the death of His only begotten Son. The Supper reminds us that we are forgiven, but it does not give us that forgiveness.

This whole negative discussion is necessary because of the rise of the "Grace Robbers." They are Christians who mean well, but whose view of the Eucharist steals the grace of Christ away from us. And in its place, they insert the "earn-your-own-blessings" system. This tends to rob Christ of the glory He deserves as the God of all grace. And this ought to concern us; it is a life-and-death issue. For the grace of God is the very essence of our faith and hope. It is the foundation of Christianity.

Without grace, the Church is destroyed. This precious and comforting doctrine, that God forgives sinners who believe in Christ apart from works (Romans 3:28), is the most vital teaching in God's inerrant Word. Alexander

Campbell saw this clearly when he quoted the following words from Martin Luther:

> Luther said that the doctrine of justification, or forgiveness, was the test of a standing or falling church. If right in this, she could not be very far wrong in anything else; but if wrong here, it was not easy to suppose her right in any thing. I quote from memory, but this was the idea of that great reformer. The reformer also said, "If the article of justification be once lost, then is all true Christian doctrine lost.[2]

But how have the Grace Robbers harmed this precious doctrine? What are they declaring about the Lord's Supper that tends to "nullify the grace of God" (Galatians 2:21)? For centuries people have argued over this question, "Does the Christian receive the forgiveness of sins each week in the Lord's Supper?" The Lutherans and Catholics answer with a resounding "Yes," whereas most other church groups deny it. But the Grace Robbers have added a new twist to this debate.

They have maintained that unless the Christian takes the Eucharist every week, the sins committed in the previous week are left unforgiven. That is, the Supper is the main way our sins are cleansed through the blood of Christ. Notice these typical quotations from their literature:

One preacher among them exclaims, "Whatever happens to repenting sinners' sins when they are baptized into Christ's death happens to our sins when we have communion of the blood and body of Christ in the Lord's Supper."

Another one affirms, "Communion is to the saved sinner what baptism is to the lost sinner." He goes on to write, "communion is essential to the forgiveness of sins of the

---

2. Alexander Campbell, *Christian System* (fifth edition; Cincinnati: Standard Publishing Company, 1901 reprint), p. 153.

Christian, and must be taken each week, or you cease to be under the New Covenant." In fact, he even points out that unless you believe the Lord's Supper is for the forgiveness of sins, you receive no blessing from taking it, except what one would expect from merely drinking some grape juice.

In their zeal to glorify the Supper of the Lord, the Grace Robbers have ruined the grace of God. Their error is refuted by seeing the Biblical meaning of the following elements: 1) "justification," 2) "this is My blood" (Matthew 26:28), and 3) the "communion" of Christ's body and blood (1 Corinthians 10:16).

The Biblical Meaning of Justification

The very meaning of the doctrine of justification by faith refutes their position about the Supper. We are justified or "declared not guilty" by grace through faith in Christ's blood (Romans 3:28; 5:1, 9; Ephesians 2:8-9). This forgiveness occurs initially at baptism (Titus 3:4-7; 1 Peter 3:21; Mark 16:15-16; Acts 2:38; 22:16), and remains with us throughout the rest of our life if we continue trusting in Christ's blood and confessing our sins to Him in prayer (Ephesians 3:17; Colossians 1:21-23; 1 John 1:8-10).

But our good works are not involved whatsoever in this justification. It is without or apart from good works (Romans 3:28; Ephesians 2:8-9; 2 Timothy 1:9). We cannot save ourselves. We cannot add anything to the already perfect work of Christ on the cross. We simply let Him save us as we trust in His blood and submit to baptism for the forgiveness of our sins. Baptism is not our good work, but is rather the God-ordained time when He promises to meet us and to justify us. At baptism, God works upon our sinful heart, forgiving our sins, recreating us in His holy image (Colossians 2:11-13). And this is grace.

We become clothed with Christ and united with Him in baptism (Galatians 3:27); thus we come under the cleansing blood of the Redeemer (Romans 6:3-5). And this union with Christ is a *continuing state maintained by faith* (Ephesians 3:17). We remain in *constant contact* with Christ's blood by faith (1 Peter 1:2; 1 John 1:7). This comes forth loud and clear in 1 John 1:7. When it says the blood of Jesus *cleanses* us from all sin, the Greek word that is translated "cleanses" is in the present tense, meaning continuing action in the present. Therefore, the blood of Christ is *continually* cleansing the Christian—all the time. Therefore the Christian has the forgiveness of sins as a *continuing possession,* as long as faith remains (1 Peter 1:5; Hebrews 3: 12); but he can still lose his salvation if he rejects Christ through unbelief.

Since forgiveness is the Christian's continuing possession, *nothing* can be contributed or added to it by the *Lord's Supper!* This logically follows from the doctrine of justification by faith. Although that simple yet profound feast is a marvelous means of grace to us, it cannot and should not cleanse from sin. It was not designed for that. That was not its purpose. It was not given us to take away sins, but to remind us of the glorious fact that all our sins are cleansed through the finished work of Christ at Calvary. This is obvious from our Lord's Words of Institution: "Do this in remembrance of Me" (Luke 22:19). It reminds us of sins forgiven. Period.

To say that the sins of the previous week are unforgiven until we eat the Eucharist, is to make a travesty of the doctrine of grace. Besides this, where is such a teaching found in the Word of God?

222

The Biblical Meaning of "This Is My Blood" (Matthew 26:28)

Some of the Grace Robbers allege that the phrase, "This is My blood" (Matthew 26:28), proves that the Lord's Supper must be eaten for the forgiveness of sins. One of their advocates argues this point by declaring, "Jesus held the cup and said clearly, 'This is My blood.' And if the blood was shed for the remission of sins, and the cup is the blood, then the cup is 'for the remission of sins.'"

But is this preacher actually saying that Christ's blood "is poured out" (Matthew 26:28) every time the Supper is eaten throughout church history? I am positive that he would not believe this. Yet that seems to be the logical conclusion of his argument. If the blood was shed for remission of sins, and the cup is the blood, and the cup is for the remission of sins, then it must follow that this preacher believes Christ's blood is shed at every Communion service. For if the words "remission of sins" may be connected with the cup so that the cup gives the remission of sins (as he affirms), then why cannot the words "poured out" also be joined with the cup? What is good for the goose ought to be good for the gander.

Most probably he would say that in Matthew 26:28 the phrase, "is poured out," has nothing to do with the cup itself. Rather "poured out" simply goes with the words "My blood." And I agree. That is the only common-sense way of interpreting those words. But why can't he see that his argument cuts two ways? If "poured out" does not go with the cup, then neither does "remission of sins" go with the cup. "Poured out" surely refers to the blood shed in A.D. 30 on Mount Calvary—not to the cup itself. The cup is not for the remission of sins. But instead the cup is the symbol reminding us of the blood poured out for the remission of sins.

223

Therefore, his whole syllogism breaks down. The cup is not for the remission of sins—the blood of Christ is. The Eucharist does not give us the remission of sins, but instead it reminds us through the bread and cup that full remission of sins was accomplished in A.D. 30 at the cross by our Savior Jesus Christ.

The Biblical Meaning of the "Communion" (1 Corinthians 10:16)

When the Apostle Paul proclaimed that the Lord's Supper is a "communion" (*koinonia:* sharing, fellowship, participation) in the blood and the body of Christ, did he mean that a Christian receives the forgiveness of sins therein? Some of the Grace Robbers believe that he did (some who are not Grace Robbers also think this). They maintain that at the Supper the benefits and fruits of Christ's blood and body are given to the saints. And if this is so, one of those benefits is the forgiveness of sin.

As we endeavor to understand this difficult text, we can see that the very least Paul meant was this: in some way as we partake of Communion, we receive a share in the body and blood of Jesus (along with other Christians). But precisely what does that mean? It cannot mean that we literally "eat the deity" for that would involve the gross sin of cannibalism. And I have already refuted that error in chapter four.

I believe the key is in that term "communion" (*koinonia:* sharing, fellowship, participation). Always in the New Testament it refers to the fellowship or sharing of persons with persons. If this be true, Paul means that at the Lord's Table we enjoy a deeply personal fellowship of Christians with other Christians (and with Christ) as together we remember the Savior's death (His "body" and His "blood"). Together we share in remembering that our sins have already been forgiven through Christ's body and blood. We share together in realizing anew that the forgiveness of sins is a continuing possession guaranteed to us by faith in Christ (justification by faith). In this manner, we share in the blood and body of Christ.

Needless to say, the idea that Communion itself forgives us of sins committed during the past week is foreign to this passage. That error would inevitably lead to an even worse one, extreme unction: at one's death the Lord's Supper must be administered or how else would any remaining sins be forgiven? Thank God, grace delivers us from such legalistic errors!

In conclusion, Scripture never says the Lord's Supper will do for Christians what baptism does for alien sinners. This meal is not some celestial "Blood-Blanket," the main way that we receive the weekly forgiveness of our sins after baptism. No. That view, advocated by the "Grace Robbers," ruins the Biblical doctrine of grace. For when we turn the Lord's Supper into the primary means of receiving forgiveness, we are implying that sins are cleansed by something we ourselves are doing (by eating and drinking), rather than through Christ's works. If we receive forgiveness through faith in Christ as a *continuing possession,* then that Feast can add nothing to our salvation.

Please do not misunderstand me. The Supper can and will increase our growth in Christ. Yes, that is most certainly true. This whole book is devoted to that grand theme. But the Feast is not primarily designed to give us the forgiveness of sins. That is already ours as a free gift of divine grace through faith in the death of Christ.

When we daily confess our sins, God will forgive us completely (1 John 1:8-10). Never does the Word say this concerning the Breaking of the Bread.

The Eucharist was designed to do only one thing. It stimulates us to remember that we have already been forgiven through the death of our Lord. This is grace.

The precious doctrine of grace is too important to lose. In our zeal for magnifying the Lord's Supper, may we never rob the Church of its pearl of great price—*amazing grace.*

8

THE THINGS SIGNIFIED—COMMUNION

The Supper of the Lord is a time of sweet communion with Christ and with His people—the Church. "Communion" (*koinonia*) means the act of sharing something in common among two or more persons. And in the Eucharist we gather together with saints of like precious faith. We share together the blessings of Christ. We enjoy blessed fellowship with our Lord and with the Church as we commune around His Table. Together we share in the sweet knowledge that Christ's blood has already saved us from all sin. And together our souls are richly fed by Christ's grace.

At the Holy Communion we not only have Gospel benefits offered to us and accepted by us. That it is a "communion" can be seen by what the Apostle says about it in 1 Corinthians 10:16. It is a time of "communion" or "fellowship" or "participation" in Christ's body and blood.

When Paul speaks of the body and blood of Christ in 1 Corinthians 10:16, he refers to all those precious benefits and privileges which were purchased for us by Christ's death. These are assured to us through the Gospel terms of pardon.

When we say that the sun in the heavens is with us during a hot summer's day, we do not mean the physical body of the sun but instead we are referring to its rays and beams that stream down upon us to give us light and warmth. In this manner, the sun communicates with us; it touches us and comes into contact with us. And so it is at the Table of the Lord. We are partakers of Christ; He comes down to us and communicates with us in sweet and blessed *communion*. This communion is not of His literal body and blood (that would be senseless and absurd, not to mention gross and unhuman), but of His spiritual power that streams down from heaven to bless us. We do not need to reach up to the skies and bring Christ down, for He communes with His people in the Breaking of the Bread.

But people cannot carry away from the Table any more than they can collect in the vessel of faith. If one wishes to gain blessings from this holy banquet, he must be prepared to receive them through earnest and holy meditation.

What benefits come to those who reverently partake of these elements in the Lord's Supper? There are five of them: 1) We receive the assurance of forgiveness; 2) we receive the assurance of our adoption as children of God; 3) we receive peace and satisfaction; 4) we receive plentiful supplies of divine grace for living in holiness; and 5) we receive the guarantee of heavenly bliss and joy forever.

In this chapter, we will study each of these five benefits. We will see that all humble and penitent believers partake of the blessed fruits of Christ's death, "His body and blood," for their food, their medicine, their life, their all.

THE ASSURANCE OF OUR FORGIVENESS

The Lord's Supper means Communion, a sharing with Christ. We have fellowship in the blessed benefits of Christ's body and blood. And the first benefit we receive is the assurance that all our sins have been forgiven through His death.

Truly the greatest blessing of the New Covenant in Christ is the pardon and cleansing of our transgressions. "You were washed, you were sanctified, you were justified in the name of the Lord Jesus Christ" (1 Corinthians 6:11); "in Him we have redemption through His blood, the forgiveness of our trespasses, according to the riches of His grace, which He lavished upon us" (Ephesians 1:7-8); "for He delivered us from the domain of darkness, and transferred us to the kingdom of His beloved Son, in whom we have redemption, the forgiveness of sins" (Colossians 1: 13-14); "obtaining as the outcome of your faith the salvation of your souls" (1 Peter 1:9); "behold, days are coming . . . when I will effect a new covenant . . . and I will be their God, and they shall be My people. For I will be merciful to their iniquities, and I will remember their sins no more" (Hebrews 8:8, 10, 12); "and their sins and their lawless deeds I will remember no more" (Hebrews 10:17). These precious Gospel promises are ours through Christ alone. All our sins are gone; God remembers them no more for they are covered by the blood of Christ (Romans 4:7-8). This is the great blessing that Christ died to purchase for us: His blood was poured out for many, for the forgiveness of sins (Matthew 26:28).

And over and over again throughout the New Testament the Christian is assured that he is truly forgiven. But at the Lord's Supper he receives a special confirmation of that fact. Here I receive further assurances of the forgiveness of my sins, and further comfort arising from those assurances.

I come to the Table of the Lord to hear again the voice of joy and gladness from my Lord: "Be of good cheer; your sins have been forgiven." As a returning prodigal son, I come to receive my heavenly Father's kiss, which seals my pardon, and silences all my doubts and fears (Luke 15:20).

When I come to the Lord's Supper, I seek the assurance that all my sins have been pardoned. And this is what I receive. It strengthens my soul and encourages my heart for the coming week. Through it I realize that all my sins have been forgiven through the cleansing blood of Christ. This fact is sealed and confirmed and guaranteed to me in the Breaking of the Bread. The Supper does not give me forgiveness, but it gives me the assurance that I am forgiven.

THE ASSURANCE OF OUR ADOPTION

The Lord's Supper means Communion, a sharing with Christ. We have fellowship in the blessed benefits of Christ's body and blood. The second benefit we receive is the assurance that we, who were once lost and alienated from God's love, are now the adopted sons and daughters of God. This adoption by divine grace is sealed and confirmed and guaranteed to us in the Breaking of the Bread.

Christ's New Covenant full of grace not only frees us from the doom of criminals, but it elevates us to the dignity of His own royal children. Not only our sins are gone, but our status is changed. We are no longer aliens and strangers, but the very family of God. What a blessing! The very reason that "God sent forth His Son" was "that He might redeem us" and "that we might receive the adoption as sons" (Galatians 4:5). "For you are all sons of God through faith in Christ Jesus" (Galatians 3:26). "For all who are being led by the Spirit of God, these are sons of God. For you have not received a spirit of slavery leading to fear again, but you have received a spirit of adoption as sons" (Romans 8:14-15). "See how great a love the Father has bestowed upon us, that we should be called children of God" (1 John 3:1).

And the Spirit of God assures us over and over again throughout our Christian walk that we are the adopted sons and daughters of God the Father (Romans 8:16). And one of the most important ways He does this is through the Lord's Supper. There our sonship is confirmed and sealed to us. There we are called the beloved children of God. Nor is this an empty title that is given to us, but real advantages and blessings of unspeakable value are lavished upon us in that name. He encourages us to call Him "our Father."

The eternal God here says it and seals it to every true believer: "Fear not, I will be a Father to you, an ever-loving and ever-living Father. Leave it to Me to provide for you; on Me let all your burdens be cast; with Me let all your cares be left, and to Me let all your requests be made known. My kingdom shall be your guide, My power your support, and 'underneath are the everlasting arms' (Deuteronomy 33:27). You shall have My blessing and My love, the smile of My face, and in the arms of My grace will I carry you to glory, as the nursing Father does the tiny child. Does anything grieve you? 'Shout for joy, O heavens! and rejoice;

231

O earth! Break forth into joyful shouting, O mountains! For the Lord has comforted His people, and will have compassion on His afflicted' (Isaiah 49:13). As one whom his mother comforts, so will the Lord your God comfort you. Does anything terrify you? 'Do not fear, for I have redeemed you; I have called you by name; you are Mine! When you pass through the waters, I will be with you; and through the rivers, they will not overflow you. When you walk through the fire, you will not be scorched, nor will the flame burn you. For I am the Lord your God, the Holy One of Israel, your Savior' (Isaiah 43:1-3). Are you in doubt? Consult Me and I will instruct you in the way that you should go; I will guide you with My own eye."

At the Table, our heavenly Father assures us that all these precious privileges are ours because we are His children by adoption. He calls us by name; He cleanses us from shame; He gives us promises to claim. What a blessing we receive from the Supper of the Lord. It is the time of real fellowship and communion with our Lord and Savior. Here He feeds our souls.

PEACE AND SATISFACTION

The Lord's Supper means Communion, a sharing with Christ. We have fellowship in the blessed benefits of Christ's body and blood. And the third benefit we receive is peace and satisfaction.

One of the most enjoyable gifts of God's grace to His Church is peace. As the God of all hope, He fills us "with all joy and peace in believing," so that we "may abound in hope by the power of the Holy Spirit" (Romans 15:13).

Christ speaks comfortingly to our hearts as we gather around His holy Table. He says, "Peace I leave with you,

my peace I give to you" (John 14:27). It is such a glorious
peace that the world can neither give it or take it away. Sur-
passing all comprehension and understanding, it guards our
hearts through the coming week (Philippians 4:7). We need
it desperately; and Christ gives it abundantly when we remember His death for our sins in the Supper of the Lord.

At His feast we realize that if we have been reconciled to
God through the death of His beloved Son, then we have
also been reconciled to ourselves. If God has forgiven us,
we can forgive ourselves. This is the sweet repose of the
soul in God. It is the peace of Christ. The guilt of sin lays the
foundation for trouble, uneasiness and anxiety. When that
is removed by pardoning mercy, there is peace. When the
God of all peace makes us hear joy and gladness, the raging
storm ceases; there is calm and quiet. The mind that once
was disturbed with the dread of God's wrath is now quieted
by the tokens of His favor and love—the bread and cup of
the Eucharist. Here I am waiting to hear what God will say
to me, and hoping that He, who speaks peace to His
Church, will speak that peace to me.

We find peace at the Lord's Supper for the following
two reasons: 1) because this Feast is a seal or guarantee of
the promise of peace; and 2) because this Feast is the di-
vinely-provided way of obtaining that peace.

The Supper as the Seal of the Promised Peace

At the Lord's Supper God assures us that His thoughts
towards us are thoughts of peace and favor. He does this
by reminding us that Christ's blood has reconciled us to
Him. Our sins separated us from God's love and tender
fellowship (Isaiah 59:1-2; Ephesians 2:11-12). But through
the cross we have been reunited to Him. We are no longer

His enemies, but His friends. We have been restored to loving fellowship with our Creator. The death of His Son cleansed us from sin; Jesus endured the fullest extent of divine wrath in our place for our sins. Therefore, we are now at peace with God and with ourselves.

In the Feast, all these glorious facts come forth to us in brilliant array so that it seals or confirms this peace to our hearts. It confirms in me that I am at peace with God. Before I came to the Supper, I may have known that anyway; but after communing there, that conviction is even stronger. Now I am absolutely certain that I am forgiven, a member of God's adopted family, and in a peaceful relationship with the Father. This sacred feast vividly portrays before my very eyes the peace and satisfaction I already have in Jesus. It guarantees that I am at peace with God. Now there is no doubt about it.

This comforts our troubled minds. It is that rest to the soul which Christ promised to all who come to Him and take His yoke upon them (Matthew 11:28). It comes to us in many different ways, and the Eucharist is one of them.

The Supper as the Way of Obtaining the Promised Peace

The Lord's Supper not only guarantees that I am at peace with Christ, but it also gives me that peace. It is far more than a "mere memorial." It truly communicates divine peace as I receive the bread and cup.

When the Lord Jesus appeared to His disciples after His resurrection, the first recorded words He spoke to them were: "Peace be with you" (John 20:19, 21, 26; Luke 24: 36). And He says the same thing to us at His holy Supper. Life's raging storms will surely beat upon these hearts of ours. Heart-ache and distress bombard our lives weekly.

234

And we come to the Eucharist pleading, "Master, Master, we are perishing!" (Luke 8:24). And in this blessed banquet He says to us in loving tones, "Hush, be still" (Mark 4:39). And our soul is calm and serene once more. For "the wind died down and it became perfectly calm" (Mark 4:39).

Our Host is the Prince of Peace at the Banquet of Peace, providing our hurried, harried souls with the peace they desire.

PLENTIFUL SUPPLIES OF GRACE FOR HOLY LIVING

The Lord' Supper means Communion, a sharing with Christ. We have fellowship in the blessed benefits of Christ's body and blood. And the fourth benefit we receive is the power for living the victorious Christian life. We get plentiful supplies of divine grace for holy living.

We ought to come to the Feast with anticipation, expecting rich blessings to strengthen these weak souls of ours.

Through the Father's work, in this simple meal Jesus Christ has become to us not only "righteousness and redemption," but also "sanctification" (1 Corinthians 1:30). He is not only our Savior, but also our Life and Holiness. He saves us from sin, and He also saves us for godliness. He justifies us, but He also sanctifies us. In "sanctification" the Christian is progressively conformed to Christ's holy image (Romans 8:29). We are transformed gradually into miniature Christs. We are set apart for God's service and actually made pure. This not only refers to our status in Christ (set apart, devoted), but also to our lifestyle for Christ (truly pure, overcoming sins). This progressive process is accomplished in the Christian by the Holy Spirit.

This differs from "justification." For in justification the sinner who believes in Christ and is immersed for the forgiveness of his sins is *declared* "not guilty" by God the *judge*. It is a legal act outside us. It is the work of Christ *for* us. In sanctification, however, the Christian is *made* or *created* righteous by God the *surgeon*. It is the work of Christ *in* us. We receive a spiritual "heart transplant," empowering us to live the life of holy purity. Sanctification is the slow, progressive process of becoming transformed more and more into Christ's holy likeness.

So the Christian life involves both elements: justification and sanctification. We are declared righteous and made righteous. We are not guilty and we are conquering sins daily. The guilt of sin is gone, and the power of sin is broken.

In the Lord's Supper, both elements come forth. We have already studied how this meal reminds us of our justification through the blood of Christ; but it also empowers us for sanctification as well. And in this section, we will study that second theme.

It is certain that we have as much need of the Spirit's influences to equip us for our duties, as we have of the merits of Christ's death to cleanse us of sin. We have as much need of divine grace to carry on the good work as to begin it. All by ourselves we are without strength for doing righteousness. Satan is just too powerful for us. He is smarter, quicker, faster, and stronger than we by our own strength could ever hope to become. In Christ alone have we both righteousness and strength for conquering sin, the flesh, and the devil.

And so we come to His Supper to gain that divine power for living the sanctified life of righteousness, holiness, and purity. From the fulness that is in Jesus Christ, in whom it pleased the Father that all fulness should dwell, we are at the Table of the Lord waiting to receive grace upon grace, the abundance of grace and of the gift of righteousness. For where there is true grace, there is need of more, since the very best of Christians are not totally sanctified in this life. Therefore, with a deep sense of our own weaknesses and needs, and a total dependence upon God's precious promises, we by faith come to receive the rich supplies of divine strength flowing from this Feast.

At the Lord's Supper, the rich supplies of divine grace equip us for the following four tasks: 1) for the confirming of godly habits that they may be more deeply rooted; 2) for the strength to perform gracious acts that they may be more surely accomplished; 3) for the wisdom to know how to order our Christian lives in a manner pleasing to God; and 4) for the hour of our death. We come to this meal expecting to receive grace for these four elements.

Grace for Confirming Our Godly Habits

Let us here receive divine strength for the confirming of godly habits that they may be more deeply rooted in us. We are certainly conscious of great weakness in grace. Our Christian power during the week at times seems like a grain of mustard seed, as a bruised reed or smoking flax. We are weak in our knowledge and tend to make mistakes. We are weak in our affections and tend to be cold. We are weak in our decisions and resolutions and tend to waver. How weak is our heart!

But here is bread that strengthens man's heart and soul and life. It is a communion that gives us the divine power we crave for living the abundant Christian life.

We find there is much lacking in our faith, in our love, and every grace; here, therefore, we prepare to receive from Christ such gifts of the Holy Spirit as will be mighty through God to increase our faith. In this manner, faith's discoveries of divine things will become more clear and distinct; its assurances of the truth of them will become more certain and confident. And all that increases our faith will also enflame our love and make it as strong as death in its desires towards God and resolutions for Him.

At the Lord's Supper, we wait to be strengthened with all might by His Spirit in the inner man. This heavenly banquet empowers us to suffer patiently for Him and work diligently for Him with all joyfulness. Here the rich supplies of divine grace are given to us for confirming our godly habits.

Grace to Perform Godly Acts

At the Table of the Lord, we come seeking the divine power to furnish us for every good word and work as the duty of each day requires. Not only are godly habits confirmed so that they may be more deeply rooted in us, but also we gain strength to perform godly acts so that they may be more surely accomplished. What Christ said to His servant Paul, He proclaims to His servants at the Lord's Supper: "My grace is sufficient for you" (2 Corinthians 12: 9). We come away from the Supper singing, "I can do all things through Christ who strengthens me" (Philippians 4:13).

Grace to Receive Wisdom

At the Eucharist, the penitent Christian receives the divine wisdom to know how to order his life in a manner pleasing to God.

238

When we go about any duty of solemn worship, we find that we are not able of our own selves to do it acceptably. Our "confidence we have through Christ toward God. Not that we are adequate in ourselves to consider anything as coming from ourselves, but our adequacy is from God" (2 Corinthians 3:4-5). Of ourselves, we are nothing. We lack both the power and the wisdom to know how to pray, to study Scripture profitably, and to worship God in spirit and in truth. All our sufficiency for these services is from God and from His free grace. And that grace we receive at the blessed Table where we hold sweet communion with our Lord. Of course, that is not the only time we receive such wisdom; it comes through other ways from God. But still, at the Lord's Supper we truly receive this grace. It provides us with the necessary wisdom to know how to worship God acceptably.

When an opportunity offers itself for doing good to others (comforting them when they hurt, strengthening them when they falter, cheering and encouraging them when they sigh), I need God's wisdom to know how to fulfil this ministry prudently, faithfully, successfully, and so to please God through it. I require His guidance. In fact, I need His wisdom for doing anything well in the Christian life. Where shall I go for it but to wisdom's feast, whose preparations are not only good for food and pleasant to the eye, but also greatly to be desired to make me wise? At His Table, Christ Jesus the Lord becomes to me "wisdom from God" (1 Corinthians 1:30) as well as righteousness, redemption, and sanctification.

When we are assaulted by Satan's darts and daggers, and we are struggling with temptations from him, we find how weak and ineffective our resistance has often been.

239

But we find grace to help us in time of need when we receive the broken bread and the cup. This sacred meal fortifies us against all those assaults that we may not be overcome by them. Here we receive the full armor of God that we may stand and withstand all that the devil may hurl against us in the evil day (Ephesians 6:12-13). If we are told to look to Jesus the Author and Perfecter of our faith in order to cast aside the sins that so easily surround us (Hebrews 12:1-2), where else can we see Him so clearly and dramatically than at His Supper? It empowers us to run with perseverance the race that is set before us. We gain strength to conquer even the "pet" sins that have plagued us for so long!

When we are burdened with heavy afflictions and worries and cares, we find it hard to bear up under the tremendous strain. We lack the wisdom to know how to comfort others in their distress and to encourage ourselves when we suffer. We sometimes even collapse under the load. We grieve; our hearts are filled with tears and fears in the day of trouble. But at this Feast we come to receive rich grace sufficient to support us under the calamities of this present time. Whatever we might lose, we will never lose our comfort; and whatever we suffer, we shall not sink. This is the gift from communing with our Lord at His Table. When flesh and heart fail, we may find God the strength of our heart and our portion forever (Psalm 73:26). As our day is, so shall our strength be, thanks to the Supper of the Lord. For here we know that our loving Father is for us, at our side, and suffering along with us as we endure the afflictions of this present vale of tears. We remember the death of Jesus and how God the Father was with Him during His period of affliction and pain and anguish. And He will be with us too.

In all these ways, we gain divine wisdom to know how to order our Christian lives in a manner pleasing to our Father in heaven. This is the bountiful result of communing at the Lord's Supper.

Grace for the Hour of Our Death

How near death is to us we cannot tell. We are not sure that we shall live to see another opportunity of receiving the Eucharist. But this one thing we can be sure of: it is a serious thing to die. It is a work that we never did before; and so when it comes, we will need a strength that we never possessed before. And as we think of Christ's death through the Lord's Supper, we gain the grace we need to prepare us for our own and to carry us safely through that dark valley.

In these four ways, the Feast is a blessed time of communion in which our Lord showers upon us plentiful supplies of grace for holy living. He feeds our souls at His Table. The high time of any week for the Church is when we meet together around that Table. As one holy body we fellowship with our Savior whose grace is sufficient for every day and all the way. His amazing grace is abundantly poured forth upon our weakened souls, strengthening and equipping them to live the victorious Christian life.

THE GUARANTEE OF HEAVENLY BLISS AND JOY FOREVER

The Supper also assures us that we are saved by God's grace and on our way to heavenly glory. As the crown and center of all Gospel promises, heaven is the perfection of all the good contained in them. All the blessings of the New

241

Covenant lead us to those pearly gates where we shall see His face and serve Him forever and ever. And as we commune with our Savior at His sacred Feast, He blesses us with the sweet assurance that we are bound for the Promised Land. In the Lord's Supper, we remember the blood of Christ that saved us from sin and for heaven. Here Christ guarantees that we are surely going to eternal life in the New Jerusalem. His grace stimulates our hope to look forward to the time when He shall return to take us home. With confidence we affirm in this sacred meal that we belong to heaven, that our citizenship is in heaven (Philippians 3:20). And we are sure that we are going there when we die. This comes as the result of communing with Christ at His Supper.

At this Feast our Lord says to me as he did to Abraham, "Now lift up your eyes and look from the place where you are" (Genesis 13:14). Take a view of heavenly Canaan, that land which eternally flows with far better things than mere "milk and honey." It is Immanuel's land. Open the eyes of faith as you eat the broken bread and drink the fruit of the vine and behold the pleasures and glories of that world as they are described in Scripture. Throughout the time of your meditation upon the death of Christ, read reverently and devotionally the "heavenly chapters" of Revelation 21-22. Know for certain that this land is yours! "Do not be afraid, little flock, for your Father has chosen gladly to give you the Kingdom" (Luke 12:32). Keep that precious and magnificent promise in mind as you commune around the Lord's Table.

Come and see a door opened into heaven. Look in and see the heavenly blessings awaiting your arrival. It is all yours through the grace of Christ whom you remember at the Lord's Supper.

Let this Feast do something of the work of heaven upon your heart. For God has designed this food to make you hunger for heaven. In heaven you will be separated from all sin. Therefore, let this meal make the distance all the greater. In heaven you will be filled with love for God. Therefore, let this meal stimulate your love for Him all the more. In heaven you will enter the joy of your Lord. Therefore, let this meal be your strength and song. In heaven you will possess perfect holiness. Therefore, let this meal fill you with the Holy Spirit and His wonderful fruit (Galatians 5: 22-23).

In conclusion, the Lord's Supper is a time of sweet communion. It will give us five thrilling blessings: 1) the assurance of forgiveness, 2) the assurance of being adopted into God's holy family, 3) peace and satisfaction, 4) grace for living the life of holiness, and 5) the assurance of heavenly joy forevermore. Truly these blessings make this meal worth all our time and attention.

9

THE THINGS SIGNIFIED—COVENANT

The Lord's Supper has tremendous meaning for the Christian. What is that meaning? This Feast is a time of Commemoration, of Confession, of Communion. We have already studied these in chapters six through eight. And now in this last chapter of Part Three, we will investigate its Biblical meaning as a Covenant.

In Luke 22:20, our Savior tells us that the cup in the Lord's Supper is the New Covenant. Therefore this Feast is somehow intimately connected with the whole concept of Covenant.

THE DEFINITION OF "COVENANT"

What does the term "Covenant" really mean according to Scripture? So often we hear the notion from people who ought to know better that a Covenant is an agreement or contract between two equals, God and mankind, both of whom possess equal power in drawing up the terms of the contract. According to this definition, God tells us what he expects from us; and then we tell Him what we want from Him. A bargain is reached and away we go. Here mankind has as much say in the Covenant process as God.

This definitely is not what the Bible means by a Covenant. The Greek term usually translated "Covenant" in the New Testament (*diatheke*) in the first century A.D. meant that one party possessing full authority prepared all the terms of the contract. This contract was then offered to another party that could accept or reject the terms, but could never alter them.[1] And that is the kind of "Covenant" that God has made with mankind. It is His own contract; its terms are drawn up by Him alone and offered to us by grace. Man can accept or reject God's terms, but can never change them. Through Jesus Christ, God has entered into a Covenant relationship with us by faith. The Church is the body of believers who are the children of this Covenant. We have been washed in the blood that has sealed and ratified this Covenant.

This is the Biblical definition of a "Covenant." In it, God stands supreme and sovereign over His creation. He makes the rules, and we follow them. There is no bargain struck. By faith without works we submit to this contract drawn up by Him.

THE CUP AS THE SEAL OF
CHRIST'S NEW COVENANT

Though God is our Sovereign Lord and owner and we are in His hand as clay in the hand of the potter, yet He has

---

1. J. H. Moulton and George Milligan, *The Vocabulary of the Greek New Testament* (Grand Rapids: Wm. B. Eerdmans Publishing Company, 1963 reprint), p. 148.

condescended to deal with us through the Covenant. In this way those who are saved may be all the more encouraged and comforted, while those who are lost may be rendered all the more inexcusable. The motto of this Covenant is, "Believe on the Lord Jesus Christ and you shall be saved" (Acts 16:31). Therefore salvation is the promise of this New Covenant, believing in Christ the grand condition of this contract.

Now this cup is the covenant, that is, it is the seal of the Covenant. This seems to refer to that solemn occasion in which Moses read the Book of the Covenant in the audience of Israel, and they openly consented to it, saying, "All that the Lord has spoken we will do, and we will be obedient!" Then to ratify or confirm that solemn agreement or contract with Yahweh, "Moses took the blood and sprinkled it on the people, and said, 'Behold the blood of the covenant, which the Lord has made with you in accordance with all these words.' " (Exodus 24:7-8). Thus the Covenant being made by sacrifice and the blood of the sacrifice being sprinkled both upon the altar of God and upon the representative of the people, both parties did interchangeably seal the terms of the contract. It was now binding. They entered formally into Covenant relationship with the Lord of hosts. Here the blood set the Covenant into motion and confirmed it.

And so in an infinitely higher way, the blood of Christ is fittingly called the blood of the Covenant. Through His shed blood, our Lord set the New Covenant into motion; He ratified it. His propitiatory sacrifice on the cross created that holy contract. And the cup in the Lord's Supper signifies that blood by which the New Covenant is sealed and confirmed.

Therefore the Covenant in Christ is a covenant never to be forgotten. It is eternal, settled in the heavens. And the Eucharist was instituted to assure us, that we may never forget it. It is the seal of the New Covenant.

What is the meaning of the Lord's Supper as a Covenant? What Covenant promises and pledges does God give to us through the Eucharist? And what promises and pledges do we make to Him? These vital questions will be answered throughout the rest of this chapter.

God Promises to Be Our God

Whenever we partake of the Communion, we ought to realize that here God makes a solemn Covenant with us. He hereby promises to be our God. He renews His Covenant pledge to us that He will be our Guide forever. This is His royal grant and kingly pledge to His People: He gives Himself to us forever. He empowers us to call Him our own God.

What He is in Himself, He will be to us for our own good and blessing. His wisdom will be ours to counsel and direct us. His power will be ours to protect and to support us. His justice will be ours to justify us and declare us "not guilty." His holiness will be ours to sanctify us and make us pure. His goodness will be ours to love us and to shower us with blessings. He will be to us a "Father," and we shall be to Him the "sons of the Most High," dignified by the glorious privilege of adoption into the divine Family. Our Maker is our Husband. The Lord is our Shepherd, and the sheep of His pasture shall lack nothing. God Himself is the Portion of our inheritance in the next world, as well as our cup in this world. He has prepared for us a marvelous city, and so He is not ashamed to be called our God (Hebrews 11:16).

248

The Church Promises to Be His People

Whenever we partake of the Communion, we ought to realize that here we make a solemn Covenant with God. We hereby promise to be His own People. We resign, surrender, and give up our whole selves—body, soul, and spirit—to God—Father, Son, and Holy Spirit, covenanting and promising that we will serve Him faithfully and walk closely with Him in all manner of holy obedience all our days.

We Solemnly Promise to Oppose All Sin

If ever we are to have a holy hatred against all sin, it is here at the Table of Christ. Do not let the Lord's Day pass us by without reaffirming this zealous resolution to get rid of all iniquity—no matter how small it may be. Here at His Table we pledge our utter loyalty to Christ. We promise Him that we will ever be the enemies of sin and will do all within our power (as the Holy Spirit aids us) to purge it from our lives. We want to present our bodies as living sacrifices, holy and pleasing to Christ. And we make that desire firm and sure as we partake of the Communion.

1. We must solemnly promise Christ that we will not indulge in any sin. Though sin may remain, it shall not reign in us. Though sin may oppress us as a tyrant, we will never own it as our rightful prince, nor give it a peaceful and undisturbed dominion over us. We pledge to fight and struggle against any sins that may assault us. I may not be able to say that I never sin, but I can surely declare that I never love to do it. Vain and sinful thoughts may bombard my mind, but I will never invite them in, nor entertain them once they enter. As John Wesley once put it, "I may not be able to keep the birds from landing on my head, but I can

249

surely keep them from building nests in my hair." Corrupt desires and passions may disturb me, but they shall never have the quiet and peaceable possession of me; no, whatever wars against my soul, by the grace of God, I will war against it, hoping eventually to get the mastery over all sin.

2. We must solemnly promise Christ that we will never yield to any gross sin, such as lying, injustice, uncleanness, drunkenness, profaning God's holy Name. I pledge to rid myself of all scandalous sins that mar and stain the white face of Christ's Church. I have no reason to be ashamed of the Gospel, and therefore it shall be my constant endeavor not to be in anything a shame to it. Since it is an honor to me, I shall strive never to dishonor it. I promise never to do anything that would cause the enemies of the Lord to blaspheme His sacred Name on account of me.

3. We must solemnly promise that we will keep ourselves from all "pet sins." We all have them. They are those little sins that get the best of us so easily. These are the ones that we cuddle and coddle close to our hearts, the ones that surround us so easily.

Was it pride or passion? Was it distrust of God, or love of the world? Was it an idle or gossiping tongue? Whatever it was, let the spiritual forces of righteousness be set forth in battle array against that "pet sin." Here at the Table, we pledge to cast away from us all false gods and idols that would hinder us from worshipping God alone. Anything that gets in the way of giving Christ first place in my heart is really my idol. It may be a VCR, a car, a job, or a hobby. So at the Lord's Supper, we promise to rid ourselves of all sins, but especially those that we are most prone to commit.

4. We must solemnly promise Christ that we will abstain from every appearance of evil, not only from that which is clearly sin, but from that which merely looks like sin and

even borders upon it. May we never make that to be sin which God has not made so. And yet when we are in doubt, it must be our covenanted duty to keep to the safer side and to be cautious of that which looks suspicious. Even if we are not sure that something is sinful, yet if it seems to ensnare us to be an occasion for sin, or a blemish to us, or a terror to us when we reflect upon it, or an occasion of grief or fear, then we ought not to do it. At the Lord's Supper, we promise our Lord that we will abstain from any activity that even "smells" of sin or even appears sinful.

5. Finally, we must solemnly promise Christ that we will stay away from all sinful company. We will have no fellowship with the world of sinners who love not the Lord Jesus Christ. We live in a corrupt and degenerate age, in which iniquity greatly abounds. Our business is not to judge others. But we must preserve ourselves and the purity and peace of our own minds. For "do not be deceived: bad company corrupts good morals" (1 Corinthians 15:33).

This does not mean we are to have nothing to do with non-Christians, however. Quite the contrary, we are to touch their lives with the love of Jesus, trying to save them from their sinful ways, showing them that we love them and care for their souls with the compassion of our Lord Himself. We must live as the light of the world and the salt of the earth, permeating our sinful age with Gospel light and holy life (Matthew 5:14). Christ has sent us into the world to shine forth as lights among a sinful, crooked generation (Philippians 2:15-16). We must rub shoulders with sinners.

Although we are to maintain *redemptive friendships* with non-Christians to evangelize them, we must never have *brotherly fellowship* with them. We should never treat them as close companions and brothers with whom we agree and follow. For there is nothing they have in common

251

with us. They live in darkness, but we live in the Light of Christ. They love sin, but we despise it. Jesus is the very center of our lives, but not theirs. See 2 Corinthians 6:14-7:1.

"How blessed" is the Christian who not only delights "in the law of the Lord" and "meditates" on it "day and night," but also "who does not walk in the counsel of the wicked, nor stand in the path of sinners, nor sit in the seat of scoffers!" Only "he will be like a tree firmly planted by streams of water, which yields its fruit in its season, and its leaf does not wither; and in whatever he does, he prospers" (Psalm 1:1-3). In order for David to "give heed to the blameless way," he must "hate the work of those who fall away"; however, his "eyes shall be upon the faithful of the land, that they may dwell with" him (Psalm 101:2, 3, 6). We are to have no loving fellowship and intimate communion with the workers of darkness.

And as we partake of the Communion loaf and cup, we renew this Covenant of purity with Christ. We make the Psalmist's pledge our own. We promise to keep ourselves pure from those who would ruin our spiritual growth in Christ. Though I cannot avoid being sometimes in the sight and hearing of such sinners, yet I will never take them for my chosen companions and "bosom buddies" in this world. I would rather fellowship with the lowest saint than with the highest unbeliever. Having chosen God for my God, His people shall always be my people. This we pledge to Christ at His Holy Feast.

We Solemnly Promise to Fulfil All Duty

At the Lord's Supper, we solemnly pledge to obey Christ no matter how much it costs us. We promise to fulfil all

Christian duties. For it is not enough that we depart from evil. We must also do good. Christ wants us to separate ourselves from the service of sin and to shake off Satan's bronze yoke of slavery. But our Lord also commands us to devote ourselves to His service and to put our necks under His sweet and easy yoke (Mathew 11:28-30). And this we promise to do at the Table of the Lord.

1. We promise to make Christianity our business—our only business. Our great business and goal in this world is to serve the Lord Christ. For Jesus is all the world to us. He is our reason for living. His religion must be our calling; the calling we resolve to live in and hope to live by. In His service we must be ever faithful and diligent. When we serve Him, we are in our own element. As a fish must live in water and a bird in the air, so we must live in the sphere of obedience to our Lord. Jesus gets first place in our life. To crown Christ as King is the only reason for my life. Other things must give way to this, and must be made to help us attain this goal.

And this must be our Covenant with God at His Feast, that from now on we will make Christianity the one thing needful. We will not be lazy in our obedience to Christ. We will be red-hot, zealous, always serving Him (Romans 12: 10-11). Here at His blessed meal, I make Christ my all in all, the One who engages my cares, fills my thoughts, commands my time, and gives law to my whole being. Let this matter be eternally settled here and now as I eat the loaf and drink the cup.

2. We promise to make inward godliness the very rule of our lives. Having already convenanted to give God our hearts, which is what He demands, we now resolve to employ them for His honor and glory. Here we are talking about *inward* godliness. For heart religion is what matters

253

most to God. "Watch over your heart with all diligence, for from it flow the springs of life" (Proverbs 4:23). God wants to have my heart. He wishes to rule there. This therefore we resolve to do as we commune with Christ around His sacred Feast. Here we make a solemn Covenant with Him that we will surely guard our hearts with all diligence, to keep them fixed, fixed upon God. We promise to make the desire of our souls ever towards Him. Our hearts shall be lifted to God in every prayer and their doors and gates thrown open to admit His Word—the Bible. In this manner, our constant concern will be for the hidden man of the heart which is incorruptible to present ourselves to God as workmen who do not need to be ashamed (2 Timothy 2:15). We will seek to have a godly heart.

3. We promise to live a life of communion with God. At the Table of the Lord, we make a solemn pledge to set Him always before us, having an eye to Him with love and gratitude, as the first cause and last end of all things that concern us.

What does this life of communion really mean? It involves much more than merely promising to read our Bible and pray every morning, though that is definitely involved in such a lifestyle. It also involves these comprehensive activities: we receive the common comforts of each day with love and thanksgiving; we bear the common crosses and afflictions and disappointments of each day, as ordered by His will, with patience and joy; we constantly offer to Him our heart's affection by praying unceasingly to God; we commit each day to Christ and manage its business for His glory, having a constant habitual reverence for Him in everything we do or say or think. This is what it means to live in communion with God.

When I receive the Eucharist, I promise to live in such communion with God. This is my solemn Covenant with Him. Here I resolve to live more earnestly a life of confidence in God, in His beauty, bounty, and blessing; a life of dependence upon God, upon His power, providence, and promise; a life of devotedness to God, to the command of His Word, to the conduct of His Spirit, and to the working of His will.

4. We promise to keep heaven in our mind. As we take the Communion, we pledge to set our hope completely on that future grace to be brought to us at the revelation of Jesus Christ (1 Peter 1:13). We are made for another world, and we must resolve to set our hearts upon that world and have it always in our eye, seeking the things that are above (Colossians 3:1-2) and living here on earth as citizens of heaven itself (Philippians 1:27; 3:20). The Lord's Supper is the glorious time when I realize that my treasure is in heaven—my Head and hope and home are there, waiting for me to arrive. I shall never be well until I get there. My heart right now yearns for those spacious mansions Christ has prepared for me (John 14:1-3). Therefore fixing our eyes on the joy set before us in that better world, let us run with perseverance the race that is set before us in this world. And we pledge to do this at the Breaking of the Bread.

> "Feast after feast thus comes and passes by,
>   yet passing points to that glad feast above,
> Giving sweet foretaste of our festal joy,
>   the Lamb's great bridal feast of bliss and love."

Sacred Promises to God After We Leave the Lord's Table

In order to emphasize the Covenant nature of this Feast, we not only make solemn promises to God before and during the time of Communion but also (and especially) afterwards. The emblems have been distributed. We have received them with love and thanksgiving. Christ's death and all it means to us has been uppermost in our mind as we ate the Feast. We have pledged our full loyalty to Christ at this service. The closing benediction of the worship hour has now been given. We leave the church service. But is that it? Is that all there is to it? Do our Covenant pledges stop once we get into our cars and drive home?

No! To get all we can from this marvelous means of grace, we ought to continue making our Covenant pledges to Christ even after we leave the Table of the Lord. We ought to be just as zealous to leave it in the right manner, as we were to approach it in the right manner. Why observe the Feast only half-way? Why not strive to receive all the blessings we possibly can from this simple meal? This will truly enrich our worship experiences all the more. Yet we never hear of this in our church services. I trust that this sad condition will exist no longer.

But what sacred vows and pledges should we make to God after we leave the Table? Allow me to suggest a few general guidelines. They are by no means intended to be exhaustive. I am sure that you can (and should) add many more to the list. These Covenant promises provide rich resource material for Sunday morning Communion meditations.

1. We should come from this Supper much revived to do every good work with additional zeal. Let the Covenant that we have renewed and the comforts we have received make us even more prepared and ready to put Jesus first in our life. After the Communion is over, we pledge ourselves to do the work of Christ more zealously and more actively for the glory of God, the service of our generation, and the

welfare and prosperity of our own souls. We really mean business now. We are done flirting with sin and Satan. We are sold out to give Jesus our all. And we mean it this time!

In Genesis 29:1 there is a most interesting phrase. It occurs right after Jacob had made a solemn vow to the Lord. In most English versions, the verse reads something like this: "Then Jacob went on his journey." But in the Hebrew text it says, "Then Jacob lifted up his feet." After that comforting night in Bethel when God graciously visited him, Jacob departed with a great deal of cheerfulness. That spirit strengthened his weak hands and confirmed his feeble knees so that he literally "lifted up his feet"! And in a much higher way, the Supper of the Lord ought to enlarge our hearts and fill them with cheer to run the way of God's commandments (Psalm 119:32). After celebrating the Lord's Supper, we should lift up our feet in the way of God, abounding in the work of the Lord!

After the Supper is over, pledge that you will meditate more intently, pray more earnestly, resist sin more resolutely, keep the Lord's Day more cheerfully, do good more readily.

After the Eucharist is finished, is the Covenant still uppermost in our minds? On the Lord's Day—Sunday, after the worship service is over, after we have gone home, after the Sunday meal is finished, what are we doing? Are we still remembering those Covenant pledges made during the Communion time? Are we still promising God that we will more zealously live this week for Him who died for us and arose from the dead? May the Spirit of God revive us to do this not only on Sunday, but also every day, every week, every month, every year!

2. We should come from this Supper much resolved to stand our ground against Satan himself. After the Communion, we ought to pledge solemnly to God that we will

be more watchfully aware of the devil's schemes. "For we are not ignorant of his schemes" (2 Corinthians 2:11). We promise to be more prepared this week to conquer the Prince of Darkness. Whatever comfort and encouragement we have already received from the Eucharist, we must still remember that is but preparation time before the real battle. As we partake of the loaf and cup, we are putting on our armor for "battle royal" against the demons—the principalities and powers (Romans 8:38; Ephesians 6:12). We take Communion to strengthen us against Satan's hosts this week. God has graciously promised to crush Satan under our feet (Romans 16:20). But the devil will do all he can to defeat us. So after the Supper is over, we must constantly promise Christ that we will fight with all the Spirit's might against the Old Serpent. When we return to the world again, we must remember that we go among snares and traps, set by Satan himself, and so we must be ready for them. This requires wisdom and fortitude.

It means that we must do two things: fear and fix. That is, 1) we are to have a watchful and healthy fear of demonic attacks, and 2) we are to fix our hearts upon serving Christ and defeating the devil all our days. We need to look at these two areas more closely.

Let us therefore fear. He who travels with a rich treasure about him is in most danger of being robbed. The plane that is carrying great wealth and important persons is the terrorist's prize. If we come away from the Lord's Table filled with the goodness of God's House and the riches of His precious Covenant, we must expect the assaults of our spiritual foes. Scripture constantly pleads with us to be on guard, to watch and pray, to beware of Satan's schemes (1 Peter 5:8; James 4:7-8; 2 Corinthians 2:10-11; Matthew 26:39-41). We dare not let our guard down for one hour. We cannot rest for one minute. We must ever be ready against the Prince of Darkness who is masquerading as an angel of light (2 Corinthians 11:13-14). If we relax upon our spiritual sofas and forget that we are in a life-and-death battle, the demons will destroy us. A strong guard was constantly kept upon the Jerusalem Temple, and there needs to be an even stronger one upon our living temples (1 Corinthians 6:18-20; 3:16-17; 1 Peter 2:4-6). Christians in this world are in a military state, and the followers of Jesus must be His soldiers. They who work the good work of faith must fight the good fight of faith (1 Timothy 6:12; 1:18; Philippians 1:30). We need to fear because our Adversary will usually attack right after we have performed some great service for God or enjoyed some grand blessing from God. It was so in the life of Jesus. Right after He had performed the great service for God of being immersed in the Jordan River by John the Baptist, our Lord was led away into the wilderness to be tempted by the devil (Matthew 3:13-4:11). Immediately after Jesus had enjoyed the grand blessing of receiving the Eucharist with His disciples, He told them plainly that Satan desires to own and control them (Luke 22:31). And later on that same night, the Master counselled His sleepy disciples in the Garden of Gethsemane to watch and pray so they will not enter into temptation (Matthew 26:39-40). Therefore we see that after we enjoy the bountiful blessings of the Eucharist, the devil will bombard us cruelly, brutally, and swiftly. We must watch and pray; we must fear him; we must be on our guard against his wily schemes. Yes, we must even double our guard against temptations to rash anger, and study to be more than ordinarily gentle. We should watch against the entrance of worldly cares and fears, so that they may never descend upon us after the Supper is ended and ruin the blessings we had received there. But especially we must beware of demonic temptations to spiritual pride. When our Lord had celebrated the Feast with His disciples on the night in which He was betrayed, they were so elevated with the honor of it that they began arguing among themselves. They actually were quarrelling over who would be the greatest (Luke 22:24)! Believe it or not, it really happened. And if it could happen to them, it most certainly can happen to us. Therefore, we must beware of Satan's crafty schemes. We ought to have a holy and healthy fear of his awful strategies. After we partake of the Communion, we pledge to be on our guard against Satan. This we promise to do.

Let us therefore fix our minds upon Christ. This is the second thing we need to do if we are to conquer the devil after we have taken the Lord's Supper. Let our hearts be established with the grace we have already received from this sacred meal. What we have done there, we must go away firmly resolved to abide by all our days. I am now fixed immovably for Christ and holiness, against sin and Satan. The matter is settled, never to be called into question again: "I will serve the Lord." Just to pledge to be against the devil is not enough. We must also be for Jesus— completely. No room is left to mess around with temptation. I am a Christian, a confirmed and steadfast Christian. By the grace of God, I will live and die a Christian. And therefore, "Away from me, Satan" (Matthew 4:10) is my answer to anything the Adversary wants to say to me. My resolutions, in which before I wavered and was unsteady, are now come to a head. The die is cast. I have crossed that proverbial Rubicon River and I cannot turn back. This is it! By the help of the Spirit, I am determined to go forward and not so much as even look back or wish for a release from my duties. I stand for the Lord Jesus. I will not go back on my word. I am His. Period!

3. We should come from this Supper much resolved to pray more earnestly than ever before. Even after we have received the Lord's Supper, we solemnly pledge to God that we will lift up our hearts to Him in fervent prayer. We promise to be a people of prayer, devoted to the practice of speaking often with our Lord.

And in this prayer-covenant with God, we ask for these two things: 1) that God will fulfil the promises *He gave* to us at the Lord's Table; and 2) that God will enable us to fulfil the promises *we gave* to Him at the Lord's Table. We find that King David of old provides us with the words we are to use. Let us study these two petitions more carefully.

First, after the Supper is ended, we must pray that God will fulfil the promises that He gave us at the Breaking of the Bread. David prayed for this: "Now therefore, O Lord God, the word that Thou hast spoken concerning Thy servant and his house, confirm it forever, and do as Thou hast spoken" (2 Samuel 7:25; see 1 Chronicles 17:23). God's promises in His inerrant Word are designed to be our pleas in prayer. When we pray, we appeal to the promises. We pray that He will do for us what He has already promised to us. And we waste the Word and receive the grace of God in vain when we do not use these "precious and magnificent promises" (2 Peter 1:4) in prayer. They form the very foundation of all prayer theology.

And this practice of praying the promise of God is often emphasized throughout God's Bible, but especially in that glorious Psalm 119. "Establish Thy word [or promise] to Thy servant, as that which produces reverence for Thee" v. 38). "May Thy lovingkindnesses also come to me, O Lord, Thy salvation according to Thy word [or promise]" (v. 41). "Lord, remember the word to Thy servant, in which Thou has made me hope" (v. 49). "I entreated Thy favor with all my heart; be gracious to me according to Thy word [or promise]" (v. 58). "O may Thy lovingkindness comfort me, according to Thy word [or promise] to Thy servant" (v. 76). "I am exceedingly afflicted; revive me, O Lord, according to Thy word" (v. 107). "Sustain me according to Thy word [or promise]" (v. 154). "Deliver me according to Thy word [or promise]" (v. 170).

Therefore, after we leave the Table of the Lord, we ask God to fulfil His Covenant promises to us. We say, "Lord, is not this the word which you have spoken: 'sin shall not be master over you, for you are not under law, but under grace' (Romans 6:14); 'and the God of peace will soon crush Satan under your feet' (Romans 16:20); 'no temptation has overtaken you but such as is common to man; and God is faithful, who will not allow you to be tempted beyond what you are able, but with the temptation will provide the way of escape also, that you may be able to endure it' (1 Corinthians 10:13). O Lord, be it done to me according to Your Word: 'and we know that God causes all things to work together for good to those who love God' (Romans 8:28); 'if God is for us, who is against us?' (Romans 8:31); 'for the Lord God is a sun and shield; the Lord gives grace and glory; no good thing does He withhold from those who walk uprightly' (Psalm 84:11); 'I will never desert you, nor will I ever forsake you' (Hebrews 13:5). Now Lord, let those words which you have spoken to your servant be confirmed forever, and do as You have said; for they are the words upon which You have caused me to hope." This is how we pray the promises after the time of Communion is over.

But we pray that God will not only fulfil His word to us, but also that He will enable us to fulfil our promises to Him.

262

This is our second petition after we leave the Breaking of the Bread. And here again we use David's own words. He prayed for this: "O Lord, the God of Abraham, Isaac, and Israel, our fathers, preserve this forever in the intentions of the heart of Thy people, and direct their heart to Thee" (1 Chronicles 29:18). He asks God to enable the Israelites to do what they promised. And after we have received the Eucharist and have returned to our homes, we offer that very same petition to the Father. We ask Him to help us fulfil our Covenant promises. Have there been some good desires and "intentions of the heart" and resolutions that we made at the Breaking of the Bread? Then pray to God that He will "preserve" them in us, that He will give us the necessary strength to do what we have promised. We are so apt to forget those resolutions. And even if we remember them, we are often so weak in fulfilling them. We need to pray for divine strength. This is what the Apostle Paul prayed for as well: "To this end also we pray for you always that our God may . . . fulfill every desire for goodness and the work of faith with power" (2 Thessalonians 1:11).

Prayer is important. After the Communion service is finished, we make a solemn Covenant with God that we will pray more than ever before. And those prayers involve two primary petitions: 1) that God will do for us what He promised; and 2) that God will enable us to do what we have promised. For when we leave the Lord's Table, we return to a cooling, tempting, distracting world of sin and depravity. It surrounds us. It bombards us. It tries to cram its wickedness down our throats. "Here, O my Lord, I see Thee face to face" at the Lord's Table. But then I return to the world; it greets me with its sin, as when Moses was greeted with the idolatry and immorality of Israel after he had just spent forty days and nights with God on Mount Sinai (Exodus 32:6, 15, 19; Deuteronomy 9:15-18). In the midst of such sorrows and snares, we shall find it no easy matter to preserve the peace and grace which we hope we have obtained at the Lord's Supper. We must therefore put ourselves under the divine protection through earnest, persistent, fervent prayer.

4. Finally, we should come from this Supper much resolved to love one another. Such fervent affection must be a loving, giving, and forgiving love.

We come from the Feast endeavoring to love our fellow Christians from the heart. Here we see how dear they were to our precious Savior, for He purchased them with His blood (Acts 20:28). And from here we may see how dear they should be to us. Shall I hold a grudge against those who are intimately acquainted with Christ? Shall I treat with coldness those who are Christ's friends? Shall I be indifferent to those for whom Christ has so much concern? No. Since we who are many, being one bread and one body (1 Corinthians 12:12-13), my heart shall be more closely knit in love to all the members of that one body, who are revived and strengthened by that one Spirit. I have here beheld the beauty of my glorious Lord, and therefore I must love His image wherever I see it on His sanctified ones. I have here joined myself to Him in an everlasting Covenant, and I thereby have joined myself in love to all those who are in the bond of that same Covenant. I have here bound myself to keep Christ's commandments, and this is His commandment, "that we love one another," and that brotherly love continue (John 13:34-35; 1 John 3:23; Hebrews 13:1).

We should come from this Supper with a desire to give to the poor and needy, according as our ability and opportunity is. If at the Table of the Lord our hearts have been opened to Christ, we must show this by being open-handed to poor Christians. If we have here given ourselves to God in solemn Covenant pledges and promises, we have also automatically devoted all we have to His service and honor, including our money in almsgiving.

We must come from this Supper with a desire to forgive those who have been provoking us. Patience is a blessed result of rightfully receiving the Eucharist. Leaving the Table of the Lord ought to make it natural for us to forgive others. The great argument for the forgiving of injuries, when we come from the Eucharist, is taken from the grace of God revealed at the cross of Christ, which we celebrate in this sacred Feast. Let the death of Christ, which we have here commemorated, not only slay all enmities and hostilities, but also tear down all walls of separation; not only forbid revenge, but also remove all unfriendliness; and let all our feuds and quarrels be buried in His grave. Has our Master forgiven us that great debt, and a very great debt it was, and ought we not then to have compassion on our fellow-servants?

PART IV

THE
IMPORTANCE
OF
THE LORD'S SUPPER

10

THE FREQUENCY OF THE LORD'S SUPPER

Concerning the Lord's Supper, our Lord declared: "This do in remembrance of Me" (Luke 22:19). However, neither He nor His Apostles ever explicitly said *how often* we should do it. Does the Bible give any guidance for us on this issue? Yes, I believe that it does. There is ample evidence that God intends us to observe the Lord's Supper every Sunday.

This question has been hotly debated by the Church for generations. But why? Doesn't it seem terribly sad that I should even have to present arguments urging Christians to take the Lord's Supper every week? How decadent the state of Christendom has become! When you lose some of your appetite for physical food, you are obviously sick. And so it is in the spiritual realm: only sick Christians would be satisfied with anything less than weekly Communion. All

Holy Spirit-filled Christians earnestly desire to feast with their Master around His Table as often as they possibly can! If anything, they would rather be guilty of receiving the Supper too much than too little, too often than too seldom. For this is the nature of Christianity; it produces a spiritual hungering and thirsting after righteousness; "as the deer pants for the water brooks, so my soul pants for Thee, O God" (Psalm 42:1). This is precisely the reason that Bickersteth remarked:

> Yet it has been justly remarked, that in the accounts which we have of those most distinguished for piety, never any one excelled in the virtues of the Christian life, but was accustomed frequently to nourish his soul with 'the banquet of this most heavenly food.'[1]

A healthy, vigorous Christian and the weekly observance of the Lord's Supper go together like lock and key. You cannot have the one without the other. And on the other hand, by receiving Communion on a weekly basis, you can find revival; you will increase in Christian power and maturity.

The evidence for weekly Communion will be presented in the following three ways: 1) the Biblical evidence; 2) the Historical evidence; and finally 3) the Theological evidence.

THE BIBLICAL EVIDENCE FOR WEEKLY OBSERVANCE

The Holy Scriptures teach that the Church ought to celebrate the Holy Communion at least once every week. It does this through the typology of the Old Testament feasts and through the evidence of New Testament practice.

---

1. Edward Henry Bickersteth, *A Treatise on the Lord's Supper* (London: L. B. Seeley and Son, 1825), p. 2 of the Preface.

The Evidence of the Old Testament Type of the Lord's Supper

Christianity teaches that in the Bible we have what is called "typology." This means that certain New Testament persons, places, and things are prefigured by similar Old Testament persons, places, and things, for the Old Testament is "a shadow of the good things to come" in the New Testament (Hebrews 10:1). For instance, we find from Romans 5:12-14 that Adam was a type of Christ. Both persons are so very similar to each other that Adam is the Old Testament "shadow" or "type" of what Jesus is in the New Testament. The study of typology covers a tremendous amount of ground.[2] To discuss it any further would take us far away from the main issue at hand.

So what Old Testament feast is the type or shadow of the Christian Eucharist?

The Position of Herbert W. Armstrong

According to some groups, including the "The Worldwide Church of God" governed by Herbert W. Armstrong, the Jewish Passover is the pattern for the Lord's Supper. This seems harmless in itself, but Mr. Armstrong carries it too far. Since the Passover was observed only once a year, he concludes the same for the Lord's Supper. In his churches,

---

2. I recommend the following works on the subject of Typology: Patrick Fairbairn, *The Typology of Scripture* (N.Y.: Funk and Wagnalls, 1900); Jean Danielou, *From Shadows to Reality* (Westminster, Maryland: Newman Press, 1960); Leonard Goppelt, *Typos: The Typological Interpretation of the Old Testament in the New Testament* (Grand Rapids: Wm. B. Eerdmans Publishing Company, 1982); Norman L. Geisler, *Christ the Key to Interpreting the Bible* (Chicago: Moody Press, 1968); J. S. C. Frey, *A Course of Lectures on the Scripture Types* (N.Y.: Fanshaw, 1841).

271

they receive the Eucharist only one time each year, on the fourteenth day of Nisan. [3]

To support his position, he appeals to Exodus 12:14 and Acts 20:6-7. Since Exodus 12:14 declares that the Passover was to be celebrated "forever" (olam), he maintains that the Lord's Supper is really a continuation of the Passover and must be observed only once a year just like the Passover was.

Concerning Acts 20:6-7, Mr. Armstrong denies that verse 7 refers to the weekly observance of the Lord's Supper ("And on the first day of the week, when we were gathered together to break bread"). In fact, he denies that it refers to the Lord's Supper at all. It merely means they ate an evening meal. It could not possibly mean the Lord's Supper because of what verse 6 says: "And we sailed from Philippi after the days of Unleavened Bread." According to Mr. Armstrong, this verse proves the Christians at Troas had already received the Lord's Supper for that year—at the Passover during the Feast of Unleavened Bread. They would not celebrate it again until the next year on the fourteenth day of Nisan. It was not a weekly feast at all.[4]

The Fallacy of Armstrong's Position

Herbert W. Armstrong is right when he claims that the Old Testament Passover Feast is the type or shadow of the New Testament Eucharist. It is likely that the Last Supper was a Passover meal, and that the Lord's Supper is in many

---

3. Herbert W. Armstrong, "Does Easter Commemorate the Resurrection?" *Tomorrow's World*, 4 (March, 1972), pp. 11, 32; *How Often Should We Partake of the Lord's Supper?* (Pasadena, California: Ambassador College Press, 1952).

4. Herbert W. Armstrong, *How Often Should We Partake of the Lord's Supper?*, pp. 5-8.

ways similar to the Passover Feast. This is true especially with regard to its commemoration aspect. I have already explained the close relationship between both feasts in chapters one (pp. 31-41) and four (pp. 142-146).

Mr Armstrong is wrong, however, when he uses this similarity to claim that the Lord's Supper must be observed only once a year. I think he stretches the typology too far. Several points could be used to refute him. For instance, in Exodus 12:14, the Hebrew word, *olam,* does not necessarily require a "forever" idea. It may mean simply that the Passover will continue in Israel for a period of indefinite duration until God decides to end it. All modern scholars agree that this Hebrew term can and sometimes does carry such a meaning throughout the Old Testament. Most modern English versions of the Bible translate *olam* in Exodus 12:14 to mean "a permanent ordinance," but not "eternal ordinance."

Also, even if *olam* means "forever" in that text and the Eucharist is a continuation of the Passover Feast, it does not necessarily follow that everything in the Passover must be carried over into the Lord's Supper. Yes, they are similar, but not exact duplicates. For there are some important differences between them. They are not the same in all points. Unless the New Testament clearly teaches otherwise, we are not locked-in to the position that the Eucharist must be observed only once a year merely because the Passover was.

But most of all, the fallacy of Mr. Armstrong's approach is to assume that the Passover Feast is the *only* Old Testament type of the Lord's Supper. That is the main problem with his argument based on Exodus 12:14. He assumes what he needs to prove, that the Passover meal was the only type of the Eucharist. Truly the Passover is a type of the Eucharist, but not the only type. As we shall see, the Old Testament Table of Showbread is also a type for the Lord's Supper.

The Table of Showbread as a Type of the Lord's Supper

A very important Old Testament type of the Eucharist is the Table of Showbread or the "Bread of the Presence" in the Holy Place of the Temple (see Exodus 25:23-30; 26: 35; 37:10-16; 39:36; 40:22-23; Leviticus 24:5-9; 1 Kings 7:48; 2 Chronicles 4:8; Matthew 12:4; Hebrews 9:2).

The church of Jesus in general and in many of its particular practices is the direct and spiritual counterpart of the Old Testament Temple (see 1 Peter 2:5; Hebrews 9: 1ff.). And therefore the sacred furniture of the Jewish Sanctuary is a type or shadow of certain New Testament institutions.

And this principle applies to the Table of Showbread. For every Sabbath day twelve fresh loaves were placed on the table in the Holy Place of the Temple, and the priests ate the old loaves in a sacred meal (Leviticus 24:5-9). This provides the divine pattern for the *weekly* observance of the Eucharist. Just as the Old Testament priests ate this holy meal every Saturday, so all Christians as God's "priests" (1 Peter 2:5; Hebrews 13:15-16) partake of the Lord's Supper every Sunday.

Mr. Armstrong wants to emphasize *olam* in Exodus 12: 14 to make the Passover an "eternal" ordinance that continues to exist in the Lord's Supper, which must be observed only once a year. However, for the sake of the argument I could place that same emphasis upon the Table of Showbread. For it is called "an everlasting covenant"

274

(Leviticus 24:8). And so I could make it an eternal ordinance that continues to exist in the Lord's Supper, which must be observed every week—not merely once a year! But I would say this only for the sake of argument. Actually, I believe the Passover and the Table of Showbread passed away when our Lord died. He nailed them to the cross (Colossians 2:14-20; Ephesians 2:15; Galatians 4:9-10; Hebrews 8:6-13). They were never designed by God to serve as eternal feasts, but were to last only for an indefinite period of time.

The Lord's Supper is a beautiful combination of both feasts, the Passover and the Table of Showbread. As a *commemorative* meal celebrating God's redemption of His people in the *past,* the Passover is a type of the Eucharist; and as a *weekly* meal celebrating God's presence among His people ("Bread of the Presence") in the *present,* the Table of Showbread is a type of the Eucharist.

Therefore we see from the evidence of Old Testament typology that regular, weekly observance of the Lord's Supper is Biblical. Next we look at the New Testament evidence.

The Evidence of New Testament Practice

The Authoritative Nature of Apostolic Precedent

In the New Testament, Christ's people discover God's will for their lives. There Jesus commands His people.

Jesus does this through the following two methods: *direct commands* and *apostolic precedent.*

Sometimes we know God wants us to do a certain thing because the New Testament directly commands it (1 Thessalonians 5:17). For instance, He specifically tells us in His

Word to pray without ceasing (1 Thessalonians 5:17). This is direct command.

But at other times we find God's will for His people by studying the practices of early Christians recorded in the New Testament, especially the Book of Acts. The Apostles were guided into all truth by the work of the Holy Spirit (John 14:25-26; 15:26-27; 16:12-15). Christ promised this to them. And they in turn guided their congregations into all truth. The Apostles taught the churches to do all the Lord commanded. Whatever, then, the churches did by the appointment or approval of the Apostles, they did by the commandment of Jesus Christ Himself. Whatever acts of religious worship the Apostles taught and sanctioned in one Christian congregation, they taught and sanctioned in all Christian congregations, because all are under the same government of one and the same King. By going to the New Testament and following the practices of those churches, we find what God wants us to do today. This is Apostolic precedent.

Having said this, we see clearly that Apostolic precedent is fully authoritative. It is just as binding upon us today as direct command is. Both are found in His authoritative Word. Apostolic precedent comes from the Lord of hosts just as surely as if He had directly commanded us. This is a basic principle of Biblical interpretation that all Christians throughout church history have followed.

The Apostles Taught Their Churches to Commune Weekly

The Apostles were led into all truth by the Holy Spirit. They taught those truths to their congregations. Their churches followed that teaching. Since these facts are true, the churches in the Book of Acts reveal to us what the

Apostles commanded them. What things they did and how often they did them can show us what the Apostles told them.

And the Book of Acts tells us that the early Christians celebrated the Lord's Supper *every Sunday*. That was their established practice. The Apostles commanded them to do that.

1. In order to see this truth, let us take two texts together and see what they tell us: Acts 2:42; 20:7.

In Acts 2:42, Luke records for us the practice of the very first Christian church, the congregation at Jerusalem: "And they were continually devoting themselves to the apostles' teaching and to fellowship, to the breaking of bread and to prayer." Here we see that they observed the Breaking of the Bread or the Lord's Supper as regularly and faithfully as they did any other part of the Christian worship. All four items fit together as one giant chain. As often as they met together for the Apostles' teaching and fellowship and prayers, the Jerusalem Christians met together for "the Breaking of Bread." This is plainly what Acts 2:42 teaches us. No other conclusion from this text is possible. They continually devoted themselves to all four acts of worship. Therefore Acts 2:42 tells us that the Lord's Supper was a stated part of the worship of the disciples in their meetings.

Now we come to our second text, Acts 20:7, which briefly describes a Christian worship service at Troas. And we are expressly told that the disciples at Troas met on Sunday for the purpose of "breaking bread," that is, receiving the Eucharist. It says, "And on the first day of the week, when we were gathered together to break bread, Paul began talking to them, intending to depart the next day, and he prolonged his message until midnight." What one church did by the authority of the Lord, as a part of His instituted worship, they all did. This is the principle of Apostolic precedent. And the purpose for which this church met together was to receive the Lord's Supper ("to break bread"). Two obvious truths appear from this text: 1) that it was an established rule for the Christians to meet together on the first day of every week or Sunday; and 2) that the primary purpose of their meeting together in worship was to break the bread (receive the Communion).

Now, when we join these two texts together, notice the result: from Acts 2:42 we learn that the Lord's Supper was a regular, stated part of the worship of the disciples in their meetings. And then from Acts 20:7 we learn that Sunday was the stated time for those meetings and that the Lord's Supper was the stated purpose for those meetings. This provides us with a solid Biblical basis for declaring that Jesus wants His Church to celebrate Communion every Sunday.

Some people, however, would deny that the Lord's Supper is even referred to in Acts 20:7. We saw that Herbert W. Armstrong feels this way. He believes it refers only to a common meal—not the Eucharist.

But that view is weak. For the context of Acts 20:7 proves conclusively that nothing else but the Lord's Supper could be meant by the phrase, "to break bread." The context points to the first day of the week as a day of worship (1 Corinthians 16:1-2) during which the Christians in Troas met together. And this indicates more than merely a common fellowship meal.[5] Many (if not most) Bible scholars concur with the words of M. W. Smith: "The expression 'break bread,' in this context, almost certainly refers to an

---

5. Alfred Plummer, "The Lord's Supper," in *A Dictionary of the Bible*, edited by James Hastings and others (1902), 2:144.

observance of the Lord's Supper."[6] Also, the context reveals that even though Paul was evidently in a great hurry to get to Jerusalem in time for the Feast of Pentecost (Acts 20:16; cf. 19:21; 20:22; 1 Corinthians 16:8), yet he and his companions tarried in Troas for seven whole days (Acts 20:6). But why? So he could eat a common meal with the brethren of Troas? That seems highly unlikely and borders on the ludicrous. He would not need to wait seven days in Troas before he could eat an ordinary lunch with some Christians! Is it not more in harmony with the context to maintain that he stayed this long at Troas to celebrate *The Lord's Supper* with the Christians there, which, by the way, they were accustomed to receive *every Sunday?* If the phrase, "to break bread," in Acts 20:7 means nothing more than a common fellowship meal, the entire Troas visit is shrouded in confusing mystery. But if it refers to the Eucharist, then everything makes perfect sense. And for that reason, few have adopted Armstrong's interpretation. If the phrase, "the Breaking of the Bread," does not refer to the Lord's Supper, then in the Book of Acts the Church never celebrates it. And this would be quite amazing, since

---

6. M. W. Smith, *On Whom the Spirit Came* (Philadelphia: Judson Press, 1948), p. 163. See also W. J. Conybeare and J. S. Howson, *The Life and Epistles of Saint Paul* (Hartford, Conn.: The S. S. Scranton Company, 1914), p. 594; Albert Carver, *The Acts of the Apostles* (Nashville: Broadman Press, 1916), p. 200; F. F. Bruce, *The Acts of the Apostles* (Grand Rapids: Wm. B. Eerdmans Publishing Company, 1951-1953), p. 374; J. W. McGarvey, *Acts of Apostles* (Cincinnati: Standard Publishing Foundation, 1892), Part 2, pp. 177-180; M. R. Vincent, *Word Studies in the New Testament* (Wilmington, Delaware: Associate Publishers and Authors, 1972 reprint), p. 272; Matthew Henry, *Commentary on the Whole Bible* (Wilmington, Delaware: Sovereign Grace Publishers, 1872), 2:866; Adam Clarke, *The Holy Bible Containing the Old and New Testaments . . . with a Commentary and Critical Notes* (New York: Abingdon-Cokesbury Press, 1831), 5:851; R. J. Knowling,

Jesus commanded His disciples to keep the Lord's Supper in His memory! It is obvious that Acts 20:7 must refer to the Eucharist.

Others, however, contend that though the Eucharist is referred to in Acts 20:7, Luke does not say the Christians as Troas observed it *every* first day of the week. Therefore that text cannot be used to defend weekly Communion.

This common objection needs to be exploded once for all. First, it is inconsistent. When they are arguing with someone like a Seventh-Day Adventist who believes Saturday is the divinely-appointed day for public worship, they will use Acts 20:7 to prove that Jesus wants us to worship Him on *every* first day of the week (Sunday)—not on Saturday. The Adventist will respond that the text does not say *every* first day of the week. But that does not matter to them. They point out, and rightly so, that the wording of the text itself strongly favors an *every*-first-day-of-the-week interpretation, even though Luke does not say those precise words. But yet, when these same people are talking about *how often* we ought to observe the Lord's Supper, they inconsistently forget all their own arguments and adopt those previously used by the Seventh-Day Adventist! They begin saying that the text does not say the Troas disciples

---

6. (cont.) "Acts," in *The Expositor's Greek Testament,* edited by W. Robertson Nicoll (London: Hodder and Stoughton Limited, n. d.), 2:425; M. Baumgarten, *Acts of the Apostles or the History of the Christian Church in the Apostolic Age* (Edinburgh; T. and T. Clarke, 1863), pp. 319-323; Albert Henry Newman, *A Manual of Church History* (Philadelphia: American Baptist Publication Society, 1899), 2:137; Jules Lebreton, *History of the Primitive Church* (N.Y.: Macmillan Company, 1949), 1:344; William Jacobson, "Acts," in *The Bible Commentary* [sometimes called *The Speaker's Commentary*] edited by F. C. Cook (N. Y.: Charles Schribner's Sons, 1887), 2:370 of the New Testament.

celebrated the Eucharist *every* Sunday. How inconsistent, then, are they who make Acts 20:7 an express precedent for attending church every *Sunday* when arguing with Adventists, and then they turn right around and tell us it will not prove that the early Christians kept the Supper *every* Sunday! "O consistency, thou art a rare jewel!" If it does not prove the one, then it does not prove the other. For the weekly observance of Sunday as the stated day of Christian worship, and the weekly observance of the Lord's Supper at those worship meetings, stand or fall together. This is quite evident from the verse itself. Hear it again: "And on the first day of the week, when we were gathered together to break bread." Did you notice that Luke used the very same terms to describe the frequency with which the disciples met together for worship as he did to describe the frequency with which they broke the bread? If the one was done eighty times or only twice, the other one was done just as frequently. This is the obvious import of Luke's wording in Acts 20:7. Therefore they are inconsistent who deny that Acts 20:7 teaches weekly Communion.

Secondly, when Acts 20:7 mentions "The first day of the week," the definite article here is not merely describing one day alone, but a stated or fixed day. This is so in all languages that use a definite article. Allow me to illustrate this with our Fourth of July holiday. Suppose that in the year 2023 the annual observance of that day had stopped. But in 2358 someone wishes to resurrect that day from the ash-heaps of antiquity. He wants to see it celebrated just as it was during those glorious days of early American purity and patriotism. Suppose none of the records of the eighteenth century had expressly stated that it was a regular and fixed custom for American citizens to celebrate the fourth day of July. But a few incidental glimpses of it appeared in the ancient biographies of the leading men of the republic. And those casual references described it in much the same way that Luke recorded the meeting at Troas in Acts 20:7. For instance, this American researcher found that in the life of John Quincy Adams, it is written (1823): "And on the 4th of July, when the republicans of the city of Washington met to dine, John Q. Adams delivered an oration to them." Would not he find clear and forceful evidence in these words that it was an established custom in America during the first century of its existence to celebrate the 4th of July *every year?* And would it not also indicate that the primary purpose for which they met together on every 4th of July was to *dine?* For that is exactly what the document says. And if anyone disagreed with him, he would point out that the narrative does not say on "A" 4th of July, as if 1823 were the only year they ever celebrated the fourth day of July; but rather it says on "*the*" 4th of July, thus indicating a fixed and stated day of celebration *every year.* That is the force of the definite article ("the") in English. At any rate, he could not fail to persuade even the slowest of listeners that these Americans met *every* 4th of July for the purpose of *dining.* Whatever might be the frequency or the intention of that dinner, it must be confessed, from the words cited above, that they *met to dine.* And the same is true of Luke's words in Acts 20:7. He does not say on "A" first day of the week, but on "*the*" first day of the week; this shows that the Christians met *every Sunday.* And he states the primary purpose for which they met: "to break bread," that is, to receive the Lord's Supper. The very style used by the inspired historian proves that it was the established rule of all Christians in the first century to meet every first day of the week to celebrate the Eucharist. This is the only view that does full justice to the wording of Acts 20:7.

Therefore, Acts 20:7 stands. It shows the early Christians meeting each first day of the week to receive the Lord's Supper. All those who deny this are inconsistent and do not see the importance of the definite article ("the") in that text.

2. That the Apostles taught their churches to receive the Eucharist weekly is proven not only by combining Acts 2:42 with Acts 20:7, but also by seeing what the New Testament says about the church at Corinth. That congregation met the first day of every week (every Sunday) to show forth the Lord's death until He comes. To prove this, we notice first of all 1 Corinthians 16:1-2. "Now concerning the collection for the saints, as I directed the churches of Galatia, so do you also. On the first day of every week let each one of you put aside and save, as he may prosper, that no collections be made when I come." Here we see that they truly met on the first day of every week (every Sunday). Everyone agrees on this point. With this in mind, we have only to notice 1 Corinthians 11:20. "Therefore when you meet together, it is not to eat the Lord's Supper." Since the brethren at Corinth had made a shambles of the Lord's Table through gluttony, selfishness, and greed, they really were not eating the Lord's Supper—even though they ate a little bread and drank some grape juice. To act in this way, says the Apostle, is really not to eat the Lord's Supper. It is not to show forth the Lord's death. By writing in this manner, Paul shows that eating the Lord's Supper is the main purpose for which the Corinthians ought to be meeting. When a public school teacher scolds his pupils for wasting time, he cannot remind them more forcibly of the purpose for which they come to school than to say, "When

you act this way, this is not to assemble to learn." And this is exactly what Paul means in 1 Corinthians 11:20. "When you assemble in this way, this is not to eat the Lord's Supper." The very way in which he condemns them shows that he had commanded them to keep the Eucharist *every Sunday;* that is the primary reason for which they ought to meet together as the church. Anyone can see this. Paul here is not commanding them to abstain from eating the Supper every Sunday. Rather he is condemning them because they are ruining it by the way they are eating it *every Sunday.* Therefore, we have seen that the Corinthian church met every Sunday; and when they assembled in one place it was to eat the Lord's Supper. This is the clear, definite, unmistakable meaning of the Apostle's words. It is agreed by all that whatever the congregations did with the approval of the Apostles, they did by the authority of the Apostles. For the Apostles gave them all the Christian institutions. Now, as the Apostle Paul approved the meeting of the Corinthians every Sunday in one place to show forth the Lord's death and only condemned their departure from the *meaning* of that sacred institution, his words provide the highest possible authority for weekly observance of the Lord's Supper.

But when Acts 2:42 and 20:7, 1 Corinthians 11:20 and 16:1-2, are combined, it appears that we act under the influence of apostolic teaching and precedent when we meet every Sunday for the breaking of the loaf.

3. Notice a third Biblical argument that proves the weekly observance of the Lord's Supper. If it is not our duty and privilege to assemble on the first day of every week to receive the Lord's Supper, it will be difficult, if not impossible, from either Scripture or reason, to show that it is

our duty or privilege to meet monthly, quarterly, semi-annually, annually, or indeed at all, for this purpose. For those very reasons and Scriptures that prove we ought to receive it weekly. This argument is extremely strong.

4. Finally, we observe the Lord's Day to honor the resurrection of Christ. Should we honor the *death* of our Lord—through the Supper of the Lord—any less freqently?

By using the sound principle of Apostolic precedent, we have seen four Biblical arguments that prove Christians ought to observe the Lord's Supper every Sunday. We proceed next to the Historical arguments.

THE HISTORICAL EVIDENCE FOR WEEKLY OBSERVANCE

Having studied the Biblical evidence, we now investigate the verdict of church history on this question. We will include the testimony of early Christian writers and of modern Christain scholars. Although the Biblical evidence is all-authoritative, the historical evidence is not to be slighted. It sheds light upon our interpretation of the Biblical evidence.

The Testimony of the Early Christian Writers

The consistent testimony of the early Church (post-Biblical) is that the Christians observed the Supper every week. And church historians are fully agreed on this matter as well. They record that the practice of the early Christians was to gather at the Table of the Lord every Sunday.

Justin Martyr (about A.D. 140) says in his first Apology 1:67,

285

On the day called Sunday, all who live in cities or in the
country gather together to one place . . . . Then we all rise together and pray, as we before said when our prayer is ended,
bread and wine and water are brought . . . and there is a distribution to each, and participation of that over which thanks has
been given, and to those who are absent a portion is sent by
the deacons.[7]

Justin does not say that they celebrated the Eucharist
every third Sunday of the month, or every other month, or
every three months. No; he mentions nothing of a monthly
or quarterly or semi-annual observance. Rather you get the
distinct impression from his words here that whenever the
Christians met on Sunday morning—every Sunday morning, they received the Supper of the Lord. His words
strongly imply a weekly observance of the Feast.

Also, Tertullian says in his treatise entitled "On Prayer"
that those who are in a period of fasting must not abstain
from the Lord's Supper.[8] This passage could be understood
only if the Christians at the beginning of the third century
were celebrating the Eucharist every Sunday. This passage
would make no sense if the Church had been taking the
Lord's Supper only once a year or semi-annually or monthly.

The third witness for a weekly observance of the Eucharist by the early Christians appears in the Didache or The
Teaching of the Twelve Apostles (about A.D. 110). Since it
proclaims the same truth that Justin Martyr has already
expressed, I will not take the time to quote it in full.[9]

---

7. Justin Martyr, *First Apology*, 1:67; in *The Ante-Nicene Fathers*, edited by
A. Roberts and J. Donaldson (Grand Rapids: Wm. B. Eerdmans Publishing
Company, 1885 reprint), 1:186.

8. Tertullian, *On Prayer*, 19; in *The Ante-Nicene Fathers*, 3:681-91.

9. *The Didache* (or *The Teaching of the Twelve Apostles*), in *The Ante-
Nicene Fathers*, 7:381.

These three witnesses provide us with solid evidence that for the first three centuries all Christians kept the Eucharist every Sunday.

Weekly Communion was prepared in the Greek church until the seventh century; and, by one of their canons, "such as neglected three weeks together were excommunicated."[10]

In the fourth century, when all things began to be changed by baptized pagans, the practice began to decline. Some of the councils in the western part of the Roman Empire, by their canons, attempted to keep it up. For instance, the church councils held at Illiberis in Spain (A.D. 324) decreed that "no offerings should be received from such as did not receive the Lord's Supper" (Canon 28).[11]

Then the council of Antioch (A.D. 341) decreed that "all who came to church, and heard the Scriptures read, but afterwards joined not in prayer and receiving the sacrament, should be cast out of the church until such time as they gave public proof of their repentance."[12]

But what caused this decline? The answer must be pride, superstition, covetousness, and carnal indifference, for the Eastern hermits, retiring from the society of men, had taken up their residence in deserts and mountain caves. This secluded existence made it difficult for them to go where the Eucharist was administered. And so they seldom received it. As an excuse to justify this neglect, they said their high reverence for the Lord's Supper kept them from weekly observance. According to them, if one received it

---

10. Alexander Campbell, *The Christian System* (Nashville: Gospel Advocate Publishing Company, 1964 reprint), p. 287.

11. Campbell, p. 287 (1964 edition).

12. Campbell, p. 287 (1964 edition).

every Sunday, the Feast would lose its meaning. Since the Eastern churches highly respected these hermits, this imaginary holiness became the rule of all. Out of superstitious respect for Christmas and Easter, most of the people celebrated the Lord's Supper only on those holy days. Eventually the practice of weekly Communion died out, even though its decline was strongly condemned by John Crysostom.[13]

Then the Council of Agatha in Languedoc (506) decreed that "none should be esteemed good Christians who did not communicate at least three times a year—at Christmas, Easter, and Pentecost."[14] This soon became the standard of holiness (?) for the next seven centuries. To take the Eucharist more often than this was considered unnecessary.

But matters went from bad to worse; even three communications per year seemed too burdensome for most. And so the infamous Council of Lateran (1215), which decreed Auricular Confession and Transubstantiation, also announced that "an annual communion at Easter was sufficient."[15]

As we leave the testimony of the early Christians, we see that weekly Communion was the standard for all churches during the first three centuries of Christianity. No one during that time even questioned the practice. But then in the fourth century, this Biblical norm began eroding away, until at last it reached the very bottom of the barrel in the thirteenth century when Christians were told that only once a year was sufficient.

---

13. John Brown, *Hints on the Lord's Supper; and Thoughts for the Lord's Table, Original and Selected* (Edinburgh: William Oliphant and Sons, 1856), pp. 34-35.

14. Campbell, pp. 287-288 (1964 edition).

15. Campbell, p. 288 (1964 edition).

The Testimony of Later Christians

Beginning with the Reformation Movement of the sixteenth century, Christians began to restudy this question. How often does God want us to receive the Lord's Supper? In this section I will list some of the most important contributions by Christian scholars. We will find that a large number of important theologians and Biblical scholars have agreed with the Presbyterian, Matthew Henry, when he said concerning Acts 20:7, "In the primitive times it was the custom of many churches to receive the Lord's Supper every Lord's day."[16] These men have encouraged their churches to adopt this practice. And their testimony becomes all the stronger when we see that they belong to churches that do not favor weekly Communion.

John Calvin (1509-1564), the renowned Reformer of Geneva, strongly advocated weekly Communion. He was among the earliest to do this. During the sixteenth century, in general practice the Mass was frequently celebrated, but few people actually received the elements. Communion received monthly was regarded as "frequent" in the Middle Ages, and the Catholic preachers tended to discourage their congregations from frequent participation. In fact, the Catholic Church did not start the reverse trend until the year 1643 when the Jansenist, Antoine Arnauld (*De la frequente communion*), advocated weekly Communion.[17] Therefore, Calvin's words are all the more amazing. He

---

16. Matthew Henry, *Commentary on the Whole Bible* (Wilmington, Delaware: Sovereign Grace Publishers, 1872), 2:866.

17. John T. McNeill, in John Calvin, *Institutes of the Christian Religion*, edited by John T. McNeill and translated by Ford Lewis Battles. The Library of Christian Classics (Philadelphia: Westminster Press, 1960), 2:1421, note 39.

was a lone voice in the wilderness, calling on all the churches to receive the Eucharist every Sunday. Listen to his words:

> Now to get rid of this great pile of ceremonies, the Supper could have been administered most becomingly if it were set before the church very often, and at least once a week.[18]
>
> What we have so far said of the Sacrament abundantly shows that it was not ordained to be received only once a year. . . . Rather, it was ordained to be frequently used among all Christians in order that they might frequently return in memory to Christ's Passion, by such remembrance to sing thanksgiving to God and to proclaim his goodness. . . .
>
> Luke relates in The Acts that this was the practice of the apostolic church, when he says that believers ". . . continued in the apostles' teaching and fellowship, in the breaking of bread and in prayers" (Acts 2:42). Thus it became the unvarying rule that no meeting of the church should take place without the Word, prayers, partaking of the Supper, and almsgiving. That this was the established order among the Corinthians also, we can safely infer from Paul (1 Cor. 11:20). And it remained in use for many centuries later.
>
> Hence arise those ancient canons attributed by them to Anacletus and Calixtus, that, after consecration is finished, all who do not wish to be outside the precincts of the church should partake. And in those old canons which they call "apostolic," we read: "Those who do not stay until the end, and do not receive the sacred communion, should be corrected as disturbers of the church." In the Council of Antioch, also, it was decreed that those who enter the church and hear the Scriptures and abstain from communion should be removed from the church until they correct this fault. Although this was softened or at least set forth in milder language at the First Council of Toledo, still it was also decreed there that those who, having heard the sermon, have been found never to communicate are to be warned; if, after warning, they still abstain, they are to be excluded.[19]

Plainly this custom which enjoins us to take communion once a year is a veritable invention of the devil, whoever was instrumental

---

18. John Calvin, *Institutes of the Christian Religion*, 2:1421.
19. Calvin, 2:1422-1423.

in introducing it. For there is not the least doubt that the Sacred Supper was in that era set before the believers every time they met together; and there is no doubt that a majority took communion. . . . The Lord's Table should have been spread at least once a week for the assembly of Christians, and the promises declared in it should feed us spiritually.[20]

The next author who advocated weekly observance of the Feast is William King (1650-1729), the esteemed Archbishop of Dublin, Ireland. In the year 1695, he wrote an essay entitled, *A Discourse Concerning the Inventions of Men in the Worship of God.* In it he compared the scriptural worship of God with the anti-scriptural practices of those religious groups in his day. Listen to his words:

Christ's positive command to do this in remembrance of him, etc., must oblige us in some times and in some places; and there can be no better way of determining when we are obliged to do it than by observing when God in His goodness gives us opportunity; for either we are then obliged to do it, or else we may choose whether we will ever do it or no; there being no better means of determining the frequency, than this of God's giving us the opportunity. And the same rule holding in all other general positive commands, such as those that oblige us to charity, we may be sure it holds likewise in this. Therefore, whoever slights or neglects any opportunity of receiving which God affords him does sin, as certainly as he who, being enabled by God to perform an act of charity, and invited by a fit object, neglects to relieve him, or shuts up his bowels of compassion against him concerning whom the Scriptures assure us that the love of God dwells not in him. And the argument is rather stronger against him who neglects this holy ordinance; for how can it be supposed that man has a true love for his Saviour, or a due sense of his sufferings, who refuses or neglects to remember the greatest of all benefits, in the easiest manner, though commanded to do it by his Redeemer, and invited by a fair opportunity of God's own offering.

---

20. Calvin, 2:1424.

It is manifest that if it be not our own fault, we may have an opportunity every Lord's day when we meet together; and, therefore, that church is guilty of laying aside the command, whose order and worship doth not require and provide for this practice. Christ's command seems to lead us directly to it: for "Do this in remembrance of me" implies that Christ was to leave them; that they were to meet together after he was gone; and that he required them to remember him at their meetings whilst he was absent. The very design of our public meetings on the Lord's day, and not on the Jewish Sabbath, is, to remember and keep in our minds a sense of what Christ did and suffered for us till he come again, and this we are obliged to do, not in such a manner as our own inventions suggest, but by such means as Christ himself has prescribed to us; that is by celebrating this holy ordinance.

It seems then probable, from the very institution of this ordinance, that our Saviour designed it should be a part of God's service in all the solemn assemblies of Christians, as the passover was in the assemblies of the Jews. To know, therefore, how often Christ requires us to celebrate this feast, we have no more to do but to inquire how often Christ requires us to meet together; that is, at least every Lord's day.[21]

The next author who advocated the weekly observance of the Eucharist is John Mitchell Mason (1770-1829), the eminent Presbyterian minister of New York City. In the year 1798, he wrote a brief treatise (113 pages) to the members of the Associate-Reformed Church in North America; it was entitled, *Letters on Frequent Communion.* Listen to his words:

It is notorious, that during the first three centuries of the Christian era communions were held, with the frequency of which, among us, we have neither example nor resemblance. It is also notorious, that it has been urged as a weighty duty by the best of men and the best churches, in the best of times.

---

21. William King, *A Discourse Concerning the Inventions of Men in the Worship of God* (third edition; London: Printed for W. Keblewhite, 1696), pp. 125-127.

Weekly communions did not die with the Apostles and their contemporaries. There is a cloud of witnesses to testify that they were kept up by succeeding Christians, with great care and tenderness, for above two centuries. It is not necessary to swell these pages with quotations. The fact is indisputable.

Communion every Lord's day was universal, and preserved in the Greek church till the seventh century; and such as neglected *three weeks* together were excommunicated.

In this manner did the spirit of ancient piety cherish the memory of the Saviour's love. There was no need of reproof, remonstrance, or entreaty. No trifling excuses for neglect were ever heard from the lips of a Christian; for such a neglect had not yet degraded the Christian's name. He carried in his own bosom sufficient inducements to obey, without reluctance, the precepts of his Lord. It was his choice, his consolation, his joy. These were days of life and glory; but the days of dishonor and death were shortly to succeed; nor was there a more ominous symptom of their approach, than the decline of frequent communicating. For as the power of religion appears in a solicitude to magnify the Lord Jesus continually, so the decay of it is first detected by the encroachments of indifference. It was in the fourth century, that the church began very discernibly to forsake her first love.[22]

The next author who advocated the weekly observance of the Lord's Supper is John Wesley, the founder of modern Methodism. As a younger preacher, he had delivered a short sermon to the students at Oxford University. It was called, "The Duty of Constant Communion." In it he emphasized the need for all Christians to receive the Eucharist every Sunday. And after fifty-five years' reflection upon that message, Mr. Wesley remarked that he still believed every word of it. Listen to him:

It is no wonder that men who have no fear of God should never think of doing this. But it is strange that it should be neglected by any that do fear God, and desire to save their souls; and yet

22. John Mitchell Mason, *Letters on Frequent Communion* (N.Y.: T. & J. Sword, 1798), pp. 34-38, 52.

nothing is more common. One reason why many neglect it is, they are so much afraid of eating and drinking unworthily, that they never think how much greater the danger is when they do not eat or drink at all.[23]

When he advocates a "constant" communion, he means the weekly celebration of the Lord's Supper—every Sunday, as opposed to the "frequent" observance—so common in his day and ours—in which the Supper was received monthly or less often. He declares,

> I say *constantly* receiving; for as to the phrase *frequent* communion, it is absurd to the last degree. If it means anything else but constant, it means more than can be proved to be the duty of any man. For if we are not obliged to communicate *constantly*, by what arguments can it be proved that we are obliged to communicate *frequently*? yes, more than once a year? or once in seven years? or once before we die? Every argument brought for this either proves that we ought to do it constantly, or proves nothing at all. Therefore, that indeterminate, unmeaning way of speaking ought to be laid aside by all men of understanding. Our power is the one rule of our duty. Whatever we can do, that we ought. With respect either to this or any other command, he that, when he may obey if he will, does not, will have no place in the kingdom of heaven.[24]

Besides all of this, in 1784 Mr. Wesley sent a letter to the elders in his American churches: "I also advise the elders to administer the supper of the Lord on every Lord's day.[25]

Other authorities could be quoted, but I think this is enough. The verdict of history is clear. For the first three centuries of Christianity, the Lord's Supper was celebrated

---

23. John Wesley, *The Works of John Wesley* (reprinted from the 1872 edition; Grand Rapids: Zondervan Publishing House, n.d.), sermon number 101 in the second series, 7:147.

24. Wesley, *Works*, 7:149-150.

25. Quoted in Campbell, p. 286 (1964 edition).

every Sunday. Only when the churches began to backslide from the pure faith, did they slip away from that original practice. Scholars throughout church history agree that we ought to receive the Communion every Sunday.

THE THEOLOGICAL EVIDENCE

So far in this chapter we have studied the Biblical and the historical evidences for the weekly observance of the Lord's Supper. The Bible teaches it. History shows us that the early Christians practiced it. And many scholars have recognized it.

The final argument, the theological evidence, will now be presented. Here I list the objections that some have offered. And then I refute them by Christian theology.

Objection Number One:
The Meaning of the Supper Is Ruined

Many churches have objected to the weekly observance of the Supper. Why? Because, they claim, if we receive it that often, it loses much of its meaning and effectiveness. This is the most common objection used by many today.

However, once we consider what the Lord's Supper really means, it is obvious that just the opposite is true. Weekly celebrations make it all the more meaningful to us. In fact, taking the Eucharist less often really ruins its meaning and effectiveness for our lives.

The Lord's Supper is a commemoration of Christ's death: can we honor His death too often? Can anyone tell me why Christians should celebrate the Lord's resurrection fifty-two weeks a year, and His death only once, or twice, or twelve times? This piece of sophistry must be exposed immediately. It simply makes no sense whatever. Besides all this, if the weekly celebration of it is taught in the Scriptures and practiced by the Christians of the first three centuries of the church, then the monthly or quarterly observance of the Eucharist must be from man—not God. How can a human invention improve the divine plan? How can the Supper become less meaningful when we observe it as often as God says and more meaningful when we do it man's way?

The Lord's Supper is a confession that Christ's blood has already saved us from all our sins: can we confess this too often? Do we not need to remember this vital event every week?

The Lord's Supper is a communion: do we not need frequent and weekly communion with our Lord? Are we not spiritually weak and in constant, weekly need of Christ's strengthening grace and power? Spiritual health as well as physical health depends upon food. It is required for physical health that the food not only be nutritious in its nature and sufficient in its quantity, but that it be received regularly at the proper intervals. And is it otherwise with our moral health? Is there no analogy between the bread that perishes and the Bread of Life? Is there no analogy between natural and spiritual life—between natural and moral health? I believe there is. Therefore if the original disciples of the Lord only enjoyed good moral health when they assembled weekly to show forth the Lord's death through the Eucharist, we cannot enjoy good moral health who meet only monthly or quarterly or semi-annually for this purpose.

The Supper is a covenant: how we need a formal renewing of our covenant with every week!

As an act of worship, why should weekly observance make the Supper any less meaningful, when it does not do the same for prayer, singing, the offering, or preaching? All churches among us hear preaching every Sunday; they take up the offering every Sunday; they engage in public prayer every Sunday; they sing holy songs to the Lord every Sunday. Do those acts of worship suffer because we do them every week? Do they become less meaningful to us when we perform them each Sunday? Is their effectiveness ruined by frequent participation? Of course not. In fact, all agree that the more we have such activities in our weekly services of worship, the more they mean to us—the more they bless us—the more effective they become. We would never tolerate a church where preaching was heard only once a month. What preacher would permit the offering to be collected only once every three months? What Christian would belong to a congregation that sang hymns of praise to God only once every four months? We all desire to do these worshipful acts every Sunday—if not more often! And why should the Eucharist be any different?

Besides, if our infrequent receiving of the Eucharist makes it more solemn, more meaningful, more effective, then does it not become even more so if received only once in seven or ten or twenty or thirty or sixty or a hundred years? Shall we not find that those who pray only once a year have their minds far more in tune with doing the Lord's will, than those who pray seven times a day and hear one hundred sermons within the year? If our objectors are right, then this would have to be true. But is it? In reality, just the opposite is true. Those who pray less do not get more out of prayer than those who pray more. Rather, those who pray less are blessed less; those who pray more are blessed more. Those who read their Bible less do not enjoy it more than those who read it every day; rather just the reverse is true: those who study the Scriptures daily are the only ones who enjoy the Scriptures supremely.

Therefore, this objection just simply is wrong. It cannot be true. To say that the Feast loses its meaning for us if we receive it weekly, is to deny all that we know of Christian worship. Rather, the meaning of the Supper is greatly increased when we celebrate it every Sunday. This has been proven over and over again throughout the history of Christianity.

Objection Number Two:
It Was Needed for the Early Christians

Those who object to the weekly observance of the Lord's Supper say that the original Christians celebrated it weekly because of the continual persecutions that then raged among them. However, since we today suffer no such dangers in our Christian lives, we do not need to take the Feast so frequently. It was easy and necessary for the first century disciples to take it each week, but today it is not needed.

This objection at best is but a lame excuse. Shouldn't we still live as if every Sunday were our last? Have we now a new lease on life more than the early Christians had?

Also, is it true that the early Christians were ALWAYS under savage persecution during the first three centuries? No it is not. For church history shows they were under persecution only one-third of the time that weekly Communion was observed. Tribulation was not the primary reason they received the Lord's Supper every Sunday. The early Christians celebrated it each week because their Apostles taught them to do it. And therefore, just because we in the twentieth-century church are not persecuted all that much, is no reason to receive the Feast less than every week. This issue of persecution has nothing to do with the question of frequency.

Suppose, for the sake of the argument, that the early saints had been exposed to the cruelest persecution and suffered far more than we are now. Then this second objection becomes even more absurd. If they gathered every week around the Lord's Table at great peril to their own lives, does it follow that now, when God gives us greater and better opportunity for it, we ought to omit it? Surely God requires greater work from us when He grants us greater opportunities. If they received it weekly during harsh and difficult times, should we be content with receiving it monthly during easy times? Or does God require less work, when He gives greater opportunity to do it? If this be so, what an irrational Master is our Lord!

And who is to say that we in the twentieth-century Church are persecuted any LESS than those in the first-century Church? This is the main weakness of objection number two. Christians today may not be boiled in oil or fed to hungry lions or burned at the stake as were the early Christians. However, is PHYSICAL suffering the only form of persecution used by the devil against God's flock? Of course not! We today suffer greatly from the demonic lusts of the flesh, lusts of the eyes, and the boastful pride of life (I John 2:15-17). We need protection from the world's smiles as much as from its frowns. This objection assumes that the only danger from the world is physical persecution; spiritual suffering is not perilous at all. But this is a Satanic lie. The Prince of Darkness would love for us to believe such a myth. We need the weekly celebration of this holy meal to strengthen us from the devil's traps as much as the early Christians did.

Therefore, this second objection cannot refute those who receive the Lord's Supper weekly.

Objection Number Three:
It Was Natural for the Early Christians

Finally, those who object to the weekly observance of the Lord's Supper say that the original Christians lived during

299

seasons of tremendous spiritual growth and revival; therefore it was quite easy and very natural for them to receive the Eucharist every Sunday. But today those conditions no longer exist. We live in a decadent age of coldness and indifference. So for us the weekly celebration of this Feast would be unnatural.

However, if this proves anything, it shows we ought to receive the life-giving nourishment of the Eucharist all the more so! If we truly do live in the midst of a sin-loving generation, then we definitely need the Lord's Supper every Sunday. Ought we to go seldom to the wells of salvation, because we can bring but little water at once from them? Ought we seldom to endeavor to fill our pitchers at the fountain of living waters, because they are small? Is not this Feast a glorious and loving invitation for restoring the faint, strengthening the weak, recovering the sick, and reviving the dying believer? Therefore, is it not the epitome of lunacy for us to say that fainting, weak, sick, and dying believers must not have the Lord's Supper often given to them just because they are not in perfect health? That is like saying the physically sick should not go to the hospital because they are not healthy enough!

Away with such tomfoolery; the Eucharist should be given to the Church every Sunday for this very reason: we need it. We live in a perverse and crooked and degenerate generation; we therefore must have the strengthening nourishment God wants to give to us at the Table of the Lord.

When we miss the Lord's Supper, these two consequences result: 1) deliberate absence from it is a sin, but it does not leave our other sins unforgiven. 2) Most important: the Eucharist is a means of staying close to Christ and of growth as a Christian. Missing it (like abusing it—1 Corinthians 11:30) results in spiritual weakness and death.

In conclusion, God has told us how often we are to receive the Lord's Supper. He wants us to take it each and every Sunday. Three reasons have been offered to prove this point: the Biblical, the Historical, and the Theological evidence. I believe the Bible deems this an important issue; it is definitely not in the mirky realm of opinion; it is a matter of faith. Although it should not be made a test of fellowship, it is what the Word of the Lord teaches. We are to commune around the blessed Table of the Lord every week. May we follow the will of our Savior in this matter.

11

THE HELPS FOR THE LORD'S SUPPER

In chapters 6-9 you will find an abundance of devotional material. They provide you with resources for GIVING Communion meditations, and they also equip you for RECEIVING the Communion in the right spirit. I encourage you to use them as you eat the Lord's Supper.

But I want to enrich your worship experiences even more. So permit me in this last chapter to expand and elaborate upon the devotional use of the Lord's Supper. These devotions will help to improve the quality of our meditations around the Lord's Table. They will help any Christian to prepare properly for the Lord's Supper.

This chapter will be divided into the following sections: 1) Scripture Texts Selected for Meditation, 2) Questions for Self-Examination, 3) Hints for Regulating the Mind During the Communion Time.

SCRIPTURE TEXTS SELECTED FOR MEDITATION

As you prepare to give a Communion devotion before the Church assembly or as you prepare to receive the Communion, open your Bible to these texts and meditate on them earnestly and prayerfully. This practice will greatly increase the blessings you receive from this means of grace. The Spirit thus teaches you from His infallible Word how to commune properly with Jesus. The Word and the Supper work together in a marvelous way.

The Love of God: John 3:16; 1 John 3:16; 4:10; Romans 5:8; 8:32; Isaiah 63:7; 49:15-16.

The Love of Christ: John 15:13; Romans 5:10; Ephesians 3:18; 5:2; John 15:9; 2 Corinthians 5:14; Revelation 1:5-6.

The Sufferings of Christ: Isaiah 52:14; 53:3, 10; Matthew 26:38; Hebrews 12:1-2; Luke 23:33; John 19:34; 1 Corinthians 15:3; Luke 24:26.

The Atonement of Christ: Isaiah 53:6-7; Matthew 20:28; Romans 4:5; 5:6; Ephesians 1:7; 1 Timothy 2:5-6; Hebrews 9:28; 1 John 2:1-2; Revelation 5:9; Exodus 12:23 with 1 Corinthians 5:7-8; Romans 5:10; Colossians 1:19; Hebrews 2:17.

The Work of the Holy Spirit: John 15:26; 16:8; Romans 8:9; 5:5; 1 Corinthians 12:3; John 16:7; 2 Corinthians 3:17; 3:18; Galatians 5:22-23.

The New Covenant: Hebrews 8:6-13 (Jeremiah 31:31-34); Hebrews 12:22-24; Jeremiah 32:40-41; Matthew 26:28; Galatians 4:21-31.

Faith in Christ: John 6:29; 11:27; 6:68; Romans 4:20-21; Galatians 2:20; Ephesians 3:17; John 1:12; Hebrews 12:1-2; Romans 3:25.

Repentance: Zechariah 12:10; Romans 2:4; Acts 5:31; Luke 24:46; Isaiah 55:7; Jeremiah 3:22; Hosea 6:1; 2 Corinthians 7:10-11; Luke 13:1-3; Psalm 51.

The Forgiveness of Sins: Psalm 130; Daniel 9:9; Psalm 32; 1 John 1:9; Colossians 2:13-15; Matthew 9:6; 1 John 2:12; Micah 7:18-19; Psalm 51.

Justification: Romans 3:23-24, 28; Romans 4:2, 5, 24-25; 5:1; 8:31-35; Galatians 2:16; 5:6; Acts 13:38-39; Isaiah 53:11.

Sanctification: Ezekiel 36:25-27; 1 Peter 1:2; John 17:19; Romans 7:4; Hebrews 13:20-21; 1 Thessalonians 5:23; Ephesians 5:25-27; Hebrews 12:14; Colossians 1:12-14.

Devotion to God: 1 Corinthians 6:18-20; 2 Corinthians 5:15; Romans 12:1-2; Titus 2:14; 1 Peter 1:17-19; 1 John 1:7.

Love for the Brethren: 1 John 4:7-11; John 13:34-35; 1 John 3:14; Hebrews 10:24-25; Romans 12:10; 1 Thessalonians 4:9-10; 3:12-13.

Communion with Christ: Luke 24:30-32; John 14:21; Philippians 1:21; Colossians 2:6; 1 Corinthians 1:9; 1 John 1:3.

Communion with the Saints: Ephesians 4:4-6; Philippians 2:1-2; 1 John 1:1-4; Ephesians 2:19-22; 1 Corinthians 12:25-27.

Dying to Sin: Galatians 2:20; 5:24; Romans 6:5-6, 10-11; 8:13; Colossians 3:1-5.

Strength According to Our Needs: Deuteronomy 33:25; Philippians 4:13; Isaiah 43:1-3; 2 Timothy 1:12; 2:1; Hebrews 4:14-16.

Victory Over Temptation: 1 John 5:4-5; 1 Corinthians 10:13; James 1:12; Hebrews 2:18; Romans 16:20; 1 Corinthians 15:57; Matthew 12:20-21; James 4:7-8.

Eternal Life: Romans 6:23; John 6:51; 17:3, 24; 1 Thessalonians 5:10; Revelation 7:15-17; chapters 21-22.

This is not an exhaustive listing. I trust that you will enlarge it to enrich your Communion time even more.

QUESTIONS FOR SELF-EXAMINATION
The Holy Law of God (Mark 12:30-31)

Do I love the Lord my God with all my heart, with all my mind, with all my soul, and with all my strength? Do I know anything of His glorious perfections and the blessings which he has bestowed upon me? With what feelings do I regard His word, His house, His day, His commandments, and His people? Is my mind in general alienated from God and forgetful of Him? Do I think much and frequently of Him, and am I zealous for His glory and praise? Do I enjoy communion with Him when I pray to Him or do I desire this? Do I strive to become like Him? Is my entire soul devoted to giving Him affectionate, intelligent, sincere, and resolute service?

Do I love my neighbor as myself? Do I know that all mankind is entitled to my benevolence and love and compassion? Am I free from all malice, ill-will, hostility to every human being? What grudges am I bearing against anyone today? Do I follow the golden rule daily, treating others the way I would want to be treated? Am I actively desiring and seeking the good of all around me, even as I desire and seek my own? Is my love to others like that of Christ to me? Do I love not only in word, but also in deed and in truth? Have I spoken evil of anyone in the past week? Do I gossip? Am I a tale-bearer? What am I doing for the relief of the needy and poor? Am I seeking the salvation of my fellows?

Has the Law of God taught me my own sinfulness, and as a schoolmaster led me to Christ? And does the knowledge of Christ stimulate me constantly to fulfil the Law of my God?

The Gospel (Romans 1:16-17)

Have I deeply felt my corruption, sinfulness, and guiltiness before the All-Holy God? Have I seen my own helplessness to save myself? Do I know and believe that the Gospel of Christ is the appointed and only and complete way of salvation? Do I truly believe that it is the power of God for everyday living? Am I so believing in Jesus as to rely upon Him as my only Savior? Do I know that God declares me righteous and not guilty through faith in Christ's death? Am I seeking righteousness in this way—by faith and not by merits? Is my life, as it regards spiritual things, not a life of sight and sense, but of faith? Am I truly grateful to God for His great salvation? Am I demonstrating this gratitude by striving to please Him in all things?

Repentance and Faith (Acts 20:21)

Do I repent of my iniquities? Am I acquainted with, and do I love, the strictness of God's holy law? Have I any knowledge of the Divine purity, justice, and goodness? Have these things led me to see my own great sinfulness? Have I therefore felt grieved because of my sins? Have I determined to forsake all sin, however dear it may be to me? Have I confessed my own sinfulness before God? Have I actually turned away from my sins? Is sin exceedingly sinful to me? Do I hate it as that which sent my wonderful Savior to the cross?

Do I believe in Jesus as my only Savior? Have I seen my danger on account of sin? Do I know what the Scriptures say of Christ as able to save? Have I seen that He is full of grace and truth? Do I rely on Him for pardon and for strength to serve Him? Do I make use of Him in all His offices as Prophet, Priest, and King?

The Beatitudes (Matthew 5:3-10)

Am I "poor in spirit"? Am I sensitive to my lost and un-done condition without Christ? Do I feel that I am unable to help myself? Am I acquainted with the workings of my own evil heart? Do I think of myself as truly "poor" and in need of Christ for all? Am I humble and lowly in mind, affection, and manner of life?

Do I "mourn" over my sins? Do I see what dreadful evil sin has produced? Do I know that the wrath of God is against all sin? Does the suffering Savior, crucified for sin, affect my heart with godly sorrow? Am I grieved for my own repeated transgressions?

Am I "gentle" or "meek"? Do I contend with my proud and unholy tempers? Am I patient under crosses, trials and injuries? Am I willing to suffer reproaches for Christ's sake? Do I quietly submit to God's painful blessings and "severe mercies"? Do I endeavor to unite ardent zeal with patient gentleness?

Do I constantly "hunger and thirst after righteousness"? Am I deeply aware of my lack of righteousness? Do I earnestly desire to obtain that righteousness which is through faith in Christ? Do I supremely desire to be wholly free from the dominion, pollution, and power, as well as from the guilt of sin?

Am I "merciful"? Have the miseries of others called forth compassion and efforts to relieve them? Have I sought to find out the poor and the afflicted? Do I pray fervently for those who suffer? Have I shown a merciful attitude towards all who come to me?

Am I "pure in heart"? Do the sins of my heart grieve me? Do I avoid all those occasions which I have found to be temptations to impurity? Is my eye single and my heart one for God? Am I striving to destroy all carnal, sensual, and sinful desires?

Am I one of the "peacemakers"? By my own conduct do I pacify all contention and disputes, and do I influence others to be full of love and unity? Have I, as much as I could, promoted brotherly affection and union in my own family? Do I seek to unite those who have quarrelled? Am I laboring to spread the Gospel of peace to all the world?

Am I "persecuted for righteousness' sake"? Is my religion contrary to the course of this sinful age? Is my righteous conduct the only thing that causes others to dislike me? Do the ungodly laugh at, revile, or oppose my religion? Have I ever suffered any loss for conscience' sake?

Am I looking forward to the blessed rewards that Jesus has graciously promised to all who follow these beatitudes? Am I ever striving to live in harmony with these holy attitudes?

The Flesh and The Spirit (Galatians 5:22-23)

Have I learned to distinguish between the actions of the flesh (sin-loving attitudes) and of the Spirit (righteousness-loving attitudes from the Holy Spirit)? Am I endeavoring to live under the influence, power, and holy guidance of the Spirit? Do I experience an inward conflict between the flesh and the Spirit? Have I crucified the flesh with its affections and lusts? Particularly do I yield to any of the following sins in thought, word, or deed (Galatians 5:19-21):

Adultery	Enmities	Factions
Fornication	Strife	Envying
Impurity	Jealousy	Drunkenness
Sensuality	Outbursts of Anger	Carousing
Sorcery	Disputes	Etc.?

Do I cultivate and seek to demonstrate all holy dispositions and affections, and especially do I bring forth the fruit of the Holy Spirit as follows:

Love	Patience	Faithfulness
Joy	Kindness	Gentleness
Peace	Goodness	Self-Control?

The Christian Graces (2 Peter 1:4-7)

Do I receive the promises of the Bible as altogether sure? Do I view them as "precious and magnificent"? Have they led me to fly from the corruption that is in the world through lust? Have they changed my heart and made me a partaker of the divine nature? Am I using diligence to add all other Christian graces to my "faith" in the promises? Have I "moral excellence" ("virtue") in doing that for which God created me? Is my "knowledge" of God so rich that I have not only head-knowledge but also HEART-knowledge? Have I added "self-control" by restraining my sensual appetites and being moderate in all things of this world? Am I "patient," quietly yielding to God, meek towards the ones who injure me and persevering in the midst of my difficulties and distresses? Do I possess a "godliness" which sanctifies all my daily labors, so that I practice God's presence and walk with Him? Do I practice "brotherly kindness," truly and fervently loving my fellow Christians? And to all of these, do I add "love" for mankind, turning even my enemies into my friends through unselfish kindness to all?

Earthly and Heavenly Wisdom (James 3:15-17)

Am I showing forth "jealousy" and "selfish ambition" in my daily life? Am I looking mainly for "earthly" distinctions or seeking worldly advantages rather than God's favor? Do I yield to "natural" (or "sensual," "unspiritual") and carnal desires and passions? Have I any tendencies to that which is "demonic," proud, ambitious, and self-conceited? Do I look to God alone to give me that "wisdom from above" and to deliver me from that which is "earthly, natural, demonic"? Do I possess the true wisdom, "pure" in its goals, motives, and tendencies? Is my conduct "peaceable, gentle, reasonable ["willing to yield"], full of mercy and good fruits"? Am I free from "hypocrisy"?

310

The Talents Entrusted to Us (Matthew 25:15)

Have I ever seriously thought that I am accountable to God for all I have? Have I considered what gifts He has bestowed, and how I may use them for His glory? Am I using the powers of my body and mind in His service? Are my time, health, influence, authority, and property devoted to Him? Do I use my talents, carefully estimating how they can be most effectively employed for the divine glory? Do I thus act from love and not from fear, or any idea of meriting either heaven or grace by works?

Christian Love (1 Corinthians 13)

Do I count love the best gift and the necessary companion or fruit of true faith? Are the following characters of true love seen in my daily lifestyle:

It is patient and is kind,
  is not jealous,
  does not brag,
  is not arrogant,
  does not act unbecomingly,
  does not seek its own,
  is not provoked,
  does not take into account a
    wrong suffered,
does not rejoice in unright-
    eousness,
rejoices with the truth,
bears all things,
believes all things,
hopes all things,
endures all things?

Is it my grief that I have so little of such a spirit? Is it my constant aim to possess more of this great gift that "never fails"? Am I seeking and praying for it?

Christian Morality (Philippians 4:8)

Do I think on the things that are true, honorable, just, pure, lovely, and of good report? Do I endeavor more constantly to practice them? And yet do I view myself as an unprofitable servant and depend on Christ alone (see Luke 17:7-9)?

The Chief Matters of the Law (Matthew 23:23)

Am I primarily concerned to practice "justice" so that I wrong no one in any matter? Do I cheerfully show "mercy" in dealing with all my fellow creatures, and particularly with the poor and the afflicted, and those who depend on me? Are all my actions marked by "faithfulness" and reliability so that I am a trustworthy servant of both God and mankind? As I have tried to live by these weightier matters, do I now feel my own sinfulness and shortcomings so that I fly to Christ for pardon and strength?

The Lord's Prayer (Matthew 6:9-13; cf. Luke 11:2ff.)

"Our Father"

Do I know that God is a reconciled Father, through the death of His dear Son? Do I look up to God with child-like confidence for instruction, provision, and protection, knowing that He is my "Father"? Do I love Him better than the dearest relations on earth? Have I a brotherly affection for God's people as being children of one Parent? Do I regard all mankind as my brethren by creation?

"Who art in heaven"

Do I stand in awe of God's power and majesty, so as to revere and obey Him? Have I a constant recollection that His eye is ever upon me? Am I longing to be where He more immediately manifests Himself—that is, in Heaven?

"Hallowed be Thy name"

Is the promotion of His honor and glory the great object of my life? Do I seek to know God more myself and to spread the blessed knowledge about Him throughout all the world?

"Thy kingdom come"

Is the kingdom of righteousness, peace, and joy in the Holy Spirit, established in my own heart? Are the interests of that kingdom and its progress among all people zealously promoted by me? Am I looking forward to the heavenly kingdom with hope and joy?

"Thy will be done, on earth as it is in heaven"

Do I rejoice in the unlimited government of God? Do I strive to know and to follow His revealed will, copying Jesus and His holy angels? Have I cheerfully submitted to His chastening rod as I suffered trials and tribulations? And am I laboring that all may know and do His will?

"Give us this day our daily bread"

Do I receive all temporal and spiritual blessings as from God? Am I delivered from anxiously looking after future provision and do I gladly leave that to God? Am I living by faith in a daily and simple dependence upon God? How often do I remember that every good and perfect gift comes down from the Father of lights with whom is no shadow of turning (James 1:17)?

"And forgive us our debts, as we also have forgiven our debtors"

Am I deeply aware of my daily and numerous trespasses, do I earnestly seek forgiveness? Do I rest on the only ground of my forgiveness: redemption through the blood of Jesus Christ? Do I show forth the consistent temper of those who have been forgiven: the forgiveness of others? Am I manfesting good to those who are evil, liberality to the needy, and love towards all?

"And do not lead us into temptation, but deliver us from evil"

Do I carefully avoid known occasions and places where I have fallen? Am I so sensitive to my own weaknesses so that I watch and pray? Do I desire deliverance from sin as the great evil? Am I going forth in my own strength or rather in the strength of God alone to help and to deliver me?

HINTS FOR REGULATING THE MIND
DURING THE COMMUNION TIME

The main purpose of this specific section is to assist the communicant in regulating the general state of his mind so that he will truly commune with the Lord during Communion time. A good worship leader will make sure that all the preceding portions of the worship service will have prepared us for the more solemn act of remembering Christ's death through the Breaking of the Bread.

General Suggestions for the Worshipers

During the time of meditation just before the bread and cup are passed to you, endeavor to maintain a composed and tranquil spirit. Let us remember that we are going to a Father's table. And therefore let us strive to go with freedom and cheerfulness, as well as with seriousness and devotion.

Realize the Divine Presence. Christ is truly here at the Supper in a spiritual way. This is a solemn service in which we are engaged. Receiving the emblems unworthily (in a flippant and thoughtless manner) is both sinful and dangerous. With David, then, pray: "Search me, O God, and know my heart; Try me and know my anxious thoughts" (Psalm 139:23).

Humble yourself before God. The nearer we approach to God, the humbler we ought to be. When Isaiah saw the glory of the Lord and heard the song of the angelic seraphs— "holy, holy, holy, is the Lord of hosts," the prophet's own sinfulness rushed upon his mind. His first expressions were: "Woe is me, for I am ruined! Because I am a man of unclean lips" (Isaiah 6:5). We ought to be filled with the very same attitude as we partake of the Lord's Supper.

Make known your requests to God. It is a favorable time for prayer when we gather to break the bread and drink the cup of the Lord. First of all, pray for yourself. Sinners are now reconciled to God by the death of His Son. Consider, then, what it is you most need. Be particular in opening your heart to your heavenly Father, even as a little child would bring his requests to a kind and loving father. Pray that the service in which you are now engaged may be a means of grace to your own soul, so that you may receive all the blessings designed by this grand institution and especially an increase of faith in Christ. Pray for a simpler faith that depends more fully on His death as "an offering and a sacrifice to God as a fragrant aroma" (Ephesians 5:2). Pray also for others. Ask your Father that they all may obtain "a faith of the same kind as ours by the righteousness of our God and Savior Jesus Christ" (2 Peter 1:1). Pray for your partners in this life: wife, husband, children, relatives, work associates, neighbors. If they are unsaved, pray earnestly for their conversion to Christ. And if they are already Christians, ask that they may abound always in every good word and work. Parents, bring your own dear children before the Lord, naming them one by one and by name. Pray for the minister that while he breaks the Bread of Life to the Church, he may also richly partake of it himself. Look around at those receiving the Supper with you. Ask God to give you a forgiving heart if you bear a grudge or any feeling of ill-will towards any. Pray for the Christians all around the world.

315

Next, praise God for His many mercies. Surely the immense benefits which we are here commemorating should lead us to exclaim: "Bless the Lord, O my soul; and all that is within me, bless His holy name" (Psalm 103:1). We can never see redeeming love without a thankful heart! If Jesus has done so much for us, surely we may well offer up the reverent song of praise: "To Him who loves us, and released us from our sins by His blood, and has made us to be a kingdom, priests of His God and Father; to Him be the glory and the dominion forever and ever. Amen" (Revelation 1:5-6).

Give holy resolutions in the strength of Divine grace. Now is the time to determine more firmly to strive against all sin and more resolutely to fulfil all our duties. Deliberately, in the presence of God and of His saints, now in your secret devotions express your steadfast purpose to have no fellowship with the unfruitful workers of darkness. Vow that however assailed and attacked and tempted, we will be faithful to Him who loved us and died for our sins. Now is the time to decide to bind ourselves to love others more completely. When Zaccheus was honored with the presence of the Lord Jesus under his own roof, the tax-collector promised: "Behold, Lord, half of my possessions I will give to the poor, and if I have defrauded anyone of anything, I will give back four times as much" (Luke 19:8). Because of that sacred vow, our Lord then replied: "This day salvation has come to this house" (Luke 19:9). And when Christ comes to dwell in our hearts by faith, may we also make similar holy resolutions and promises.

Communion Meditations and Devotions

Their Nature

There are many things that should not be said at the Lord's Table. And there are some things often said that do not need to be said any more. There are some things that should be said that are rarely mentioned.

What should not be said at the Lord's Table? We should not try to condemn and to refute the denominational and sectarian errors and practices just at this time. That would tend only to enflame and confuse the minds of the simple worshipers; that would keep them from getting their whole heart into this spiritual Feast. God wants us to drink deeply into divine thoughts of a more positive and faith-strengthening nature. Although the act of refuting heresy is needed in our churches, the sermon is a much more appropriate occasion for it than the communion time.

Also refrain from all attempts at humor and funny stories. Humor may have its place in the church services, but not at the Table of the Lord. Comedy is simply out of place there. It mars the beauty, detracts from the sacredness, hinders the touching solemnity, and degrades the goodness of the Communion time. Let the remarks fit the seriousness of the occasion. It is sad to see someone who thinks he is the Apostle Peter's answer to Don Rickles get up and tell us a story that actually distracts our attention from the meaning of this Feast.

Do not scold the children of God every time you get up to give a Lord's Supper devotion. Rather make the worship so scriptural, so spiritual, so full of love, so powerful, that they cannot stay away.

Avoid giving long meditations. In giving a Lord's Supper devotion, you are not to preach a three-point sermon! Do not use unnecessary words. Oh, how beautiful it is to say the right words at the right time! Read the Scripture text, make the point and make it quickly, then sit down. No Communion meditation needs to be more than three minutes long anyway.

Avoid making random talks that just ramble on and on. What is said at the Table of the Lord should be carefully planned for the assembled congregation. Every word that is said here ought to help bring to the mind of the Christian a sense of renewed appreciation of Christ's supreme sacrifice on the cross. It ought to revive in us a deeper love for the Crucified One.

Now that we have seen what should never be said at Communion time, what should be spoken during the meditation?

What shall we say? We ought to say those things that are sure to show plainly the heavenly purpose of this grand Feast: the monument of Christ and His death for our sins.

What shall we say? It is highly recommended that we use elevated illustrations that stimulate our minds to think of Christ's sacrifice. For instance, one might make an eloquent Lord's Supper devotion out of the Washington Monument at Washington, D. C., in honor and in memory of "The Father of His Country." Also any memorial statues of great characters who lived before our time, or the Statue of Liberty, or the Jewish Passover feast, or historical anecdotes of heroic men and women who gave their lives for those they loved, would make noble and worthy topics for our communion meditations.

What shall we say? Say that which will create and develop and increase faith in the law of the Lord (Psalm 37:4; 1 John 5:3; Genesis 22).

What shall we say? Say words that encourage the disciples to continue in this communion with Christ until He comes again (James 1:25; 1 Corinthians 11:26). Refresh the brethren!

Their Substance

I here give you a few examples of some Communion meditations. Use them freely. Improve them all you wish.

318

Not all of them are original; I have gathered my materials from many different resources which you will find listed in the bibliographies at the end of this book.

1. Luke 22:19. "He died for me." Many years ago a traveller in one of the Oriental countries came one day to a very old city. As he travelled down its streets admiring the various scenes, he came to a magnificent cathedral. Out in front of the building stood a simple marble form—that of a LAMB. The inscription read: "He died for me." Being curious to know its significance, the stranger asked a passer-by what it meant. He was told that when the great building was nearing completion the frail scaffold high upon the spire gave way, and down toward the earth the painter fell. There seemed not a ray of hope for him. But a moment before he reached the ground, a little lamb dashed beneath him. The man was saved, but the lamb was crushed to death. Out of loving gratitude the man had the monument erected to the little animal that had saved his life. All the people said it was good to do this, for the lamb deserved to be remembered.

As I read this tender, touching incident, I thought of another Lamb that gave His own precious life for poor, lost, fallen man. We were fallen, lost, and in midnight darkness, without a ray of hope. But then—praise God!—Jesus, the Lamb of God, threw His body beneath us and made a way for our escape. Does He deserve to be remembered? Surely no man would dare say He does not. But the little monument He left His followers will live on in their hearts until He shall return with all His holy angels and thousands of His saints.

2. 1 Corinthians 11:24. "Do this in remembrance of Me." J. W. Brents, that great Restoration Movement preacher, tells of the time he sat by the bedside of his dying sister in a little cottage on Russell Street in Nashville, Tennessee.

Her parting words to him were, "Go and make a man of
yourself." He never forgot those words as long as he lived.
And whenever he would return to that old dear home, J. W.
Brents would always be sure to look upon her picture hang-
ing on the wall. It reminded him of those words. Then he
said, "But, brother, sister, do you know that Jesus should
be 'all the world' to us—more than brother, sister, father,
or mother? And, with our minds away from worldly men
and ungodly things, let's go back through all these fleeting
years to crucifixion day; let's see Jesus and his broken-
hearted apostles wending their way across the brook Kidron
into gloomy Gethsemane; let's see that raving, bloodthirsty
mob come and lead him away like a lamb to the slaughter
and like a sheep dumb before her shearers. See the crown
of thorns, the burdensome cross and insults heaped upon
him. Hear him, after the nails have been driven through
his hands and feet, praying: 'Father, forgive them; for they
know not what they do.' Hear him cry out: 'It is finished.'
See the Roman spear as it pierces his side. And after seeing
and hearing all this, then realize that 'it was for me that
Jesus died on the cross of Calvary.' Do these things, and
the Lord's Supper will have a new and more transcendent
meaning to you."

3. Galatians 6:14. "In the cross of Christ I glory." At
the Lord's Table we boast in Christ's glorious cross. Here
we publicly confess our faith in His blood to save us from
all sin. To the world, it is foolishness; but to us who are
saved, it is the power of God.

One of the most eloquent testimonies of faith to this
grand fact is the hymn entitled, "In the Cross of Christ I
Glory," written by Sir John Bowring. He was an eminent
British statesman, having been twice elected a member of
Parliament. He had a brilliant mind: at only sixteen years

320

of age he could speak five languages fluently and when he died he knew over two hundred languages. Due to his excellent administrative abilities as the Governor of Hong Kong, he was knighted by the Queen of England.

The history behind his writing of this hymn is most instructive. As he was sailing along the China coast, he saw in the far distance the city of Macao. It had just recently suffered the fury of a devastating earthquake. But on the shore, high on a hill, he noticed the ruins of a mission church building. A huge cross towered above the shattered debris. In a flash, he took out pen and paper and wrote: "In the cross of Christ I glory; towering o'er the wrecks of time."

Yes, behold how time has wrecked the world! Like some destructive earthquake, it has devastated our lives. And we also notice the tragic wrecks of sin. For the wages of sin is death. Truly the world seems one sad junkyard filled with human debris. Ah, but there is hope. It is the cross of Jesus Christ. For it alone towers above the shattered rubble caused by time and sin. At the cross God graciously promises to save us from sin and rescue us from death. And as I partake of the bread and the cup, I declare that "in the cross of Christ I glory."

4. Matthew 26:28. "The blood of Christ." No language can speak to us in such strong terms as the blood of Jesus Christ. It has an eloquence all its own; it has a unique power. It speaks to us in stronger terms than the blood of the Old Testament sacrifices. When Jesus shed His own precious blood, it was the royal blood of a King eternal, immortal. It was the blood of our Savior. It was the blood of our dearest Friend.

It was cleansing blood, because "the blood of Jesus Christ His Son cleanses us from all sin" (1 John 1:7).

It was washing blood, because "these are the ones who come out of the great tribulation, and they have washed their robes and made them white in the blood of the Lamb" (Revelation 7:14).

It was justifying blood, because "having now been justified by His blood, we shall be saved from the wrath of God through Him" (Romans 5:9).

It was redeeming blood, because "in Him we have our redemption through His blood, the forgiveness of our trespasses" (Ephesians 1:7).

It was a blood that draws us near to the Holy God, because "now in Christ Jesus you who formerly were far off have been brought near by the blood of Christ" (Ephesians 2:13).

It was a peace-making blood, because He "made peace through the blood of His cross" (Colossians 1:20).

It was victorious blood, for "they overcame him because of the blood of the Lamb" (Revelation 12:11).

It was the blood of the New Covenant, because "this is My blood of the Covenant, which is poured out for many for forgiveness of sins" (Matthew 26:28).

Yes, this blood was shed for you and for me. It was poured out when Jesus died on the cross that we might enter in by a new and living way to peace of soul, pardon of sins, the hope of glory and the gates of heaven. Surrounding this Table, eating this bread and drinking this cup, by the eye of faith we behold this Brother, Friend, Savior, and King, who shed His blood for us. By faith we see His broken body and shed blood at Calvary. By faith we regard these elements as tokens from heaven that He shed His blood for us.

As you eat and drink, remember Him who poured out His own blood for our salvation. And let us thank Him that by His blood we are set free from sin, adopted as sons of God, that we have washed our robes and made them white in the blood of the Lamb. Appreciate all the more deeply how much it cost our dear Lord to save us from hell!

5. Galatians 2:20. "He gave Himself for me." The most marvelous love the world ever witnessed was God giving up His only Son to die for sinners. "For God so loved the world that He gave His only begotten Son" (John 3:16). "He who did not spare His own Son, but delivered Him up for us all" (Romans 8:32).

"Delivered Him up for us all." Matchless mercy! Marvelous grace! Unspeakable love! The Savior died for me.

A certain man was once visiting a national cemetery to remember a loved one. As he stood there for several tender moments, remembering that one who had died, he noticed another man kneeling down in front of a grave-stone, strewing it with flowers and weeping. This was his story: during the Civil War, when the Conscript Act was passed, this man was drafted into the army. But a young man came to him, saying, "I'll take your place. You stay at home. You have a family to care for. If you go, you might get killed; and your wife and children would be thrown upon the charity of the world. I have no one dependent upon me. If I should be killed in the war, no one would mourn. Let me go in your place." And he did go. He was found in the thickest of the battle, bravely fighting for what he believed to be the right. The deadly bullet pierced his heart, and he fell on the field. When the war-storm had spent its fury, and peace waved her white banner over the land, the poor man whose place had been taken in the army by this friend, saved a few dollars out of his hard earnings, paid his way on the train, and sought the cemetery in which that friend lay buried. He found his grave; he knelt down; he kissed the grassy mound and covered it with flowers. He would always remember that one who had gone in his place to die.

323

Brethren, think of the sufferings and death of our Lord. Remember that He died for us. Your heart will melt and your tears will flow.

> Dear Lord, while we adoring pay
> Our humble thanks to Thee,
> May every heart with rapture say,
> The Savior died for me.

6. 1 Corinthians 2:2. "The glory of the cross." The death of Jesus Christ stands forth as one of the greatest events of all history. Its greatness is seen—

. . . in the actions of nature during His death hour. The sun was shrouded in darkness. The earth trembled, the rocks were broken, the graves were opened, and the veil of the temple was torn in two.

. . . in His surrender to the will of God. No complaint comes from Christ's lips. He thinks of others, provides a home for His mother, confers pardon upon the thief and prays for His persecutors. He teaches men how to suffer and how to die. His one ruling thought is, "Thy will be done."

. . . in the fulfillment of Old Testament predictions. The prophets foretold His death. Many of the types, figures, and prophecies of the Old Covenant meet at Calvary. That which the world desired is coming to pass. The testimonies of the ages are centered in His death.

. . . in that the cross ended the Jewish Age. He declared, "It is finished!" (John 19:30). That is, the feasts, sacrifices, ceremonies, institutions and holy days of the Old Testament are being taken away and nailed to the cross (Colossians 2:14-15).

. . . in the defeat of Satan. By His death, Jesus destroys him who had the power of death; that is, the devil (Hebrews 2:14-15).

. . . in the purpose of the cross. The Righteous dies for the unrighteous, the Just for the unjust. Jesus is shedding

His blood that we may have the forgiveness of sins. He is being pierced through for our transgressions and crushed for our iniquities. He is saving us from hell.

And therefore by partaking of these emblems do we celebrate one of the greatest events in all the world's history, the greatest of all death hours, a death in which we are most deeply interested, a death which purchases for us joy, peace, pardon and hope.

7. 1 Corinthians 10:16. "More than a memorial." The Lord's Supper is truly a memorial; and it is more than a memorial.

It is a memorial. It is a sweet habit of the heart, the remembrance of its dead. As a memorial this sacred Feast began. It was so instituted by the Lord Himself, there in the Upper Room, the night in which He was betrayed. "This do in remembrance of Me."

But it is more than a memorial. It is also a COMMUNION. It is a way not only of remembering the Lord who died, but of communing with the Lord who lives. It looks not only backward, but upward. It not only recalls an absent Lord, it also rejoices in a present Lord. It celebrates the Lord's death, but the celebration is on the Lord's Day, the day on which He arose from the dead. "The cup of blessing which we bless, is it not a participation in the blood of Christ? The bread which we break, is it not a participation in the body of Christ?" The death of Christ for sin is effective only because He arose and ever lives to make intercession for us. The body and the blood of Christ today have their benefits of redemption because of His living presence in the Gospel, with its ordinances and promises. A communion of the body and blood of the Lord is a participation in His life. According to Paul, those Christians who sit at the Lord's Table, eating the bread and drinking the cup of the Lord, have sweet communion with Him.

8. 1 Corinthians 11:26. "Till He come." The Jews celebrated the Passover until Christ came the FIRST time to die on the cross for sinners. And all Christians should celebrate the Lord's Supper until He shall come the SECOND time to put an end to the present state of things, to receive the church to Himself. This is His standing memorial and our standing obligation. In partaking of these emblems, we . . .

. . . proclaim the manner of His death. His body was broken and His blood was shed. He was scourged, pierced, mangled, crucified.

. . . proclaim the object of His death. His blood was shed for many for the forgiveness of sins. "This is My body broken for you." He was crushed for our iniquities.

. . . proclaim the innocency of His death. "Like a lamb that is led to slaughter, and like a sheep that is silent before its shearers, so He did not open His mouth" (Isaiah 53:7). He voluntarily laid down His life.

. . . proclaim our interest in His death. We become interested by believing and obeying Him. We are interested in the redemption which He purchased for us by His death.

. . . proclaim the love manifested in His death. It was the Son of God, the gem of the skies, and the Savior of the world, showing the full measure of His love for fallen humanity.

. . . proclaim the death itself. The cross, the soldiers, the nailing, the inscription above the cross, the seven sayings on the cross, the darkened sun, the trembling earth, the veil that was torn in two, all these we remember at the Lord's Table.

Thus, with judgment and understanding, with reverence and humility, with joy and gratitude, faith and love, we do proclaim His death until He comes again.

9. 1 Corinthians 11:24. "This do in remembrance of Me." Though it sounds incredible, Christians may forget Christ. If our memories were not so treacherous, there

would be no need for this loving exhortation, "Do this in remembrance of Me."

This tragedy is too often confirmed in our own Christian experience, not as a mere possibility, but as a sorry fact. It appears almost impossible that those who have been redeemed by the blood of the dying Lamb, those who have been loved with an everlasting love by the eternal Son of God, should forget that gracious Savior. But, if startling to the ear, it is quite apparent to the eye. We must confess the crime. Forget Him who never forgot us? Forget Him who poured His blood forth for our sins? Forget Him who loved us even to the death, yes, even death on a cross? Can it be possible? Yes, it is; it is not only possible, but conscience confesses that it is too sadly a fault with all of us. The cross, where one would think that memory would linger, is desecrated by the feet of forgetfulness.

It is the constant turmoil of the world, the ever-present attraction of earthly things which lures the soul away from Christ. While memory too well preserves a poisonous weed, it permits the Rose of Sharon to wither.

Let us charge ourselves to bind a heavenly "forget-Me-not" about our hearts, for Jesus our Beloved. And, whatever we let slip, let us hold fast to Him. This we promise to do by endeavoring to keep the Feast each week. Let us remember our loving Redeemer by faithfully receiving the blessed Eucharist with earnest devotion and reverent faith.

Therefore, when our Lord says: "This do in remembrance of Me," shall not our hearts respond: "Yes, Lord, we will remember You"?

10. 1 Corinthians 11:27-29. "Unworthily." The more excellent something is, the more worth it has; and the greater is our guilt for abusing it.

And if the Gospel of our Lord is His greatest gift to sinners, then the Supper of the Lord is His most EXCELLENT memorial for the saints. It possesses infinite worth! Therefore, it ought to be worthily appreciated and observed.

What is it to eat the bread and drink the cup of the Lord unworthily?

Some Christians are confused about this. They think that no one is worth enough to receive the Eucharist. However, they have misread the text. It does NOT say whosoever shall eat and drink, BEING UNWORTHY, shall be condemned. But rather whosoever shall eat and drink in an unworthy MANNER. The issue here is the WAY we take Communion —not how many sins we have committed.

Therefore, to take the Lord's Supper unworthily involves these elements:

Doing this ignorantly of Christ's nature. That is, not discerning the Lord's body (v. 29). The elements symbolize His broken body and shed blood. If we do not see this in them, we are guilty of taking this Feast in an unworthy manner.

Partaking of this meal in an unloving spirit. The rich Corinthian Christians came together with food and drink and were thoughtless of the poor (v. 22). Such an unloving attitude that is proud, haughty, and unforgiving will cause us to receive the Eucharist in an unworthy manner (see Matthew 5:23-24).

When we come to the Lord's Table thoughtlessly, without first examining ourselves (v. 28). This self-examination ought to extend to every facet of my life: my faith, my practice, my speech, my motives, my mind, my heart, and my body. If God told the Jews to eat the Passover Lamb only AFTER they had spent four days in diligent preparation, should not the Lord's Supper—the Christian Passover— be eaten only AFTER we have made a thorough, heart-searching examination?

In these three ways, we can be guilty of receiving the Eucharist unworthily. May God give us grace to overcome this sin. For the Supper is truly WORTHY of being received in a WORTHY MANNER!

11. Luke 22:24. "Strife at the Supper." Jesus has just instituted His Supper. Over the Upper Room hangs the peace of heaven. Then, like a sudden storm breaking the quiet of a peaceful landscape, a quarrel springs up among the disciples. The restful calm of the Last Supper is rudely shattered by Satan himself!

They were arguing about who should be greatest among them. The old desire for first place had not died out in their hearts (see 9:46; Mark 9:34).

And the terrible tragedy of it all appears as we realize the emptiness of the honor they were fighting about. One of the bravest French soldiers of Napoleon's army was General Neil. Throughout his career, he had one all-consuming ambition—to become the Marshal of France. One day he decided that he would receive this honor at the next battle or die in the attempt. That day of battle came. But after displaying extraordinary bravery, he was mortally wounded. When news of it reached the Emperor, he rushed to the side of the dying soldier. The Emperor took his own Marshal's badge and pinned it just above the heart of his dying General. Neil smiled with joy. His ambition was finally fulfilled. But then he died, the proud owner of an empty honor.

Honor, glory, pleasure, position, and wealth—the things most worth while. They last but a fleeting moment!

And with tears in His eyes, our Lord arose from the table, took a towel and bowl, and washed their feet (John 13:4-20). Who shall be the greatest? The one who SERVES most!

Even at the Communion time we must guard against the entrance of sinful ambitions and desires. As we receive the Lord's Supper, let us solemnly pledge to serve one another in love from the heart.

12. Mark 14:19. "Lord, is it I?" Jesus at the Last Supper spoke this startling statement: "One of you will betray Me" (Matthew 26:21; Mark 14:18; Luke 22:21). It is a lightning flash. There is a moment of tense silence among His disciples. Each one asks, "Lord, is it I?"

Usually we are quick to find sin in others. But sometimes a single sentence reveals to us the evil within ourselves. And so it was at the Last Supper. They caught a glimpse of their own wicked hearts and said, "Lord, is it I?"

Each disciple saw in himself a potential betrayer of his Lord. They dreaded sin. And so they asked, "Lord, is it I?" Am I the culprit? If we could only catch their spirit! For all too many of us, sin is a thrill to be sought after—not an enemy to be hated and destroyed. At the Communion we see how wicked our hearts can really be.

Here we must ask Jesus that same question: "Lord, is it I?" Our sins truly betrayed Him. For them He died.

As we see these disciples searching their own hearts, we should learn that sin is at home everywhere. No place is so sacred that sin will not dare to enter. It lurked in the holy precincts of the Upper Room where our Lord instituted His Feast. It had seeped into the hearts of His devoted disciples, even causing one of them to betray Him. Sin can enter even our own hearts as we participate in our Master's sacred memorial. Therefore, as we eat the bread and drink the cup, let us resolve to conquer all sin.

> Some one has turned from the Lord away;
> Some one has gone from the fold astray;
> Some one is treading the downward way;—
> Lord, is it I? Lord, is it I?

330

Lord, is it I? O the thought like a dart,
Pierces the innermost depth of the heart!
If there be one who in Thee hath no part,
    Lord, is it I? Lord, is it I? (Author unknown)

13. Psalm 78:19. "A Table in the wilderness." The Psalmist has been recounting God's redeeming faithfulness despite Israel's fickle faithlessness. Even though the Lord had saved them from Egyptian slavery, the Jews still grumbled against Him by saying, "Can God prepare a table in the wilderness?"

Well, can He? The Lord's Supper is answer enough! For here we see that God most certainly can and does spread a bountiful Table in this wilderness of life. At the Communion our starving souls are fed the Bread of Life.

In our wilderness of UNBELIEF the Lord's Table is spread. The universe is so vast that we seem a tiny speck in a huge wilderness. Unbelief creeps into our lives, and we cry to the sky: "Does anyone out there love me?" In such a bleak wilderness, the Lord's Table is spread for us; in it Jesus assures us that God demonstrated His own love for us at Calvary.

In our wilderness of SUFFERING the Lord's Table is spread. Trouble comes to us all. What comfort is there in this wilderness of grief? At the Communion, we see that "even though I walk through the valley of the shadow of death, . . . You are with me, . . . You prepare a Table before me." The assurance of divine companionship is here to see us THROUGH any suffering.

Finally, in our wilderness of SIN the Lord's Table is spread. I crave the peace of a pure heart, a conscience free from sin's guilt and stain. Here especially the Supper of Christ speaks its healing word. As we eat, we are reminded that the blood of God's own Son cleanses us from ALL SIN (1 John 1:7).

14. Mark 14:19. "Lord, is it I?" An old Negro spiritual asks, "Were you there when they crucified my Lord?" and then it answers, "Sometimes it causes me to tremble." And in the same way the question, "Lord, is it I?" ought to make us tremble, too. For if we do not rightly examine ourselves at the Lord's Supper, we may suffer punishment from Christ (1 Corinthians 11:27-28).

"Is it I, Lord?" suggests three basic facts of Christian experience.

First, it reveals HOW LITTLE I KNOW MYSELF. Not one person is sure of himself. Peter made such tremendous promises at the Last Supper! He would never deny his Lord—even if all others did! Peter was so sure of himself. Yet this majestic Apostle denied Jesus three times. Is any of us safe? We begin to see the force of Christ's prayer: "Do not lead us into temptation, but deliver us from evil" (Matthew 6:13).

Again, this question reveals HOW LITTLE I KNOW MY LORD. Those disciples loved their Master, but they understood Him so little. They quarrelled about who would occupy the chief seats. Their questions at the Last Supper show how much they have misunderstood Jesus. But what about us? Are we any better off? Is it not true that even after twenty centuries, Jesus is still a Stranger to some of His followers?

Finally, the question, "Is it I, Lord," reveals HOW DEEPLY MY LORD KNOWS ME, AND HOW DEEPLY HE LOVES. This is the essence of the Eucharist. Jesus loves me and gave His life for me. How well He knows us and loves us! He welcomes us to His Table of fellowship and mercy. He saves me from sin, because He knows me and loves me so deeply. This comforts me as I ponder this all-important question: "Lord, is it I?"

At the Supper, let us ask this question, thinking about these three facts of Christian experience.

15. Mark 10:45. "The missions banquet." The very purpose for which Jesus entered our world was to save sinners (1 Timothy 1:15). He came not to be served, but to serve, and to give His life a ransom for many (Mark 10:45). Jesus was born to die. He came not so much to reveal truths as to redeem sinners.

During the Lord's Supper, we are vividly reminded of this grand fact. He died for the whole world.

Therefore, when we reverently commune with Christ at His Table, we will realize that evangelism—missions—winning the lost—is the purpose of the Church. It lies at the very heart of this Feast. The Breaking of the Bread is truly the Missions Banquet! It is designed to get us on fire for soul-winning. At our baptism we promised God that we would endeavor to save sinners; and at the Lord's Supper we renew that sacred promise.

What we see at the Table of the Lord leads us to do all we can for the spiritual welfare and salvation of others. Did Christ think them worth His blood? And shall not we think them worth our care and pains? Shall not we willingly do our utmost to save a soul from death, and thereby cover a multitude of sins (James 5:19-20), when Jesus our Savior did so much to make it possible?

SELECT BIBLIOGRAPHIES
ON THE LORD'S SUPPER

A. General Works.

*Adamson, Robert M. *The Christian Doctrine of the Lord's Supper*. Edinburgh: T. and T. Clark, 1905.

Allmen, Jean-Jacques von. *The Lord's Supper*. Richmond, Va.: John Knox Press, 1966.

Armstrong, George Dodd. *The Sacraments of the New Testament as Instituted by Christ*. New York: A.C. Armstrong and Son, 1880.

Arndt, Elmer J.F. *The Front and the Table*. Ecumenical Studies in Worship, no. 16. Richmond, Va.: John Knox Press, 1967.

*Aylsworth, Nicolas John. *The Frequency of the Lord's Supper*. St. Louis: Christian Publishing Company, 1899.

Barclay, William. *The Lord's Supper*. Nashville: Abingdon Press, 1967.

Berkouwer, Gerritt Cornelius. *The Sacraments*. Studies in Dogmatics. Grand Rapids: Wm. B. Eerdmans Publishing Company, 1969.

*Bickersteth, Edward. *A Treatise on the Lord's Supper: Designed as a Guide and Companion to the Holy Communion. In Two Parts*. London: L.B. Seeley and Son, 1825.

*Brandt, John Lincoln. *The Lord's Supper*. Cincinnati: Standard Publishing Company, 1889.

Campbell, Alexander. "Breaking the Loaf." *Christian System*. Reprinted from the second edition of 1839. Nashville: Gospel Advocate Publishing Company, 1964. Pages 265-292.

Candlish, James S. *The Christian Sacraments*. Handbooks for Bible Classes and Private Students. Edinburgh: T. and T. Clark, n. d.

Cullmann, Oscar and F.J. Leenhardt. *Essays on the Lord's Supper*. Ecumenical Studies in Worship, no. 1. Richmond, Va.: John Knox Press, 1958.

Dimock, Nathaniel. *The Doctrine of the Lord's Supper. Two Lectures*. London: Stock, 1894.

_____. *The Doctrine of the Sacraments in Relation to the Doctrine of Grace*. London: Macintosh, 1871.

Dimock, Nathaniel. *The Hour of Holy Communion*. London: Stock, n.d. A brief pamphlet running nineteen pages.

*_____. *Papers on the Doctrine of the English Church Concerning the Eucharistic Presence*. London: Longmans, Green, and Company, 1911. Two volumes.

*Dungan, D.R. "The Lord's Supper." *The Old Faith Restated*. Edited by J.H. Garrison. St. Louis: Christian Publishing Company, 1891. Pages 231-253.

Fey, Harold Edward. *The Lord's Supper*. New York: Harper and Row, 1948.

*Griffith-Thomas, W.H. *The Principles of Theology*. London: Church Book Room Press, 1945. Pages 389-426.

Grove, Henry. *Nature and Design of the Lord's Supper*. Dedham, Mass.: Herman Mann, 1800.

Higgins, A.J.B. *The Lord's Supper in the New Testament.* Studies in Biblical Theology, no. 6. London: SCM Press, 1952.

*Hook, Norman. *The Eucharist in the New Testament.* London: Epworth Press, 1964.

Jeremias, Joachim. *The Eucharistic Words of Jesus.* Second edition. Philadelphia: Westminster Press, 1966.

Käsemann, Ernst. "The Pauline Doctrine of the Lord's Supper." *Essays on New Testament Themes.* Naperville, Ill.: A.R. Allenson, 1964.

*Lambert, John Chisholm. *The Sacraments in the New Testament.* The Kerr Lectures of 1903. Ediburgh: T. and T. Clark, 1903.

Lane, Thomas. "The Symbol, the Supper." *Christian Standard,* 112 (July 31, 1977), 687-688.

Lash, Nicholas. *His Presence in the World: A Study of Eucharistic Worship and Theology.* Dayton, Ohio: Pflaum Press, 1968.

Lehmann, Helmut T. (ed.). *Meaning and Practice of the Lord's Supper.* Philadephia: Muhlenberg Press, 1961.

*Lietzmann, Hans. *Mass and Lord's Supper.* Leiden: E.J. Brill, 1953 reprint.

Lilly, J.P. *The Lord's Supper: A Biblical Exposition of Its Origin, Nature, and Use.* Edinburgh: T. and T. Clark, 1891.

McCormick, Scott. *The Lord's Supper: A Biblical Interpretation.* Philadelphia: Westminster Press, 1966.

*Marshall, I. Howard. *Last Supper and Lord's Supper.* Grand Rapids: Wm. B. Eerdmans Publishing Company, 1980.

*Meyrick, Frederick. *Doctrines of the Church of England on the Holy Communion as a Guide to the Present Time.* Second edition enlarged. London: Rivingtons, 1888. First published in 1885.

*Moule, Handley Carr Glyn. *The Supper of the Lord:* Present Papers on Romanism, no. 1. London: The Religious Tract Society, n.d.

*Schultz, Joseph. *The Soul of the Symbols: A Theological Study of Holy Communion.* Grand Rapids: Wm. B. Eerdmans Publishing Company, 1966

Schweizer, Eduard. *The Lord's Supper According to the New Testament.* Philadelphia: Fortress Press, 1967.

Stone, Darwell. *Holy Communion.* The Oxford Library of Practical Theology. London: Longman's, Green and Company, 1904.

Thurian, Max. *The Eucharistic Memorial.* Parts 1-2. Ecumenical Studies in Worship, no. 7-8. Richmond, Va.: John Knox Press, 1961.

*Tisdall, J.J. "The Lord's Supper." *Christian Standard.* 51 (September 23, 1916), 1743—1744.

*Van Buren, James. "The Lord's Supper." *Christian Standard.* 88 (May 2, 1953-June 6, 1953).

*Vogan, Thomas Stuart Lyle. *The True Doctrine of the Eucharist.* London: Longmans, Green and Company, 1871. First published in 1849 as *Nine Lectures on the Holy Sacrament of the Lord's Supper.*

Wace, Henry. *The Doctrine of Holy Communion.* London: Longmans, Green and Company, 1900.

*Waterland, Daniel. *A Review of the Doctrine of the Eucharist, as Laid Down in Scripture and Antiquity.* Cambridge: C. Crownfield and W. Innys, 1737. Reprinted at Oxford: Clarendon Press, 1868, 1869, 1880, 1896.

Williams, L.A. "Great Convictions Concerning the Breaking of Bread." *Christian Standard.* 85 (June 3, 1950), 347-348.

B. Reference Works

Behm, Johannes. αἷμα. *Theological Dictionary of the New Testament.* Edited by Gerhard Kittel. Translated by Geoffrey W. Bromiley. 1968. 1:172-177.

_____. δεῖπνον, δειπνέω. *Theological Dictionary of the New Testament.* Edited by Gerhard Kittel. Translated by Geoffrey W. Bromiley. 1968. 2:34ff.

_____. Κλάω, Κλάσις. *Theological Dictionary of the New Testament.* Edited by Gerhard Kittel. Translated by Geoffrey W. Bromiley. 1968. 3:726-743.

Falconer, R.A. "The Lord's Supper." *A Dictionary of Christ and the Gospels.* Edited by James Hastings and others. 1917. 2:63-71.

Goppelt, L. ποτήριον. *Theological Dictionary of the New Testament.* Edited by Gerhard Kittel. Translated by Geoffrey W. Bromiley. 1968. 6:148-159.

_____. Τρώγω. *Theological Dictionary of the New Testament.* Edited by Gerhard Kittel. Translated by Geoffrey W. Bromiley. 1968. 8:236ff.

Jeremias, Joachim. Πάσχα. *Theological Dictionary of the New Testament.* Edited by Gerhard Kittel. Translated by Geoffrey W. Bromiley. 1968. 5:896-904.

Kidder, D.P. "Sacraments." *Cyclopedia of Biblical, Theological, and Ecclesiastical Literature.* Edited by John M'Clintock and James Strong. 1890. 11:212-218.

*Klappert, Bertold. "The Lord's Supper." *The New International Dictionary of New Testament Theology.* Edited by Colin Brown. 1980. 2:520-238.

*Lambert, John Chisholm. "Sacraments." *The International Standard Bible Encyclopedia.* Edited by James Orr and others. 1939. 4:2636-2637.

*Martin, Ralph P. "The Lord's Supper." *The New Bible Dictionary.* Edited by J.D. Douglas and others. 1973. Pages 748-752.

*Plummer, Alfred. "The Lord's Supper." *A Dictionary of the Bible.* Edited by James Hastings and others. 1902. 3:144-150.

Schweizer, Eduard. σῶμα. *Theological Dictionary of the New Testament.* Edited by Gerhard Kittel. Translated by Geoffrey W. Bromiley. 1968. 7:1024-1094.

*Stalker, James. "Sacraments." *The Encyclopedia of Religion and Ethics.* Edited by James Hastings and others. 1913. 10:897-915.

337

Stone, Darwell. "The Lord's Supper." *A Dictionary of Christ and the Gospels.* Edited by James Hastings and others. 1917. 2:71-76.

Workman, J.H. "Impanation." *Cyclopedia of Biblical, Theological, and Ecclesiastical Literature.* Edited by John M'Clintock and James Strong 1890. 4:521.

C. Special Studies

1. The Manner of Christ's Presence in the Lord's Supper.

*Dimock, Nathaniel. *Missarum Sacrificia. Testimonies of English Divines of the Claim of the "Massing-Priests" To Offer Christ for the Quick and the Dead, To Have Remission of Pain and Guilt.* London: Stock, 1896.

*Goode, William. *The Nature of Christ's Presence in the Eucharist: or, The True Doctrine of the Real Presence Vindicated, in Opposition to the Fictitious Real Presence Asserted by Archdeacon Denison, Mr. (late Archdeacon) Wilberforce, and Dr. Pusey: with Full Proof of the Real Character of the Attempt Made by Those Authors To Represent Their Doctrine as That of the Church of England and Her Divines.* Two volumes. London: J.H. Hatchard, 1856.

Hammond, Thomas Chatterton. *Does the Doctrine of Transubstantiation Involve a Material Change?* London: Church Book Room, 1928. 47 page pamphlet.

*Harrison, John. *An Answer to Dr. Pusey's Challenge Respecting the Doctrine of the Real Presence, in Which the Doctrines of the Lord's Supper, as Held by Him, Roman and Greek Catholics, Ritualists and High Anglo-Catholics, Are Examined and Shown To Be Contrary to the Holy Scriptures, and to the Teaching of the Fathers of the First Eight Centuries, with the Testimony of an Ample Catena Patrum of the Same Peirod.* London: Longmans, Green and Company, 1871. Two volumes.

*_____. *An Answer in Seven Tracts to the Eucharistic Doctrine of Romanists and Ritualists, in Which It Is Shown That Their Teaching Is Contrary to Holy Scripture and Unknown to the Fathers.* London: Longmans, Green and Company, 1873.

*_____. *An Exposure and Refutation of the Doctrine of the Real Presence as Held by Dr. Pusey, in Eight Lectures.* London: 1876.

Kershner, Frederick D. "This Is My Body." *Christian Standard,* 50 (May 1, 1915), 1016ff.

Matthew, Robert T. "The Lord's Supper More Than Memorial." *Christian Standard,* 20 (September 12, 1885), 289ff.

Paris, Andrew. "The Doctrine of the Presence of Christ in the Lord's Supper." Cincinnati: Cincinnati Christian Seminary M.A. thesis, 1975.

Pendleton, W.K. "Talks by the Way: The Lord's Supper Not a Sacrament." *Christian Standard,* 11 (December 30, 1876), 412.

Pusey, Eduard Bouverie. *The Real Presence of the Body and Blood of Our Lord Jesus Christ the Doctrine of the English Church, with a Vindication of the Reception by the Wicked and the Adoration of Our Lord Jesus Christ Truly Present.* Oxford: J. Parker, 1857.

Wilberforce, Robert Isaac. *The Doctrine of the Holy Eucharist.* London: Mozley, 1853.

2. Grape Juice versus Wine?

*Bury, Reginal Victor. *Vinum Sacramenti: Critical Examination of the Nature of the Wine of the Holy Communion.* Dublin: Hodges, Figgis, 1904.

*Dungan, D.R. "Bible Wines or Communion Wines." *Christian Standard,* 18 (July 14, September 15, October 27, and December 29, 1883).

Loos, Charles Louis. "Wine or No Wine." *Christian Standard,* 19 (August 9, 1884), 252ff.

Nash, Donald E. "The Beverage Was Grape Juice." *Christian Standard,* 88 (June 13, 1953), 376.

_____. "What Had the Apostles Been Drinking?" *Christian Standard,* 110 (May 18, 1975), 439-440.

*Stein, Robert H. "Wine-Drinking in New Testament Times." *Christianity Today,* 19 (June 27, 1975), 923-924.

*Thayer, William M. *Communion Wine and Bible Temperance.* New York: National Temperance Society and Publication House, 1870.

Van Buren, James. "More on 'the Fruit of the Vine.'" *Christian Standard,* 88 (July 11, 1953), 439.

3. Relation of the Passover to the Lord's Supper.

Marshall, I. Howard. *Last Supper and Lord's Supper.* Grand Rapids: Wm. B. Eerdmans Publishing Company, 1980.

Sailer, A. David. "The Significance of the Concepts $\delta\iota\alpha\theta\dot{\eta}\varkappa\eta$ and $\alpha\tilde{\iota}\mu\alpha$ Toward Understanding a Passover Background of the Lord's Supper." A Research Paper. St. Louis: Concordia Seminary, 1968.

*Skene, William F. *The Lord's Supper and the Passover Ritual; Being a a Translation of the Substance of Professor Bickell's Work Termed "Messe Und Pascha."* Edinburgh: T. and T. Clark, 1891.

4. Chronology of the Lord's Supper.

Gilmore, A. "The Date and Significance of the Last Supper." *The Scottish Journal of Theology,* 14 (September, 1961), 256-269.

Jaubert, Annie. *The Date of the Last Supper.* Staten Island, N.Y.: Alba House, 1965.

*Ogg, George. *Historicity and Chronology in the New Testament.* London: SPCK, 1965. Pages 75-96.

Pineo, B.N. "Did the Jews Eat the Passover at the Same Time with Christ?" *Christian Standard,* 28 (October 28, 1893), 864ff.

Ruckstuhl, Eugen. *Chronology of the Last Days of Jesus: A Critical Study.* New York: Desclee Company, 1965.

5. John 6 and the Lord's Supper.

Dunn, J.D.G. "John 6: A Eucharistic Discourse?" *New Testament Studies,* 17 (1970-1971), 328-338.

Meserve, Dallas. "John 6 and the Lord's Supper." *Christian Standard,* 109 (February 24, 1974), 159-160.

Paris, Andrew. "John 6 and the Lord's Supper." *Restoration Herald,* (September, 1985).

6. Weekly Communion.

*Aylsworth, Nicolas John. *The Frequency of the Lord's Supper.* St. Louis: Christian Publishing Company, 1899.

Richardson, Robert. "Weekly Communion." *Christian Standard,* 44 (July 10, 1909), 1202ff.

7. Origin of the Lord's Supper.

Higgins, A.J.B. "The Origins of the Eucharist." *New Testament Studies,* 1 (1954-1955), 200-209.

Taylor, Vincent. "The New Testament Origins of Holy Communion." *New Testament Essays.* London: Epworth Press, 1970. Pages 48-59.

8. Eschatology and the Lord's Supper.

Thompson, Fred P. "Eschatology and the Eucharist." *Christian Standard,* 100 (July 23, 1966), 497-498.

*Wainwright, Geoffrey. *Eucharist and Eschatology.* London: Epworth Press, 1971.

9. Was Judas Present at the Institution of the Lord's Supper?

Wilson, L.C. "Was Judas Present at the Last Supper?" *Christian Standard,* 28 (July 15, 1893), 564; cf. page 556.

10. Benefits to those who receive the Lord's Supper.

*Vaux, William. *The Benefits Annexed to a Participation in the Two Christian Sacraments, of Baptism and the Lord's Supper, Considered, in Eight Sermons Preached Before the University of Oxford.* The Bampton Lectures of 1826. Oxford: the University Press for the author, 1826.

D. Historical Treatments.

*Barclay, Alexander. *The Protestant Doctrine of the Lord's Supper: A Study in the Eucharistic Teaching of Luther, Zwingli, and Calvin.* Glasgow: Jackson, Wylie, and Company, 1927.

Bennett, William James Early. *The Eucharist, Its History, Doctrine and Practice with Meditations and Prayers Suitable to That Holy Sacrament.* Second edition. London: W. J. Cleaver, 1846. First published in 1837.

Brooks, Peter Newman. *Thomas Cranmer's Doctrine of the Eucharist.* New York: Seabury Press, 1965.

*Campbell, Alexander. "Testimonies of Reformers, Critics, Commentators, etc., on the Lord's Supper." *The Millennial Harbinger* (October, 1863), 460-468.

*Cosin, John. *The History of Popish Transubstantiation.* London: A. Clark for H. Brome, 1676.

Dollar, George W. "The Lord's Supper in the Second Century." *Bibliotheca Sacra,* 117 (April-June, 1960), 144-153.

_____. "The Lord's Supper in the Third Century." *Bibliotheca Sacra,* 117 (July-September, 1960), 249-257.

_____. "The Lord's Supper in the Fourth and Fifth Centuries." *Bibliotheca Sacra,* 117 (October-December, 1960), 342-349.

Dosker, Henry E. "The Lord's Supper." *The International Standard Bible Encyclopedia.* Edited by James Orr and others. 1939. 3:1924-1926.

*Dugmore, C.W. *The Mass and the English Reformers.* London: Macmillan and Company, 1958.

Elert, Werner. *Eucharist and Church Fellowship in the First Four Centuries.* St. Louis: Concordia Publishing House, 1966.

Foulkes, Edmund Salusbury. *Primitive Consecration of the Eucharistic Oblation.* London: J.T. Hayes, 1885.

*Jacob, G.A. *The Lord's Supper Historically Considered.* London: Henry Frowde, 1884.

Keating, John Kitzstephens. *The Agape and the Eucharist in the Early Church: Studies in the History of the Christian Love-Feasts.* London: Methuen and Company, 1901.

Kelley, J.N.D. *Early Christian Doctrines.* Second edition. New York: Harper and Row, 1960. See "eucharist" in the index of this book.

*Kidd, B.J. *The Later Medieval Doctrine of the Eucharistic Sacrifice.* London: Macmillan and Company, 1898.

Leitzmann, Hans. *Mass and the Lord's Supper: A Study in the History of Liturgy.* Leiden: E.J. Brill, 1953.

*McCue, J.F. "Doctrine of Transubstantiation from Berengar to Trent." *The Harvard Theological Review,* 61 (July, 1968), 385-430.

MacDonald, Allan J. *Berengar and the Reform of Sacramental Doctrine.* London: Longmans, Green and Company, 1930.

341

*_____ (editor). *The Evangelical Doctrine of Holy Communion*. Cambridge: W. Heffer and Sons, 1930.

_____. *Lanfranc, His Life, Work and Writing*. Oxford: At the University Press, 1926.

Parris, John. *John Wesley's Doctrine of the Sacraments*. Naperville, Illinois: A.R. Allenson, 1963.

Richardson, Cyril C. "Cranmer and the Analysis of Eucharistic Doctrine." *Journal of Theological Studies*, 16 (October, 1965), 421-437.

*_____. *Zwingli and Cranmer on the Eucharist*. The M. Dwight Johnson Memorial Lectureship in Church History. Evanston, Illinois: Seabury-Western Theological Seminary, 1949.

Scudamore, W. E. *Notitia Eucharistica*. London: 1872-1875.

*Srawley, J.H. "Eucharist (to the end of the Middle Ages)." *Encyclopedia of Religion and Ethics*. Edited by James Hastings and others. 1914. 5:540-563.

*Stone, Darwell. *A History of the Doctrine of the Holy Eucharist*. London: Longmans, Green and Company, 1909. Two volumes.

Swete, Henry Barclay. "Eucharistic Belief in the Second and Third Centuries." *Journal of Theological Studies*, 3 (1902), 161-177.

Turner, C.H. "*Figura Corporis Mei* in Tertullian." *Journal of Theological Studies*, 7 (1905-1906), 595-597.

Wace, Henry. *Cranmer on the Eucharist*. 1928.

*Watt, Hugh. "Eucharist (Reformation and Post-Reformation Period)." *Encyclopedia of Religion and Ethics*. Edited by James Hastings and others. 1914. 5:564-570.

E. Roman Catholic View of the Lord's Supper.

Benoit, Pierre (editor). *The Breaking of the Bread*. Volume 40 of *Concilium: Theology in the Age of Renewal*. New York: Paulist Press, 1969.

*Bernas, Casimir. "Eucharist (Biblical Data)." *The New Catholic Encyclopedia*. Edited by William J. MacDonald. 1967. 5:594-599.

A Debate on the Roman Catholic Religion Between Alexander Campbell and the Right Reverend John B. Purcell. Reprinted from the 1837 edition. Nashville: McQuiddy Printing Company, 1914. Pages 348-392.

Delorme, J. and others. *Eucharist in the New Testament: A Symposium*. Baltimore: Helicon Press, 1964.

Dewan, W.F. "Eucharist (as Sacrament)." *The New Catholic Encyclopedia*. Edited by William J. MacDonald. 1967. 5:599-609.

*Fortescue, Adrian. *The Mass: A Study of the Roman Liturgy*. London: Longmans, Green and Company, 1937.

Guzie, T.W. *Jesus and the Eucharist*. New York: Paulist Press, 1974.

Howell, Clifford. *Of Sacraments and Sacrifice*. Collegeville, Minnesota: The Liturgical Press, 1952.

Kilmartin, Edward J. *Church, Eucharist, and Priesthood: A Theological Commentary on "The Mystery and Worship of the Most Holy Eucharist."* A Commentary on John Paul II's Holy Thursday Letter of 1980. New York: Paulist Press, 1981.

* _____. *The Eucharist in the Primitive Church.* Englewood Cliffs, N.J.: Prentice Hall, 1965.

Leeming, Bernard, *Principles of Sacramental Theology.* London: Longmans, Green and Company, 1956.

Louvel, Francois and Louis J. Putz. *Signs of Life.* Notre Dame, Indiana: Fides Publishers Association, 1961.

*Maas, Anthony John. *The Gospel According to St. Matthew with an Explanatory and Critical Commentary.* Second edition. St. Louis: B. Herder, 1916. See section on Matthew 26:26-28.

Moehler, John A. *Symbolism: or, Exposition of the Doctrinal Differences Between Catholics and Protestants as Evidenced by Their Symbolical Writings.* Fifth edition. New York: E. Dunigan, 1844.

Nicholas, Marie-Joseph. *What Is the Eucharist?* New York: Hawthorn Books, 1960.

*Pohle, Joseph. "Eucharist." *The Catholic Encyclopedia.* Edited by Charles G. Herbermann, 1913. 5:572-590.

* _____. *The Sacraments.* Adapted and edited by Arthur Preuss. St. Louis: B. Herder, 1927. Volume 2.

Powers, Joseph M. *Eucharistic Theology.* New York: Herder and Herder, 1967.

Quasten, Johannes. *Patrology.* Westminster, Maryland: Newman Press, 1953. See the index in Volume 2.

Rahner, Karl and Angelus Haüssling. *The Celebration of the Eucharist.* New York: Herder and Herder, 1968.

*Raitt, Jill. "Roman Catholic New Wine in Reformed Old Bottles? The Conversion of the Elements in the Eucharistic Doctrines of Theodore Beza and Edward Schillebeeckx." *Journal of Ecumenical Studies,* 8 (Summer, 1971), 581-604.

*Schillebeeckx, Edward. *The Eucharist.* New York: Sheed and Ward, 1968.

_____. *Christ the Sacrament of Encounter with God.* London: Sheed and Ward, 1963.

Schaff, Philip (editor). *The Creeds of Christendom with a History and Critical Notes.* New York: Harper and Brothers, 1877. Volume 2.

"Transubstantiation." *Cyclopedia of Biblical, Theological, and Ecclesiastical Literature.* Edited by John M'Clintock and James Strong, 1890. 10:526-527 Excellent bibliography.

*Vonier, Dom Anscar. *A Key to the Doctrine of the Eucharist.* London: Burns Oates and Washbourne, 1925.

*Wiseman, Nicholas Cardinal. *The Real Presence of the Body and Blood of Our Lord Jesus Christ in the Blessed Eucharist Proved from Scripture.* London: Burns Oates and Washbourne, 1934. First published in 1836.

F. Lutheran View of the Lord's Supper.

The Abiding Word. An Anthology of Doctrinal Essays for the Years 1954-1955. St. Louis: Concordia Publishing House, 1960. 3:425-561.

Althaus, Paul. *Theology of Martin Luther.* Philadelphia: Fortress Press, 1970. Pages 375-403.

Chemnitz, Martin. *The Lord's Supper.* St. Louis: Concordia Publishing House, 1980 reprint of a sixteenth century classic.

Concordia or The Book of Concord: The Symbols of the Evangelical Lutheran Church. St. Louis: Concordia Publishing House, 1957.

"Consubstantiation." *The New Schaff-Herzog Encyclopedia of Religious Knowledge.* Edited by Samuel M. Jackson and others. 1949. 3:260.

*Dau, W.H.T. "Lord's Supper." *The International Standard Bible Encyclopedia.* Edited by James Orr and others. 1939. 3:1926-1928.

*Elert, Werner. *The Lord's Supper Today.* The Contemporary Theology Series. St. Louis: Concordia Publishing House, 1973.

*Engelder, Theodore and W.F. Arndt, Theodore Graebner, and F.E. Mayer. *Popular Symbolics: The Doctrines of the Churches of Christendom and of Other Religions Examined in the Light of Scripture.* St. Louis: Concordia Publishing House, 1934.

Luther, Martin. (A chronological listing of his main writings about the Lord's Supper.)

"Sermon on the Worthy Preparation of the Heart To Receive the Sacrament of the Eucharist." 1518. *Weimar Ausgabe Kritische Gesamtausgabe.* 1:325-334.

*"A Treatise Concerning the Blessed Sacrament of the Holy and True Body of Christ and the Brotherhoods." 1519. *W.A.* 2:742-775./ *The Works of Martin Luther.* The Philadelphia edition. Reprinted from the 1915 edition. Grand Rapids: Baker Book House, 1982. 2:9-31./ Also in *Luther's Works.* Philadelphia: Fortress Press, 1961. 35:49-73. Luther's first extended discussion of the Eucharist. In this he still maintained Catholic Transubstantiation.

*"A Treatise on the New Testament That Is the Holy Mass." 1520. *W.A.* 6:353-378./ *The Works of Martin Luther.* Philadelphia edition. 1:289-326./ Also in *Luther's Works.* 35:79-111. Luther's first clear discussion of the Lord's Supper, appearing just before he wrote the *Babylonian Captivity of the Church* (October, 1520) and after he wrote his *Address to the Nobility* (August, 1520).

"The Babylonian Captivity of the Church." 1520. *W. A.* 6:497-573./ *The Works of Martin Luther.* Philadelphia edition. 2:167-293./ Also in *Luther's Works.* 36:11-126. Luther's first denial of Catholic Transubstantiation.

"On the Abuse of the Mass." 1521. *W. A.* 8:482-563./ Also in *Luther's Works.* 36:133-230.

"Sermon on the Worthy Reception of the Sacrament." 1521. *W. A.* 7:692-697./ Also in *Luther's Works.* 42:171-177.

"The Eight Wittenburg Sermons." March 9-16, 1522. Especially sermons 5-7. *W. A.* 10^c:1-64./ *The Works of Martin Luther.* Philadelphia edition. 2:412-421./ Also in *Luther's Works.* 51:70-100. In these Luther risked life and limb by leaving the Wartburg to return to Wittenberg and reform the abuses caused by Carlstadt and Zwilling.

"A Beautiful Sermon on the Reception of the Holy Sacrament." 1523. *Erlangen* edition. 2:197ff./ *St. Louis* edition. 2:608ff./ *The Sermons of Martin Luther.* Reprinted from the 1906 edition. Grand Rapids: Baker Book House, 1982. 2:223-237 (for Easter Sunday).

"The Adoration of the Sacrament." 1523. *W. A.* 11:431-456./ *Luther's Works.* 36:275-305.

*"A Sermon on the Chief Article of Our Faith." For Easter Monday or Second Easter Day. 1524. *Erlangen* edition. 2:243ff./ *St. Louis* edition. 2:648ff./ *The Sermons of Martin Luther.* 2:267-281.

*"Sermon on Confession and the Lord's Supper." 1524-1525. For Good Friday. *Erlangen* edition. 2:164ff./ *St. Louis* edition. 2:582ff./ *The Sermons of Martin Luther.* 2:193-214, and especially pp. 202-214.

*"The Sacrament of the Body and Blood of Christ Against the Fanatics." 1526. *W. A.* 19:482-523./ *Luther's Works.* 36:335-361. Against Zwingli and others who maintained a non-physical presence of Christ in the feast.

*"That These Words of Christ, 'This Is My Body,' Etc., Still Stand Firm Against the Fanatics." 1527. *W. A.* 23:64-283./ *Luther's Works.* 37:13-150. Against Zwingli and others.

"Confession Concerning Christ's Supper." 1528. *W. A.* 26:261-509./ *Luther's Works.* 37:161-372.

"Abomination Concerning the Sacrament of the Body and Blood of Our Lord." 1530. *W. A.* 30^b:595-626./ *Luther's Works.* 38:97-137.

"Brief Confession Concerning the Holy Sacrament." 1545. *W. A.* 54:141-167./ *Luther's Works.* 38:287-319.

*Pieper, Francis. *Christian Dogmatics.* St. Louis: Concordia Publishing House, 1953. 2:118-279; 3:290-393.

Plass, E.M. *What Luther Says.* St. Louis: Concordia Publishing House, 1982. Three volumes. See the index concerning such entries as "sacrament," "altar," "eucharist," and "Lord's supper."

345

*Sasse, Hermann. *"This Is My Body": Luther's Contention for the Real Presence in the Sacrament of the Altar.* Minneapolis: Augsburg Publishing House, 1969.

G. Calvinistic View of the Lord's Supper.

*Barclay, Alexander. *The Protestant Doctrine of the Lord's Supper. A Study in the Eucharistic Teaching of Luther, Zwingli, and Calvin.* Glasgow: Jackson, Wylie and Company, 1927. Pages 113-293.

*Bannerman, James. *The Church of Christ.* Edinburgh: T. and T. Clark, 1868. 2:128-185.

Berkhof, Louis. *Systematic Theology.* Grand Rapids: Wm. B. Eerdmans Publishing Company, 1968. Pages 644-658.

*Calvin, John. *Calvin: The Institutes of the Christian Religion.* The Library of Christian Classics. Philadelphia: Westminster Press, 1960. 21:1276-1303 (book 4, chapter 14): 21:1359-1448 (book 4, chapters 17-18).

Candlish, James S. *The Christian Sacraments.* Handbooks for Bible classes and Private Students. Edinburgh: T. and T. Clark, n.d.

*Cunningham, William. *The Reformers and the Theology of the Reformation.* Edinburgh: T. and T. Clark, 1862. Pages 212-291.

Given, John James. "Homily: The Old Dispensation Merging in the New." Volume 2 of the *Gospel According to St. Mark.* Volume 16 of *The Pulpit Commentary.* Grand Rapids: Wm. B. Eerdmans Publishing Company, 1956. Pages 280-288.

Hastie, William. *Theology of the Reformed Church.* Edited by William Fulton. Edinburgh: T. and T. Clark, 1904.

*Hoeksema, Herman. *The Triple Knowledge: An Exposition of the Heidelberg Catechism.* Grand Rapids: Reformed Free Publishing Association, 1971. 2:557-663.

Hunter, Mitchell. *The Teaching of Calvin.* Glasgow: Jackson, Wylie and Company, 1920.

McDonnell, Kilian. *John Calvin, the Church, and the Eucharist.* Princeton: Princeton University Press, 1967.

Macintosh, H.R. "The Objective Aspect of the Lord's Supper." *The Expositor.* (March, 1903), 194ff.

*Nevin, John W. *The Mystical Presence: A Vindication of the Reformed or Calvinistic Doctrine of the Holy Eucharist.* Philadelphia: J.P. Lippincott, 1846.

*Schaff, Philip. *The Creeds of Christendom.* New York: Harper and Brothers, 1877. 3:225, 291-295, 332-333, 380-381, 428-431, 467-474, 505, 542-543, 663-667, 697, 797, 823.

*Wallace, Ronald S. *Calvin's Doctrine of the Word and Sacrament.* Grand Rapids: Wm. B. Eerdmans Publishing Company, 1957.

H. Devotional Literature on the Lord's Supper.

Andrewes, Lancelot. *The Private Devotions of Lancelot Andrewes (Preces Privatae)*. Translated by F. E. Brightman. Reprinted from the 1903 edition. Gloucester, Mass.: Roger Smith, 1978. Pages 119-124.

*Bennett, William James Early. *The Eucharist . . . with Meditations and Prayers Suitable to That Holy Sacrament*. Second edition. London: W. J. Cleaver, 1846. First published in 1837.

*Bickersteth, Edward. *A Treatise on the Lord's Supper*. Sixth edition. London: L.B. Seeley and Son, 1825. Part 2, pp. 157-296.

Blackwood, Andrew. *The Fine Art of Public Worship*. New York: Abingdon Press, 1939. Pages 204-225.

Boteler, M.M. "The Lord's Supper." *Christian Standard* (June 20, 27, August 1, 8, 1925; March 17, April 24, 1928).

Bruner, Benjamin Harrison. *Communion Meditations and Prayers*. St. Louis: Bethany Press, 1953.

Cleland, James T. *Wherefore Art Thou Come?* New York: Abingdon Press, 1961.

Cochrane, Arthur C. *Eating and Drinking with Jesus*. Philadelphia: Westminster Press, 1974.

*Dunn, Chester V. "Ten Talks on the Lord's Supper." *Christian Standard*, 70-71 (July 20, August 3, 24, September 28, October 26, 1935; January 18, February 15, March 14, September 5, December 5, 1936).

*Elliott, George Mark. "United Around the Lord's Table." *Christian Standard*, 92 (April 6, 1957), 209-210.

*Garrison, J.H. *Half-Hour Studies at the Cross*. St. Louis: Christian Publishing Company, 1895.

Goff, Charles Ray. *Invitation To Commune*. New York: Abingdon Press, 1959.

Green, Peter. *This Holy Fellowship*. London: Longmans, Green and Company, 1935.

Gritter, George. *Communion Meditations*. Grand Rapids: Baker Book House, 1984.

*Hallock, G.B.F. (compiler and editor). *Holy Communion Cyclopedia*. Garden City, N.Y.: Doubleday, Doran and Company, 1928.

Hayden, Edwin V. *Sixty-Eight Communion Meditations and Prayers*. Cincinnati: Standard Publishing Company, 1984.

*Henry, Matthew. *The Communicant's Companion or, Instructions for the Right Receiving of the Lord's Supper*. Philadelphia: Presbyterian Board of Publication, 1825 reprint of the 1704 edition.

Hoven, Ard. *Meditations and Prayer for the Lord's Table*. Cincinnati: Standard Publishing Company, 1963.

*Krummacher, F.W. *The Suffering Saviour*. Reprinted from the 1854 edition. Chicago: Moody Press, 1947.

Kuyper, Abraham. *The Death and Resurrection of Jesus Christ.* Grand Rapids: Zondervan Publishing House, 1947.

Lappin, S.S. *Communion Manual.* Cincinnati: Standard Publishing Company, 1935.

Lipscomb, A.B. *Around the Lord's Table.* Nashville: Gospel Advocate Publishing Company, 1934.

*Lockyer, Herbert. *The Man Who Died for Me.* Waco, Texas: Word Books, 1979.

Maynard, Lee Carter. *Memories of the Master.* Cincinnati: Standard Publishing Company, 1973.

*Moule, Handley Carr Glyn. *At the Holy Communion: Helps for Preparation and Reception.* London: Seeley and Company, 1909.

* _____. *The Pledges of His Love: Thoughts on the Holy Communion Devotional and Explanatory.* London: Seeley and Company, 1894.

Murray, Andrew. *The Lord's Table.* Chicago: Moody Press, n.d.

Phillips, J.B. *Appointment with God.* New York: Macmillan, 1954.

*Richardson, Robert. *Communings in the Sanctuary.* St. Louis: Christian Publishing Company, 1888.

*Rotherham, Joseph Bryant. *"Let Us Keep the Feast."* Cincinnati: Standard Publishing Company, 1911.

Scott, Robert and George W. Gilmore (editors). *Selections from the World's Devotional Classics.* New York: Funk and Wagnalls Company, 1916. Ten volumes.

Shannon, Robert. *Broken Symbols: Ten Sermons on Baptism and Communion.*

Shepherd, Massey Hamilton. *Holy Communion: An Anthology of Christian Devotion.* Greenwich, Conn.: The Seabury Press, 1959.

*Spurgeon, Charles Haddon. *Communion Meditations and Addresses.* London: Passover and Alabaster, 1894.

Skeath, William Charles. *Thou Preparest a Table.* New York: Abingdon-Cokesbury Press, 1947.

*Stalker, James. *The Trial and Death of Jesus Christ: A Devotional History of Our Lord's Passion.* Garden City, N.Y.: Doubleday, Doran and Company, 1929 reprint.

*Sutton, Christopher. *Godly Meditation upon the Most Holy Sacrament of the Lord's Supper.* London: Richard Badger, 1630. First published in 1601.

Thomas á Kempis. *The Imitation of Christ.* New York: Washington Square Press, 1964. Book 4.

*Thomas, David Owen. *At the Lord's Table.* Garden City, N.Y.: Doubleday Doran and Company, 1927.

Thomas, G. Ernest. *Daily Meditations on the Seven Last Words.* New York: Abingdon Press, 1959.

Vance, James Isaac. *In the Breaking of Bread.* New York: Fleming H. Revell Company, 1922.

*Wallis, Charles L. (editor). *The Table of the Lord: A Communion Encyclopedia.* New York: Harper and Brothers, 1958.

*Zwemer, Samuel M. *The Glory of the Cross.* London: Marshall Brothers, n.d.

Index of Scriptures

Old Testament
Genesis

INDEX OF SCRIPTURES